Maud Gonne

A Life

MARGARET WARD grew up in Belfast, where she studied political science at Queen's University before becoming a research fellow at the Institute of Irish Studies. She is the author of *Unmanageable Revolutionaries: Women and Irish Nationalism* (Pluto) and *The Missing Sex: Putting Women into Irish History* (Attic Press). She now lives in Bristol and teaches history at the University of the West of England.

MAUD GONNE MacBride

A Life

MARGARET WARD

Pandora
An Imprint of HarperCollins*Publishers*

Pandora
An Imprint of HarperCollins*Publishers*
77–85 Fulham Palace Road,
Hammersmith, London W6 8JB
1160 Battery Street
San Francisco, California 94111–1213

First published by Pandora 1990
This edition 1993
1 3 5 7 9 10 8 6 4 2

© Margaret Ward 1990

Margaret Ward asserts the moral right to
be identified as the author of this work

A catalogue record for this book
is available from the British Library

ISBN 0 04 440881 1 (paperback)
ISBN 0 04 440889 7 (hardback)

Printed in Great Britain by
HarperCollinsManufacturing Glasgow

Contents

ILLUSTRATIONS

(*Courtesy of the MacBride family*)
30 Sean MacBride at Roebuck House in 1986. The painting in the oval frame above the mantlepiece is of Sean as a baby, painted by Maud while in exile in Paris. Photo by Derek Speirs/Report. (*Courtesy of Gemma O'Connor*)

ACKNOWLEDGEMENTS

Many people have helped in the writing of this book. Without them, the immobility induced by pregnancy and babies could easily have led to despair. Mike Farrell was an invaluable source of advice and information. His generosity in sharing the fruits of his own research on the life of Sean MacBride, together with his willingness to give up much precious time in order to ensure that I acquired the illustrations I needed, is greatly appreciated. Without him, the distance between Bristol and Dublin would have been intolerable. History comes alive when one has the privilege of talking to those who have lived through eventful times. Sadly, Sean MacBride died in January 1988. It is my misfortune not to have had an opportunity for a more detailed conversation with him. My grateful thanks to his daughter, Anna MacBride White, for all the information and photographs she has so generously given, and to Tiernan MacBride and Pat Murphy for their helpfulness in arranging access to the MacBride family photographs. Thanks are due also to Louie Coghlan O'Brien and to Sighle Humphreys O'Donoghue, for sharing their memories of Maud Gonne with me. Caitriona Lawlor was most hospitable on my visit to Roebuck House, while Orla Farrell's welcome, despite an influx of Wards and Hillyards, remained as warm-hearted as ever.

Andrée Sheehy-Skeffington generously lent me a photograph at very short notice; Derek Speirs reproduced the MacBride family photograph to great effect; Noel Delaney of the National Museum in Dublin was efficiency itself; Shelley Charlesworth's help with picture research was much appreciated; Marilyn Hyndman sacrificed precious time in New York in order to send me Maud Gonne's correspondence; Peter Berresford Ellis supplied information from Lilian Dalton Soiron concerning Maud's reaction to the arrest of Dorothy Macardle; Una McMahon showed me family correspondence of the Coghlan family; Rozina Vishram supplied me with information from the India Office Library concerning the life of Madame Bhikaji Cama; Liz Curtis helped me to unravel details of Maud's involvement with the Amnesty Association and Joe Sim answered many questions concerning prison conditions. Margaret Mulvihill's encouragement and friendship has been indispensable. I would also like to acknowledge the assistance of Gemma O'Connor and Philippa Brewster, my editor at Pandora Press. The care taken over the manuscript by Sue Reid, my copy-editor, is much appreciated.

I would like to acknowledge the permission of A. P. Watt Limited on behalf of Michael B. Yeats and Macmillan (London) Limited to reproduce extracts from the *Memoirs* of W. B. Yeats and the permission of Oxford University Press in the reproduction of letters by W. B. Yeats which appear in the anthologies edited by Allan Wade and by Kelly and Domville.

Mary Hiney Loftus has kept me linked to County Mayo, Mari Ward has been a constant source of support and Sara Marshall's care of Fintan and Maeve enabled me to steal a little extra writing time.

Above all, my debt is to Paddy Hillyard for all his love, intellectual and electronic support and space to write. His presence made the task of writing this book an infinitely easier experience than I could have ever anticipated.

CHAPTER 1

THE COLONEL'S DAUGHTER

At the beginning of this century there was a woman – some claimed a goddess – with red-gold hair and passionate golden eyes, whose great height towered over those she walked amongst, and whose beauty and charm mesmerised friends and foes alike. Some of Europe's most erudite writers were reduced to hyperbole in attempting to capture her qualities on paper, no artist was ever quite successful in reproducing the features of this new Helen of Troy. Many thought she could have become a famous courtesan, consorting with the crowned heads of Europe, or a famous actress, perhaps not in the Bernhardt mould, but certainly popular with her audiences. She should at least have been an artist of some sort. And she was, but her theatre was a country and her audience all of its people.

She herself was fully conscious of that extraordinary beauty, but considered it as little more than a useful weapon, enabling her to charm into submission those she felt might be of use to one of her many causes. Other than that, she regarded it with sufficient detachment to be able to describe her young self as a 'tall girl with masses of gold-brown hair and a beauty which made her Paris clothes... unnoticeable'; a disciple sitting at the feet of John O'Leary, the old Fenian who was to have a great influence upon her and upon her friend, the poet William Butler Yeats.[1] For Yeats, this woman was 'a burning cloud', to be immortalised in some of the greatest love poetry of the twentieth century. To others in Ireland she was the woman promised in ancient legend, possessed of magical powers and the strength to free the country from the tyrannies of British rule. She became Cathleen ni Houlihan, the personification of nationalist Ireland and, by virtue of a life that spanned years of conspiracy, of rebellion, of partial victory and of continued struggle, she became the last of the romantic nationalists. Many have reason to give thanks that she rejected the seductive ease of the many lifestyles that beckoned, choosing instead to give her wholehearted commitment to a cause which became her obsession and her life: the fight for a free and independent Ireland.

Her name was Edith Maud Gonne, and she was the eldest child of
Captain Thomas Gonne and Edith Cook. The woman who was to
achieve notoriety as 'Ireland's Joan of Arc' was born on 21 December
1866, in the small town of Tongham, Surrey. Her life had begun, not
in Ireland, but in the very heartland of upper-class Victorian England.
She was the daughter of a British army officer whose family, although
she liked to claim an Irish ancestry on their behalf, were prosperous
wine importers in London. Her mother's people were rich London
drapers with world-wide connections. When Maud's great-
grandfather, the founder of the Cook dynasty, died in 1869, he left a
fortune of over £2,000,000. The Cooks were part of the leisured class,
with an army of servants to wait upon their every whim and no need
to work for a living.

Great wealth did not necessarily bring much happiness. Maud's
mother Edith, the only child of William, the eldest son, was orphaned
at an early age. No one wanted her to live with them. Her three aunts
decided to send the young girl to boarding school, a solution that
proved to be such an unhappy experience for the young girl that she
vowed never to allow her daughters to suffer the same fate.

In 1867 the Fenian Rising – the latest in a long line of failed
attempts to free Ireland – was crushed and Ireland was again saturated
by the military. One year later, Captain Gonne of the 17th Lancers
was posted to the military base of the Curragh. Fears that the secret
revolutionary society of the Irish Republican Brotherhood might
finally succeed in establishing an independent Irish republic, had led to
the sending of extra troops, to stamp out any remaining traces of
sedition. Maud's father was part of this garrison. At the age of two,
she had her first experience of Ireland, but while John O'Leary,
O'Donovan Rossa and the other Fenian leaders were jailed and exiled,
Captain Gonne and his family were living the privileged existence
peculiar to members of the Protestant Ascendancy.

Maud's recollections of that time were based upon what she, as a
child, remembered. And as children do, she remembered first seeing
snow, and how her father hammered his finger when taking down the
portraits of Maud and her mother when they were packing to move.[2]
Her brief account of those early years contains no trace of any
awareness of the political realities of Irish life. Virginia Moore,
meeting her as a very old woman, assessed Maud's personality as
'freeborn, innocent, not wholly mature',[3] and these qualities are
certainly evident in the pages of *A Servant of the Queen*, the
autobiography she wrote at the age of seventy-one. As Elizabeth
Coxhead has remarked, 'One hears her very voice, and it is the voice
of a rebellious girl, never of a septuagenarian.'[4]

Maud began the story of her life with a recollection of words which
were to have a profound effect. She was four years old and her mother
was dying of tuberculosis. Her father, whom she always called

'Tommy', was saying in a strange and far-away voice 'You must never be afraid of anything, even of death.' Although she was very frightened by the occasion, his words sank into her mind and were never forgotten. Maud took her father's urging very seriously, constantly testing herself in order to conquer the many fears of childhood. In her maturity she was convinced that if one had no fear, conscious or subconscious, one would rarely be harmed. She found herself unafraid even when rifles were raised against her. It gave her, she said, a 'strange aloof power'. Her later activities showed her to be a woman of great personal courage – recklessly courageous at times. It was a powerful weapon for a revolutionary to possess.

Her memoirs, wonderfully racy in narrative pace though they are, are not the place to go to for dates or hard facts. What Maud Gonne chose to reveal about her long and action-packed life was based on emotional reactions to what she considered significant. What she chose not to reveal was at least as interesting in content. She had, of course, many more qualities as an adult, particularly her passion for justice and her concern for the poorest sections of society. These would become more dominant as time went on, but we begin, as Maud did, by considering the events and personalities which were to have a significant influence upon the young girl.

Life in Floraville, their house in the Dublin suburb of Donnybrook, was to come to an abrupt end in 1871, as a result of the death of her mother. On the night before she died Edith had made her husband promise that he would never permit their daughters to be sent to boarding school, or to fall into the clutches of the aunts. Although she was buried in England, the Gonne family did not remain over there. Tommy's posting had not come to an end and, mindful of his promise to his wife, he brought back his small daughters to Ireland, to live with him. The motherless girls were now to lead a rather different life from the secluded, rigidly supervised existence they had previously experienced in Dublin.

Tommy had an enormous influence upon Maud. Even in extreme old age she treasured her memories of him, loving to recall the fact that they were sometimes mistaken for husband and wife, rather than father and daughter, because of the quality of their relationship. He seems to have been an exceptional father, particularly for the period, when most parents of that class were little more than remote figures of authority. When Maud was only five years old she remembered Tommy teaching her how to sow seeds and to make cuttings from plants. Both her love of gardening and her fondness for all kinds of animals were inherited from her father. Pet names as well as actual pets were a family tradition. In his letters to his daughters Tommy addressed the self-willed Maud as 'lamb', while her gentle little sister was dubbed 'bear' or 'bru'. He also wrote about all the different animals he had in his care: his beautiful Arab cavalry horses, his dog

Rover who sat beside him in his cart, and his constantly warring cat. He also told them stories of camels, elephants and jungle birds. The indifference to society's convention that was characteristic of Maud was also an attribute of her father's. In India he had 'brought down the wrath of the old general in command for going to a ball not in uniform'. He was far from apologetic, believing that the general 'made a mistake in not putting on his cool plain dress clothes' and concluded by laughing that 'even an old dad can be naughty'. Colonel Gonne's letters had another unusual quality. Instead of assuming that his children, particularly because they were both girls, would be indifferent to public events, he often shared with them his political concerns. He appears to have been unusually honest, writing from Russia that he was 'very sorry we are the direct cause of the town being destroyed'. His letters are not quoted in Maud's memoirs. In those pages Tommy is only mentioned when he is actually in the presence of his family. His life in other respects does not concern Maud. It is the egotism of the very young who cannot conceive of their parents having a life separate from themselves. But Tommy's letters were preserved by Kathleen, who then left them to her daughter Thora.[5]

Tommy appears to have had less of an effect upon Kathleen, who was two years younger than Maud. She was very much the 'baby' of the family, unlike her sister, who loved the thought of growing up to become a companion for her father. One of Maud's later regrets was that a snow-covered holly branch she had excitedly brought into the house after a walk with her father became a cause of her hurting her mother's feelings. The little girl snatched the trophy out of her mother's hands declaring 'It isn't for you, Tommy says it will melt at the fire; I want to see.' Her mother was already ill and Maud had not thought of her, and so her later memory was always of her eyes 'with a sad look in them'. That pattern of an active father and passive mother was repeated with the older and younger sister. While Maud was always restless, constantly on the move, the placidity of Kathleen's nature was reminiscent of their mother. Maud remembered Edith being 'tall like a lily and very beautiful' and she used the same imagery to describe Kathleen before her death, looking like 'a faded white lily'. Kathleen loved beauty and hated any unpleasantness, but despite their different natures, the two sisters were always very close. Although Maud was to rebel against everything that the much more conservative Kathleen believed in, they never allowed themselves to quarrel. The quiet younger sister could be very stubborn in defending Maud when the rest of the family felt inclined to cut her out of their lives.

The house in Donnybrook was too full of memories for Tommy and so after a short stay at the Curragh army camp the small family moved to 'an ugly little house' opposite the Bailey lighthouse at Howth, just north of Dublin. Maud had been coughing again and the doctor had told Tommy that she needed sea air. The motherless girls were looked after by a nurse, Mary-Anne Meridith, nicknamed 'Bow', whom Maud never thought of giving a name to in her autobiography. There she was simply 'nurse', although she would be buried with Thomas and Edith Gonne in Tongham cemetery, her tombstone bearing the inscription 'Beloved nurse of Colonel Gonne's children.'[6] It must have been Maud who arranged this, which refutes any impression of someone who didn't care enough about her nurse to name her. Tommy now came home for weekends, but for the rest of the time the girls roamed around the comparative wildness of the Howth cliffs and the heather-covered hills. The intensity of Maud's love for the land, her sensuous delight in its textures and hidden treasures had its roots in these early experiences, when she and Kathleen were free to play amongst the heather and 'make cubby houses and be entirely hidden and entirely warm and sheltered from the strong wind'.

The two girls created their own little world as welcome relief from the other aspect of their lives: the carefully ordered nursery existence of the Victorian child, where the silver christening mugs and spoons were carefully laid out at meal times and a crinolined nurse ensured that her charges did not become too familiar with the ragged children of the native inhabitants. Despite any reservations she might have had about the Irish, their nurse was a sociable woman who needed adult company and she used to visit the families who lived in the little cabins dotted around Howth. She came to be much in demand because of her knowledge of nursery remedies in times of sickness. While she chatted over a cup of tea, Maud and Kathleen were free to play with the other children and to share whatever food was going. It was a one-sided hospitality, because they were never allowed to invite anyone back home with them. Maud was very conscious of the fact that, despite their superior social status, she and Kathleen had very little advantage over the others. 'If we had better clothes, they had more learning.' Only their swimming abilities could be boasted of, as the others were better climbers and better riders of donkeys. The majority of Maud's class assumed that their position in society automatically conferred a superiority in ability. Maud had sufficiently close contact with those outside of her immediate milieu to realise that this was decidedly not the case. She also began to realise that she was part of an English garrison that had very different views to most of the Irish people. Visiting the little cabins brought her into contact with the portraits of nationalist heroes like Wolfe Tone and Robert Emmet, which were reverentially hung on the walls alongside religious pictures. When nurse was not around the old people would whisper that they were great men, the Lord have mercy on them, although they were careful not to say any more to the daughters of the English soldier.

This period of idyllic solitude soon came to an end. One Sunday Tommy took his daughters to lunch with Lord Howth. Although they were dressed in black velvet, pink silk stockings and big straw hats with ostrich feathers, all pretence at being young ladies stopped there. Tommy was told bluntly that his daughters 'were being allowed to run wild like little savages' and that they were 'quite shockingly ignorant.' A futile interlude with an English governess, dispatched by the aunts at Tommy's request, followed. But, as Maud said, it was the end of their liberty. That winter, with nurse and governess, they were sent to visit Aunt Augusta in London.

Great-Aunt Augusta Tarlton, the eldest of the maternal aunts, was the childless widow of a clergyman. She lived alone, apart from her servants and her lapdog, in a large house in Hyde Park Gardens. It was 1874 and Maud was eight. Tommy was now stationed in Aldershot and his daughters were unwilling guests of a woman whose miserliness was so great that it extended into haggling over fruit at Covent Garden market, where she used to go because it was cheaper than the greengrocer. Each evening Maud and Kathleen were brought down, dressed in starched muslin dresses and blue sashes, to share in the dessert that followed the evening meal partaken by aunt and governess. The 'measly collection' of fruit on the magnificent silver dessert-stand in the middle of the dining room table was the chief topic of conversation. While the girls were supplied with a small piece of fruit and a biscuit on hand-painted china, Maud was free to eat and to silently compare this behaviour with the generosity she had witnessed in the poor homes of the Irish. It was a lesson which was well absorbed.

Augusta's patience with her nieces was limited. After a while they were dispatched to Richmond where her brother, Uncle Frank, lived. Maud totally shared her mother's dislike of the Cook relatives. She felt that her Uncle Frank, whom she also accused of unfairly acquiring grandfather Cook's art collection, treated his Portuguese wife, Aunt Emily, abominably. Aunt Emily was Maud's godmother and the only aunt Edith Cook had loved. This firsthand experience of a wife's humiliating financial dependency upon her husband was a salutory one for Maud:

> [Aunt Emily] was old and faded when I knew her, and in her long black silk dress and mantilla moved about among all these riches and splendours like a neglected ghost. Uncle Frank would not allow her even a carriage to drive in the beautiful Richmond Park; when she occasionally visited London, she had to go in a hired fly. Her excursions to London were generally to buy magnificent dolls for us children and she never forgot her godchild's birthday; but these extravagant presents had to be kept secret from Uncle Frank and the money to pay for them had to be craftily saved from the house-keeping accounts which Uncle Frank always examined every week himself.

Her conclusion was that 'women of that generation don't seem to have had a dog's life, or to have counted for anything'. After Aunt Emily died, Uncle Frank married 'an enterprising American, imbued with distinct ideas on women's rights, who took over the keeping of accounts'. It was then Uncle Frank's turn to fade away. A just retribution, concluded Maud.

Although she never saw the new Lady Cook – Tennessee Claflin – it would have been impossible for Maud not to have been aware of some of the ideas promulgated by her new aunt. Tennessee and her sister, Victoria Woodhull, had published a radical feminist newspaper, *Woodhull & Claflin's Weekly,* which advocated spiritualism, socialism and free love. Amongst other achievements, they earned a fortune as Wall Street's first female stockbrokers. For a time, the sisters were the most talked about figures in the suffrage movement and although they were eventually expelled from the National Woman Suffrage Association because of their public declaration of women's right to sexual freedom, their articles were more well known and influential than some cared to admit. Aunt Emily might have been gratified to learn that her successor had railed against woman's economic dependence, which forced her to become little more than a sexual snare for men, and I wonder if her young niece by marriage was aware of Tennessee's insistence that women should gain their sexual freedom by defying oppressive social customs:

> It is degrading, insulting mockery to define female virtue ... in any way different from man's virtue. ... From the mere imputation of impropriety in this one particular women shrink and cower with the most abject terror. This slavery to opinion must be abolished; women must vindicate their right to an absolute freedom in their own conduct ... .[7]

Whether or not Maud was aware of these words, she did go on to live her life in a manner which would have met with Tennessee's wholehearted approval.

It was partly a tactful intervention from Aunt Emily that persuaded Tommy to uproot his little family once more. Maud's weak lungs provided the necessary excuse. This time 'home' was a small villa in France, a 'nest of flowers' situated on the road between Cannes and Grasse. It stood in the midst of orange and lemon groves, with foliage from mimosa and pepper trees hanging over its walls. Once again the setting was beautiful, but the girls were as isolated as before from the realities of ordinary everyday life. Tommy's letters provided one of their main sources of outside news. From March 1876 until October 1878 Thomas Gonne was military attaché in Vienna. He was then in Bosnia for a short time before being posted first to India and, in 1881, to St Petersburg. His children were to stay at the Villa Fleurie until April 1880.[8]

A French governess now took over their education. She was of sterner stuff than the last and soon gained both the love and respect of her two charges. It turned out to be a significant relationship. 'Mademoiselle' was a strong republican with a good knowledge of history. Many of Maud's incipient political views took shape at this time. Mademoiselle's history had a republican bias, but it was focused above all upon people. Maud always attributed whatever education she possessed to this formidable woman, who had taught her to 'love human beings and to love beauty and to see it everywhere'. Typically, she tells us the names of her teacher's cat and dog, which she must have remembered for over fifty years, but never tells us the name of the woman herself. Many years later, when she was engrossed in her political activities, Maud paid a visit to her old governess, who by this time was retired and living in the little house she had had built during the time she was with her two English charges. She was happy and self-sufficient, still keeping up to date with the newly published books and interested to hear all about Maud's work. During their conversation the old woman remarked 'Independence, *ma Chérie*, is the most precious of all things and everyone can be independent.'[9] Perhaps that was the most important lesson of all.

Maud's propensity to a weak chest remained, despite the climate of the south of France. Nurse's rheumatism was also troublesome, so in May 1880 the children, nurse and governess went to Geneva, where they stayed until October. During that time they also made a trip to Rome. Whenever he could, Tommy joined them for their travels. Much time was spent in little junk shops, searching for treasure. The expenses of their lifestyle left little over for costly purchases, but Maud said her father had sound taste and judgement. After his death she and Kathleen divided up the family memorabilia between them. Despite all her later travels and her very different lifestyle, Maud was to treasure those mementoes. Kathleen's son, visiting his notorious aunt in her Irish home, was amazed to discover the interior of that rebel home resembled the staid upper-class house of his youth.[10] What continued to unite Kathleen and Maud was their intense love of their parents' memory, which those relics represented. Maud rejected her background, but never her immediate family.

As she got older, to her great delight Tommy began to treat her more as a companion than daughter. She did her best to look the part. She was helped by her height and by the early development of those incredible looks. She was five foot ten by the age of fourteen and persuaded her nurse to lengthen her skirts and pile her masses of golden hair into great coils at the back of her head. Maud's determination to appear grown up included the usual adolescent fantasies of proposals by handsome young men. After Tommy learned that his daughter had accepted a proposal made by moonlight at the Colosseum in Rome, Maud and Kathleen were ordered to join their father at his new posting. Colonel Gonne was back in Ireland. From all the evidence, the date would have been around 1883, when Maud was seventeen years of age.

It was the end of another period of turmoil in Ireland. From 1879 until 1882 the Irish Land League had organised farmers and peasantry in a concerted battle against the high rents imposed by landlords. Michael Davitt, Charles Stewart Parnell and the other leaders were gaoled for their efforts, and for the following eighteen months Parnell's sister Anna successfully led the Ladies' Land League in a continued defiance of the government. The British government became so alarmed by the determination of the women that in May 1882, they finally released the male leaders. In return, Parnell ruthlessly insisted upon the disbandment of the women's organisation and the ending of all agrarian agitation, for which he was promised further reforms to the land tenure system.[11] But the biggest blow to any prospect of continuing the Land League struggle occurred just as the leadership was being released from jail. The new Chief Secretary, Lord Frederick Cavendish, and T. H. Burke, his under secretary, were assassinated in Dublin's Phoenix Park by a terrorist group called the Invincibles. Parnell was reduced to making almost craven apologies for this deed, which convinced many Irish people of the dangers of secret societies. A well-organised, constitutional political campaign was seen as the way forward, and what could have been a disaster turned out to be the impetus for the Irish Parliamentary Party, under Parnell's leadership, to increase its strength and influence over the next decade.

These political developments remain outside Maud's autobiography. All she says is that they arrived in Dublin the day after the departure of one Lord Lieutenant and the State entry of his successor. She was given a place at one of the windows of the exclusive Kildare Street Club, so that she could have a good view of the procession of Lord Spencer and his wife. The streets were lined with police and military and the women seated beside Maud in the windows murmured to themselves about the 'shocking state' of the country. But none of this was of any great concern to the young woman who had just come back from seeing some of Europe's most romantic sights. She was most unimpressed by the spectacle and relieved when Tommy, his military duties over, came to fetch his daughters for afternoon tea with a family from nearby Dawson Street.

For the next three years Maud lived the life of the débutante. It was, however, a less restricted existence than that experienced by her contemporaries. She was an unmarried, motherless daughter, without the inconvenience of a chaperone, and she was determined to take full advantage of the freedom of being her father's hostess. As Maud was only eighteen, people said she was far too young to be the head of the household. Disapproval made her more determined to prove the doubters wrong, while Tommy appeared unconcerned and greatly amused by his daughter's efforts at housekeeping. Neither of them appeared to be at all worried by conventional opinion. Maud soon abandoned the chore of supervising the housekeeping, leaving it in the far more efficient hands of her faithful nurse, and she and Kathleen indulged themselves in riding the numerous horses provided for them.

The daughter of the garrison did have some social obligations to perform on her father's behalf, and her execution of those revealed her to be a person with a strong sense of her physical attractiveness, well used to male company and contemptuous of the majority of army wives, who were either 'vulgarly pretentious', or 'decent, drab little creatures struggling with children and household difficulties', as she patronisingly described them. With brash insouciance she claimed to find the company of the generals of far more interest. Unlike the young officers, their conversation was not limited to sport and racing.

The triumph of Maud's court presentation was indelibly imprinted upon her memory. In her extreme old age she was still capable of describing, with no false modesty, details of her shimmering dress, embroidered to look like a fountain, with its three yards long water-lily train. Oscar Wilde met her at a party and thought she looked 'positively charming' in her water-lily outfit.[12] She typically refused to attend the customary lessons in how to curtsy, practising secretly at home instead. The six foot tall beauty with her European sophistication had no difficulty in catching the attention of the Prince of Wales. He escorted her onto the royal dais, which ensured that her photo would be in all the society papers. It also led to Aunt Mary (who was Tommy's aunt and a complete contrast to the conservative Cook aunts), inviting her beautiful niece to go with her to Germany that summer. Aunt Mary, by marriage the Comtesse de la Sizeranne, had buried two husbands and, at the age of seventy, still had a male escort. He was a young English secretary whose secretarial duties were purely fictional. As Maud, who accepted his presence with amusement, remarked, they were purely 'to explain to a conventional world his constant presence'. One of Aunt Mary's proudest moments was the reprimand she received from a hotel manager following a noisy quarrel she had had with Figlio. The manager had pointed out the impropriety of her conduct, and as she told the story of the night to her niece, who was visiting her aunt in Paris, she proudly concluded 'And I am seventy-five!' Just then the waiter brought her in a gigantic basket of red roses, from her 'adoring' Figlio. Some members of the Gonne family were anything but conventional, at least as far as personal morality was concerned.

Aunt Mary had been a noted beauty when young and one of the principal interests of her old age was the launching of professional beauties. At first, Maud enjoyed all the attention her aunt was able to manufacture. As she admitted, she was 'vain enough in some ways', but the emptiness of it began to get on her nerves. All the meticulously orchestrated entrances and carefully contrived positioning came to an abrupt end when Tommy, who had just arrived, discovered that the Prince of Wales, who was also in Germany, had expressed a certain interest in his daughter. Maud was hastily removed by a furious father, concerned that his daughter would either ruin his career by snubbing the prince, or would otherwise ruin her reputation by accepting his invitation.

Life in Ireland continued its course. But once the delight of asserting her supremacy as female head of the household had palled, a great deal of the early excitement also disappeared. Maud grew to hate the seven-course dinners given by rich Dubliners who fawned obsequiously upon their military rulers, unaware of how much they were the object of derision to the soldiers when back in the barracks. She joined in with this contempt and was rebuked by her father for her ill manners. Despite that, the pro-Unionist Dublin bourgeoisie was never a group Maud could ever have sympathy for. In her eyes, they had no redeeming features.

In later years, Maud's explanation for her eventual realisation that Ireland was suffering desperately under British rule centred around an experience which finally opened her eyes to the harsher realities of life. She had gone to stay at a country house, where she was to attend a hunt ball as the guest of the landowner's wife. During dinner her host, 'a tall red-faced man with an abrupt manner' who appeared to be in a very bad temper, suddenly announced 'That damned Land League is ruining the country', and he went on to describe seeing a tenant and his family lying in a ditch, evicted by his agent because of their support for the League. The wife didn't look as though she would live till the morning and he stopped and told her husband that his political activities were the cause of her condition. When Maud exclaimed in horror, he replied, 'Let her die. These people must be taught a lesson', and then went on eating. In a fury Maud sent a telegram to Tommy, asking him to send a carriage as she was leaving the next day. She felt she could not stay any longer in that house.

According to this version of events Maud, for the first time, had witnessed something of the cruelty of the landlord system. But she still had not seen its effects at first hand. However, on other occasions, while only a small child riding in the countryside with her father, she claimed to have seen evicted tenants standing in tears beside their ruined cottages, prevented by the police from returning to their homes. And, when telling such tales to her enthralled audiences, she would conclude by affirming that her determination to do something for Ireland had started at that time. That affirmation was pure rhetoric: there is no evidence that Maud had any political views in her adolescence, and she makes no pretence to having any in *A Servant of the Queen*. But it is difficult to believe that she could have lived in Ireland for a total of eight or nine years and yet have experienced nothing of the misery of the life of the Irish peasantry. If we accept her version in *A Servant of the Queen,* she was almost twenty years of age before she heard that particular landlord condemn the workings of the Land League. Which version of events is nearest the truth? Was her description of the eviction of Paddy Ward and his family not literally true, but a convenient shorthand to describe her final awakening and to exonerate herself from the charge of simply having ignored unpalatable truths up until that point? Had anything occurred to politicise Maud, so that she was finally ready to understand the bitter reality of life in Ireland?

One possible explanation, advanced by Conrad Balliett, is that Maud had already met her future lover, Lucien Millevoye, and through their 'alliance' was to develop her determination to free Ireland while he fought for a revival of French national pride. When confessing details of her past life to Willie Yeats during a period of deep despair, she claimed to have met Millevoye 'while staying with a relative in her nineteenth year'. After that, she returned to Dublin and to her father. All this is speculative. It is possible that she met Millevoye, perhaps while staying with Aunt Mary. Certainly Millevoye was to give her the confidence to believe in her power to effect political change: after all, how many Victorian women would have had the necessary self-belief to begin such work, alone and without any encouragement? Maud's explanation for her eventual politicisation is, as so much else, shrouded amidst romance and mystery. But the origins are of much less importance than the future deeds. And they at least are indisputable.

Maud's account of Tommy's conversion to the Home Rule cause is also open to question. She claimed that soon after her return from that fateful house party he announced his decision to resign from the army and to stand for Parliament as a Home Rule candidate. Only in her autobiography does she make that claim for him. In answers during numerous press conferences on her American tours she always admitted that her family were on the English side and opposed to her activities. In St Louis in 1897, when asked by a reporter from *The Globe* if her father had been a patriot, she replied 'No. He was on the English side, a colonel in the British army, and died when I was 20 years of age.'[13] Tommy died of typhoid on 30 November 1886. His conversion, if there had been one, was of the death bed variety. There were no witnesses to it. But it is far more likely to have occurred only in the pages of his daughter's memoirs, because she could not bear to admit that the father she described with such love was, at the same time, a prominent member of the military occupation of Ireland.

The sudden death of Thomas Gonne, at the early age of fifty-one, was devastating for both his daughters. For Maud, who had been tomboy companion and proxy wife, the loss was irreplaceable. Her bitter grief was made worse by the prospect of a dismally restrictive and loveless future life. Colonel Gonne had named his elder brother William as guardian of his daughters. William had inherited the family wine business and had grown old and crusty but not, as Maud wryly remarked, as mellow as the port wine in which he traded. He was a dour, parsimonious man, a stickler for punctuality, prayers and regular church attendance. Worst of all, he lived in London, the city in which Maud and Kathleen had been so unhappy when they were last forced to live there with relatives. Much of Maud's later attitude towards the English must have stemmed from those experiences.

All Maud wanted to do was to rebel, but the dreamy Kathleen, who hated confrontation, was not the most useful of allies. She was able to shut out what was unpleasant by immersing herself in art books and writing long letters to a boyfriend she had left behind in Dublin. Tommy had another brother, Charlie, whose two daughters, Chotie and May, had often visited their Gonne cousins in Dublin. In some respects these two sisters duplicated some of the differing qualities of their cousins. Maud described Chotie as 'the gentlest and most selfless person' she had ever met, and believed that the terrible headaches she suffered were a result of her determination not to see wrong in anyone, which led to considerable nervous strain. May, three years older than Maud, was different. She was 'more of a rebel and had fiery red hair and some of the fire of Irish and Scotch ancestors but lacked the staying power for successful rebellion'. She was, in other words, a paler version of Maud herself, and the two were often allies.

An unexpected visitor at Uncle William's provided Maud with her first inkling that the beloved Tommy had had a life quite separate from the one he had shared with his daughters. In her memoirs, the woman is called 'Eleanor Robbins'; in real life she was Margaret Wilson. She had given birth to a baby, Tommy's daughter, six weeks previously, and was now destitute. It was an awful warning of what could happen to those who transgressed moral codes. Particularly if they had no independent income. The existence of her half-sister Eileen (or 'Daphne' as Maud calls her) was not the great shock William expected. While Tommy was dying he had insisted Maud help him make out a cheque for a 'Mrs Robbins'. She now understood why. Maud was only given half a crown pocket money a week and so could be of no help, but, after heated argument, she finally managed to persuade her uncle that Tommy would have wanted his commitments to be honoured. Maud staunchly declared Tommy's mistress to be 'a brave woman and life had been unkind to her'. She later managed to get Mrs Wilson a post as governess in Russia, where she was to remain for the next twenty years, and Eileen was looked after by Bow, Maud's old nurse, after she retired. This melodramatic occasion must have been more of a shock to Maud than she admitted, but her response was to her credit. She also revealed a talent for organising people that – until then – she was perhaps unaware she possessed.

Maud and Uncle William did not get on, and the scandal of Mrs Wilson did not improve matters. With May's support the sisters were able to move to Ascot, to live with Uncle Charlie's family. While they were there William visited them, to inform them frigidly that their father's affairs were in a bad way and that there would be little money coming to them. As they were incapable of earning their living, they had no choice but to accept Great-Aunt Augusta's 'generous' offer of adoption. A 'conclave of the young' was immediately held to see if there was a way out of the crisis. For Maud and May, the family, 'at least, our family, meant stagnation, and we were determined to get out of it'. Kathleen and Chotie were against any drastic action but the other two had already made up their minds to escape. The upshot was that May enrolled as a nurse at the Charing Cross Hospital, Kathleen and Chotie agreed to attend the Slade School of Art and Maud resolved to become an actress. She had been refused a health certificate, essential for prospective nurses, because of her weak lungs and, in any case, was uninterested in nursing as a career. She had starred in numerous amateur theatricals in Dublin and had taken elocution lessons. She also had a contact in Herman Vezin, a well-known London actor, whom she promptly went off to visit. Charlie's wife Lizzie supported all these plans and arranged for the family to move to London, so that they could all live together.

According to Maud, in four months' time she had the satisfaction of seeing her name a foot high on a poster containing the information that Maud Gonne was leading lady in a theatrical touring company playing an 'abominable melodrama' and an English version of *Adrienne Lecouvreur*. Uncle William wrote to beg her to spare the family disgrace by taking a stage name. She replied that 'the name belonged to me and I thought I was honouring it by earning my bread'. The events might have been taken from the pages of any Victorian melodrama. The final denouement was to turn out very differently, but the wicked uncle was defeated after all. Maud's lungs collapsed as a result of strenuous voice projection and rehearsals in cold dusty rooms. She was forced to go to Aunt Mary for help. Aunt Mary, who had given up her place in Paris for a house in Chelsea then told them the truth. Uncle William, upset by Maud's illness, had confessed that he had lied about their inheritance. He had wanted to keep them confined within the family but he now admitted that when they came of age they would have more than enough to live on. Nancy Cardozo states that the terms of Thomas Gonne's will provided Maud, when she turned twenty-one, with half of a trust set up in 1865, along with a share of the family diamonds, land and residual income.[14]

The knowledge that Tommy had left his daughters provided for was a great relief. If Maud was going to rebel against family traditions and society's conventions, she now had the reassurance of knowing that she would have a comfortable income on which to live.

The doctor advised a holiday abroad, a cure for Maud's lung condition. She and Kathleen were off to France again, accompanied by Aunt Mary, to enjoy what amusements the fashionable spa town of Royat could offer. Frivolity was not what Maud wanted, but the knowledge that she would be twenty-one in a few more months and finally able to determine how she would live her life, was sufficient to keep her at least outwardly obedient. She was ripe for adventure and, in the sultry heat of the summer, full of premonitions that something momentous was about to occur. The scene was replete with symbolism: as a violent thunderstorm broke the oppressive heat, Maud stood looking at the havoc of rose petals scattered on the grass, and the man who was to be her greatest love and political influence entered her life.

She was, she said, convinced they had met before, so familiar did the tall, melancholy looking Frenchman seem to her. Lucien Millevoye also suffered from a lung complaint and was at Royat partly for his health, and partly to be close to his idol, General Boulanger, whom the extreme right wing in France was hailing as a new Napoleon. Millevoye was fervently patriotic, obsessed with furthering the glory of France, particularly the restoration of the lost territories of Alsace-Lorraine. Each day, Maud and he walked along the promenades of the resort, their courtship inspired by the seemingly limitless possibilities that a political alliance between them could achieve. The intensity of their infatuation was heightened by their belief in each other's high-mindedness. Maud said Millevoye initiated their alliance; 'I will help you to free Ireland, you will help me to regain Alsace-Lorraine'. She grasped his hands in acceptance, jubilantly promising 'an alliance against the British Empire and it is a pact to death'.

While staying with Uncle William Maud had defied his wishes and ventured out to Trafalgar Square to witness a mass demonstration of the unemployed, addressed by the socialist leader Tom Mann. In the surge of the crowd she had ended up at the front of the platform and Mann had asked her if she belonged to the movement. Then her answer had been that she was 'from Ireland where people also were oppressed and wanted to be free'. She was far too timid to accept his offer to make a speech. Neither did she seem to have considered the possibility that she could have anything significant to contribute. When the police advanced with batons raised the crowds disappeared. To Maud, perched up high, 'they seemed to melt, going in all directions. I couldn't understand'. A speaker with a foreign accent said 'An English crowd is always like this.' Maud wanted to work for a cause, but that one experience confirmed her belief that the English were not worthy of her assistance. At this time she still had no idea what her future role would be, and she always claimed that it was the experience of meeting Millevoye which finally convinced her of where her future destiny lay.

Theirs would be, so Maud believed, a pact of both passion and principle. It would not be a dreary marriage, bound by domestic considerations and therefore certain to stultify. Millevoye was already married, although separated from his wife (he did remain in some sort of contact with her, however, as photographs of the couple taken as late as 1910 reveal), while Maud would be away from France a great deal, fulfilling her part of their pact – the 'freeing' of Ireland. She was very much in love, finding in the sophisticated older man (Millevoye was thirty-two) a substitute for her sadly missed Tommy, yet at the same time she was realistic enough to know that she had to retain her independence. Her new ally was convinced that Maud could become Ireland's Joan of Arc. It was a heady comparison and one she desperately wanted to prove worthy of.

Once her cure was complete, Maud was free to live the life of an emancipated, independent woman. Her first venture was a holiday in Constantinople to stay with an old friend, Lilla White, whose father was the British Ambassador to Turkey. By 'considerable strategy and a few lies', she succeeded in having one free, unchaperoned day in Marseilles before sailing. It had been carefully planned. Millevoye was electioneering in the vicinity and they arranged a secret meeting. They had a 'marvellous' day, visiting the old part of town, eating in a sailors' restaurant with the traditional precocious parrot and wandering around the market place. Maud bought herself a little marmoset monkey, laughingly declaring that in respect for convention she needed a chaperone, so the monkey was promptly christened 'chaperone'. More to the point, given Maud's beauty, youth and unaccompanied status, Millevoye bought her a small revolver, telling her that no woman should ever travel without one. In her racy account of her travels, she wrote that she found herself forced to aim the revolver at some Greek sailors attempting to abduct her as she returned from an expedition ashore.

The month in Constantinople was enjoyable, enlivened by potential scandal as Maud, in reaction to the restrictions imposed upon European women, persuaded Lilla to join her in dressing up as a Turkish princess. They frequently wandered around the embassy gardens in this attire until forbidden to continue, as rumours were circulating that the ambassador was secretly keeping a harem. True to form, Maud was adept in exploiting the dramatic potential of the situation, but her interest in pursuing the fun soon waned. She knew that she wanted to do something beyond play.

In December 1887, after Maud left Constantinople, she at last turned twenty-one. She had her inheritance, and was free to live as she pleased. At Naples, on her journey home, she found a telegram from Millevoye, urgently calling her to Paris.

CHAPTER 2

A PASSIONATE ALLIANCE

Maud's first political assignment included all the essential ingredients of melodrama: secret documents, international intrigue, spies, and a luxurious train journey across Europe. She was carrying papers for the Tsar, in an attempt to enlist Russian support for General Boulanger's conspiracy against the Third French Republic. Millevoye and his friends were under surveillance, so an unknown young woman like Maud was an invaluable tool in the game of undercover diplomacy. After various adventures, which included the rare feat of managing to enter Russia without a passport (thanks to the unwitting help given by the Russian agent from Berlin, who succumbed to Maud's charms and the prospect of a long train journey in her compartment), Maud was able to report a successful mission.

During her fortnight in St Petersburg Maud met W. T. Stead of the *Pall Mall Gazette*, who was in the process of writing a book about the Tsar. Stead was well known as a crusading journalist who had exposed the horrors of the white slave trade and forcible prostitution, combining moral outrage and prurient details in a style similar to the modern tabloids. He was captivated by Maud, later writing of

one of the most beautiful women of the world. . . . Everywhere her beauty and her enthusiasm naturally make an impression and although she is hardly likely to be successful where Wolfe Tone failed, her pilgrimage of passion is at least a picturesque incident that relieves the gloom of the political situation.[1]

Maud's feelings were much more ambivalent. She was pleased to learn of Stead's support for Irish Home Rule, but hated what she felt to be his 'sex obsession', finding it 'repellent to a girl who hated such talk'. She might revel in defying convention at every conceivable opportunity, but at the same time she had also had a Victorian upbringing and in certain respects was a typical product of that era, with all its prudishness and taboos. Stead did give her one good piece of advice: if she wanted to work for Ireland, she should meet Michael

Davitt, ex-Fenian prisoner and founder of the Land League, who was now an Irish Party MP.

European intrigues were all very well, and Maud was satisfied she had helped to further her alliance with Millevoye, but she still 'wanted to get to work for Ireland quickly'. On her return to England she took Stead's advice and went to the House of Commons.

Maud stood in the great hall of the Commons, hesitating as to how to fill in the form she had been given. She wondered what to write in the space marked 'business', eventually deciding on 'important', saying to herself that fighting the British Empire was important, even though she only wanted to be told how to go about it. As she waited for Davitt, an elderly woman gave her a suffrage leaflet. Maud confessed she knew little about the issue, but quite agreed that women should be able to vote. Just then the thin, one-armed figure of Michael Davitt appeared at the other side of the barrier and Maud hurried to meet him. As they sat on one of the stone seats near the barrier she blurted out her wish to work for Ireland, telling him of her revulsion at the conduct of Irish landlords and of the usefulness of her inter-national contacts. In non-committal fashion Davitt suggested that she organise publicity abroad which could counter the British govern-ment's portrayal of the Irish campaign as being involved with crime and outrage. His suspicions of the fashionable young woman were fuelled by Maud's impulsive reply that nothing an Irishman might do in retaliation for Britain's presence in Ireland could be considered a crime: they were 'acts of war and perfectly justified'. Davitt was furious, convinced Maud must be a spy. All he offered her was a ticket for the Ladies' Gallery – the only part of the Commons where women's presence was allowed – before hurrying back to business.

Maud was very bored as she listened to the Irish Party and their interminable obstruction of parliamentary affairs. If Michael Davitt would not help, she would just have to go to Ireland and find suitable political work through her own efforts.

Ida Jameson, a member of the whiskey distilling family, was an old friend of Maud and her family. She did not share the Jamesons' unionist politics and was thrilled to hear of Maud's mission. They must have made a delightful pair: Ida rushed into town to order gold rings with Eire engraved on them which she said they must always wear. Maud said of her friend that she loved to dramatise life even more than she did herself. Although Ida was too busy fighting against her family's objections to her proposed husband, the French Vice-Consul, to be able to devote too much time to the Irish cause she did have one useful contact. Charles Oldham was a Protestant home ruler and Trinity College lecturer, whom Ida felt was engaged in 'important work' for Ireland. She arranged an introduction and Oldham, amused by the two attractive yet immensely naïve young women, agreed to take Maud to a meeting of the Contemporary Club, which he had helped to inaugurate in 1885 as an informal discussion group, open to anyone willing to debate issues of political and cultural importance. Its rooms were in Grafton Street, the heart of prosperous Dublin, where it continued in existence until the 1940s.

It was quite an entrance. Oldham laconically announced:

> Maud Gonne wants to meet John O'Leary; I thought you would all like to meet Maud Gonne.[2]

As Maud glanced round the 'cosy room ... where some twelve men were sitting smoking and drinking tea' she felt a little doubtful about the last part of the introduction, as she was well aware that women were not admitted to the club. Membership was restricted to fifty, later rising to seventy-five; all male. It was only later that a monthly 'ladies night' was instituted, a half-hearted concession to the growing numbers of women in the nationalist movement.

John O'Leary was the veteran Fenian who had been sentenced to twenty years on a charge of treason-felony for having helped to plan the Fenian Rising. In 1871, having served six years, he had been released under a general amnesty, but was not permitted to return to Ireland until 1885. Many nationalists considered him to be an inspiring symbol of Fenianism and moral leader of the separatist movement. His physical presence was very imposing and Maud responded impulsively to what she described as the 'strikingly handsome' man who came towards her with a puzzled frown on his face. She blurted out 'you are the leader of revolutionary Ireland, I want to work for Ireland, I want you to show me how'. No one could remain unmoved by such a plea and, with 'eager look', O'Leary led Maud to a sofa where she promptly began to tell him of herself and her desire to help free Ireland. O'Leary was quick to see the propaganda value of this fashionable young woman, urging her to read all the books he would lend her on Irish history and literature, so that she could then begin to lecture. Maud had no worries that she might be out of her depth, 'he soon found out ... that I was not intellectual, but I was young and he was hopeful', she blithely stated. It was the beginning of a deep and enduring friendship, despite the various political differences they would later have.

The discussion on this, Maud's first evening of Irish politics, centred around the Land League. Not realising that O'Leary himself was a small-scale landlord with property in Tipperary, she was surprised at his opposition to agrarian agitation. As the argument rolled backward and forward, all participants thoroughly enjoying themselves, Maud plucked up the courage to ask O'Leary his opinion on the Ladies' Land League, disbanded by Parnell only six years ago, and was told 'They may not have been right, but they were suppressed because they were honester and more sincere than the men.' The Ladies' Land

League had been relentless opponents of landlordism and any form of compromise with the government and so, in order to begin the process by which the Irish Party and the Liberals could develop their 'Union of Hearts', thereby pushing through Parliament a bill for Home Rule, Parnell ruthlessly got rid of the women. He and the other leaders ensured that women would not be allowed to become members of the National League which was then set up to replace the now-defunct Land League. This was to be 'an open organisation in which the ladies would not take part', as the announcement of its inauguration firmly stated. Maud was soon to discover the consequences of this enforced exclusion.

Miss Beresford, matron of the City of Dublin Hospital, was teaching Maud the basics of nursing. They were in total agreement that all women should understand nursing, although possibly in less agreement on the cause to which this skill might in future be placed. Ida and Maud decided to organise an all-Irish concert in aid of the hospital, with 'Let Erin Remember' replacing 'God Save the Queen' as the finale. Maud was to recite, making use of her dramatic training, while her friend possessed a beautiful singing voice. Charles Oldham lent them his rooms for the occasion and the packed audience included Contemporary Club members along with Maud's old Dublin friends, delighted to welcome Tommy's daughter. It was a successful evening but the omission of the anthem was predictably controversial leading, Maud claimed, to letters of protest in the *Irish Times*. It was her final act of resignation from her background and tradition. It was obviously unsuitable to continue as a guest of the Jamesons, so Maud took up temporary residence in the Gresham Hotel in Dublin's main thorough-fare. For a short while she endured the uncongenial atmosphere of priests and men from the country talking loudly and drinking too much, while fending off the advances of waiters and chambermaids whom she feared were spying on her. As it turns out, this suspicion was not without foundation. The first police report on Maud (dated August 1890) gives a vivid, if jaundiced, picture of her life at this time. The superintendent reported that she possessed a 'large share of histrionic ability', that she associated with 'a lady named Jameson . . . an advanced Nationalist', that she had taken 'rifle practice' and had given suppers 'regardless of expense'.[3] Maud's income allowed her to build up quickly a circle of acquaintances; how much easier it was to meet people if you could afford to offer hospitality. The curious came to see this unusual, exotic newcomer to the political scene. Some did little except add to the gossip about Maud, but others returned for more evenings of conversation and argument, drawn irresistibly by her freshness and her desire to learn and to contribute to her adopted cause.

Close by the National Library in Nassau Street, Maud found a flat over Morrow's bookshop. The sparsely furnished rooms with their faded carpets and none too comfortable armchairs were given an artistic touch with the addition of a low couch, coloured cushions and tall vases for green branches. As Maud's circle expanded, her friends began to call in after the library closed. Late hours were the norm in those carefree days; her visitors 'went home with the milk', she said. Many famous poems and plays were first read in those rooms, where Douglas Hyde, founder of the Gaelic League and later to be first president of Ireland, unsuccessfully attempted to teach the Irish language to Maud. She blithely declared herself to be too busy 'trying to spread revolutionary thoughts and acts to sit down to the arduous task of learning a language', but Hyde simply enjoyed being in her company, confessing to his diary 'My head was spinning with her beauty!!'[4] The meetings did not continue for long. That cool observer, Katharine Tynan, watching as Maud stunned all males she came into contact with, described how they 'were flustered by her beauty and grace. But they soon got over it. . . . Her aloofness must have chilled the most ardent lover.'[5] She thought the reason for this aloofness was Maud's passion for Ireland which led her to treat people as little more than 'pawns in the revolutionary game'. No one at this time knew of the existence of Millevoye or that Maud's lack of interest in any romantic involvement was because she was already enmeshed in a passionate alliance. Despite her appearance, Maud was not spontaneously sensual. But if she had indulged in the occasional harmless flirtation, public opinion might have been more sympathetic: she would then have been behaving as a normal young woman rather than some kind of goddess. The gossips were waiting for any opportunity to unleash their tongues.

After her triumphant evening of Irish poetry and song, Maud declared herself to have been inundated with requests to recite at literary societies. She was so pleased with the activities of the Celtic Literary Society, where she had recited the poetry of Thomas Davis, that she enthusiastically exclaimed to its secretary she wanted to become a member. A very embarrassed man called over Willie Rooney, one of the society's founders, to explain, as politely as he could, that club rules excluded women from membership. She had the presence of mind to retort laughingly that she would have to start a women's society and get all their sisters and sweethearts to join, predicting that 'they would have to look to their laurels then'. Her prediction came true: the poet Padraic Colum was to remark that it sometimes seemed as though the Celtic Literary Society was only an adjunct to the women, but that moment was many years away.[6]

For the time being, Maud was determined to continue her quest for acceptance into the heart of the Irish nationalist movement. Literary evenings and discussions were all very well, but Maud was, as she said of herself, 'young and hasty [and] felt action not books was needed'. So, as she romantically described her work in these early years, she 'drifted off to speak at other meetings held on wild hillsides, where resistance to evictions was being organised'.[7] It was not, however, quite so easy as that.

The offices of the National League were almost opposite the Gresham Hotel so one day Maud called in and informed the clerk in the outer office that she wished to subscribe and become a member.[8] First ushering Maud into the League's large meeting room, the surprised man called the secretary of the League to come out and deal with the young lady. Once again Maud was to tell an embarrassed man that she was ready to do any work suggested, and once again she was to be told that women could not join. This time Maud loftily replied 'Surely Ireland needs all her children.' She was slowly coming to the realisation that 'there was no place for women in the National movement'. However, an offer of help from such an unusual young woman, who could give the flagging movement much-needed publicity, was too good an opportunity for seasoned politicians to ignore. Views on the general desirability or otherwise of women in political life could be put to one side when the occasion demanded. The next day Tim Harrington MP, head of the National League and architect of its strategy the Plan of Campaign (by which tenants offered reduced rents to landlords and if refused, withheld their rents entirely, placing them in a collective emergency fund to help the evicted), called to see Maud. The Plan of Campaign had been running for two years but never had the full support of the parliamentary party. Agricultural depression had hit it badly, funds were low and morale even lower. Evictions were threatened in Donegal and Harrington, aware of the publicity value of Maud's presence, wanted her to attend and draw attention to what was happening. She would have a letter of introduction to the Bishop of Raphoe and a list of hotels to stay in, but he warned her that travelling and conditions would be rough. Maud was only too delighted to be entrusted with such work, but she was not going to accept this offer without voicing her dissatisfaction at the way women were treated by the nationalist movement. She reminded Harrington and his two companions of the 'splendid' work of the Ladies' Land League. Pat O'Brien agreed that they were great women who 'kept things lively' while the male leaders were all in gaol, but Harrington replied in bitter tones that 'they did too good work, and some of us found they could not be controlled'. Sensitive to his tone, Maud asked whether he disapproved of women in politics and half-jestingly he replied that their place was in the home but she was not to worry as they would find plenty of work for her. Maud was not satisfied with this concession, continuing to argue, but to little effect, that women should not be excluded from the national fight, forced to work through 'back-door influence' if they wanted to get things done. Once she began fighting evictions she soon realised that she was 'only working as a freelance', but for the moment at least, that was more than any other woman was able to do and she had the consolation of knowing that her presence did have an effect.

As soon as Harrington and the other MPs had left, Maud sent her cousin May a telegram, suggesting that she join her on a riding tour around Donegal. May was taking a holiday after passing a nursing examination and was keen to have an adventure with Maud. Accompanied by Dagda, the faithful Great Dane, the two set out for Donegal. At Letterkenny they spent the night at the home of the Bishop of Raphoe, whom Maud thought 'strikingly handsome', regretful that his politics were not as dashing as his looks. He was entertaining a number of priests, as a diocesan conference had just ended. Maud and May, 'two young heretics', learned a lot from the discussion around the dinner table. Some priests encouraged the resistance of their parishioners, a Father McFadden of Gweedore had only just been released from gaol and there were others like him, but in the presence of their bishop, conversation was discreet. Maud wanted to say that landlords should be shot, but in such 'august company' dared not voice her thought, feeling a coward for her silence. It was a useful evening and they were given a list of places to visit, with names of hotels and farmhouses for accommodation. The clerics were obviously concerned for the well-being of two young ladies travelling in such inhospitable conditions.

As they passed the huge mound of Muckish the following day, Maud tried to imagine the mountain of the pig as a benign, protecting figure, but it was difficult. It was coming on to winter and a cruel wind was blowing; as they reached the sea the rain began to fall. They had to slow their pace for poor Dagda, whose paws were cut to pieces by the sharp stones. Later, Maud got a cobbler in Sligo to make him boots to wear on their long journeys together, but on this occasion she said she was so cold she could hardly walk or speak by the time Father Kelly, the parish priest of Dunfanaghy, had helped her off her horse. Father Kelly turned out to be a supporter of the Fenians and a believer in the right to take up arms to fight oppression, although he had lost all hope of Ireland achieving its freedom in his lifetime. Maud agreed on the need for physical force to fight eviction: no other option was left to the people – stones and boiling water being no match for the guns of the bailiffs. Another priest took her to a court session where six mountainy men and boys were being tried for stealing turf from land belonging to Colonel Olpherts. The previous week the court had sentenced men who had gathered seaweed for manure. At the back of the room young Father Stephens bitterly whispered his feelings to Maud, 'there is nothing free in Ireland but the air', and the turf cutters were sentenced to a fine of 10s or one month's imprisonment. British justice meant that the proceedings were conducted in English, the plaintiffs speaking only Irish, relying on a policeman to translate for them. Maud had seen enough, she promised to return when the evictions began.

The days when the Land League was a mass fighting force had gone. The parliamentary road to freedom was now in the ascendant and the people were left to face their landlords alone. In the Falcarragh area of Donegal, Colonel Olpherts had served eviction notices on one hundred and fifty houses. He had twenty Emergency Men (a force recruited and paid by the landlord to help with evictions) to enforce the evictions with a battering ram if necessary, and he was determined that the whole miserable, barbaric proceedings would be over and done with inside a week. All the people could do was to delay matters as long as they could, to offer comfort to those made homeless and, if possible, build them some form of shelter. Maud threw herself into this work, knowing that she could at least ameliorate the situation. Journalists were enticed over, publicity obtained, energetic letters written to newspapers, the sick looked after in her little hotel bedroom and rooms rented in her name to shelter those with nowhere to go. People were terrified of taking in those evicted, for fear that Olpherts would next turn on them. She went to Dublin to persuade Pat O'Brien to come to Donegal and revive the practice of building Land League huts for the homeless. Pat had been dubbed 'little Pat the builder' because of his work in the past, and he now revived his talents. For some, the huts were better than the cabins they had lived in before and they were certainly a preferable alternative to the workhouse. Resistance meant that the process was delayed so long it became a lengthy business and for Olpherts, who had to house and feed his Emergency Men, an expensive one. But all the enthusiasm in the world could not ultimately defeat the forces that caused evictions to occur. Maud's hatred of the landlord class and her contempt for constitutional, parliamentary politics was to endure for the rest of her life, so deep-rooted were the images of desolation and utter misery witnessed by her that winter in Donegal.

She was to return to Falcarragh, but there were other aspects of her life that also had to be attended to. Millevoye was waiting in France, she was eager to tell him of her exploits, and also, while passing through London en route to Paris, there were other contacts to be made. Ellen O'Leary, the gentle sister of John, had been an organiser for the Fenians in the 1860s; now her life was devoted to the care of her brother. Maud held her in high esteem, encouraging the retiring Ellen to publish her poetry and eventually, after Ellen's premature death, getting the poems published posthumously. But at this time it was Ellen who was in a position to give assistance to Maud, writing to tell W.B. Yeats that she had given 'a new lady friend of ours and new convert to love of Ireland', a letter of introduction to his father. Ellen was sure that Maud, 'so charming, fine and handsome' would not fail to be admired by the Yeats family as she already was by the male friends of the O'Learys.[9] Two weeks later, on 30 January 1889, while passing through London Maud called at the Yeats family home in Bedford Park. The 'troubling' of Willie's life had begun.

This first meeting, so momentous for Willie and for literature generally, was much less so for Maud who always wrongly maintained that they had first met in Dublin. While she vexed John Butler Yeats by her enthusiastic praise for the merits of war, Willie annoyed his father even more by supporting this 'goddess', confessing in his memoirs that 'a man young as I could not have differed from a woman so beautiful and so young'.[10] His sisters were much less impressed with their exotic visitor. Lily hated her 'sort of royal smile' and noticed that for all her airs 'she was in her slippers'.[11] It is possible they felt excluded and patronised by someone so impatient to further her cherished ideals and so eager to gather around her any possible ally that she overlooked those who sat silently listening, not sharing the same enthusiasm. Younger sisters often suffer this experience, observing situations with merciless attention to detail. If their pride had been less hurt, perhaps they would have found Maud's obvious carelessness in dress, despite her Paris gown, to be an endearing disregard for appearance rather than evidence of some lofty intellectualism?

Willie dined with Maud that evening and each evening for the rest of her stay in London. He rapidly became infected by the excitement and bustle that characterised Maud's life. Constantly moving between Ireland, England and France, planning activities and making friends, she and her ever-present companions of caged singing birds, pet monkey and Great Dane struck Yeats like a 'Burmese gong, an overpowering tumult', the resonances of which were to last for the rest of his life.[12] For the next forty years, the poet was to immortalise his unrequited love – 'that monstrous thing' – in all its guises. We are given endless portraits of Maud, at first a 'glimmering girl' with a 'pilgrim soul', while later we see her 'high and solitary and most stern' beauty. One phrase is particularly evocative and its truth can be seen in her portraits and read of in all the eye-witness accounts, 'that proud look as though she had gazed into the burning sun'. All those poems were in the future, but Maud was aware of Willie's literary gifts – he was already the author of *The Wanderings of Oisin and Other Poems*, amongst other works – and, ever-quick to seize an opportunity, told him of her desire for a play that she could act in in Dublin. He promptly offered to write *The Countess Cathleen* for her.

All too soon, the whirlwind was gone and Willie was left to write to the O'Learys of the impression she had made upon him; 'If she said the world was flat – I would be proud to be of her party.'[13] He sounded dazed, but in writing to the poet Katharine Tynan he was on the defensive, indignantly denying rumours that he had 'taken up' with Miss Gonne. He tartly replied that 'I think she is very goodlooking and that is all I think about her', and then went on to agree with the politically conservative Katharine that Maud was rather too fond of sensation.[14] At that time he was wondering whether or not he and Katharine should be in love with each other and therefore possibly showing some discretion about his current feelings. For her part, Katharine made her views on Maud's lifestyle quite plain, 'No woman who was not very emancipated drove on an outside car unaccompanied by a male escort. Miss Gonne drove on a car quite alone, with only her bulldog for escort.'[15]

Maud was back in Paris with Millevoye. Here too was excitement. General Boulanger had been victorious in the Paris by-election of January and his followers were urging him to march on the Elysée Palace to seize power. But the brave general hesitated and all their hopes ended in comic-opera fashion as he fled the country after being threatened with arrest. The final ignominious climax came two years later when Boulanger committed suicide over the grave of his mistress. He was not the Napoleon they had hoped for, but Maud and Millevoye's personal and political alliance continued to flourish. That autumn Millevoye was elected to the Chamber of Deputies and the following year, on 11 January 1890, their son George was born.[16]

Coincidentally, the O'Shea divorce scandal had broken in December, and as the facts concerning Parnell's love affair with Katharine O'Shea hit the headlines the Irish Parliamentary Party split into two, while Irish political life was ripped apart into the bitterest of factions. Families and friendships disintegrated as politicians and bishops took their sides in the dispute. More than ever, Maud must have been reminded of the necessity of keeping her private life well hidden in France. In October, while six months pregnant, she had travelled back to London to nurse her sister Kathleen, who was very ill with 'congestion of the liver', as Maud explained in a letter to John O'Leary, apologising for her slowness in expressing her sympathies over the death of his sister Ellen.[17] Significantly, she had not notified Willie of her presence in London – possibly because her time was preoccupied with Kathleen, but also very probably because she would by then have been highly conscious of her pregnancy and the difficulties of concealment. Hearing by chance that Maud was in London, Willie rushed off at once, seeing her for a mere five minutes before she set out for Paris once more. It wasn't long enough for him to register any significant changes in his beloved.[18]

The birth of her son did not deter Maud from continuing her political work in Ireland. As someone used to nurses and nannies in her own childhood, she continued the tradition by leaving the baby in Paris when he was a few months old. She could never have settled to a purely domestic life, but nor could she vent her political energies exclusively in France. She could get support for the Irish cause in France certainly, when she lectured to audiences and drew tears with the emotional power of her oratory, but for that to be effective, it had to come from the heart; and that meant being there, seeing at first hand the hunger and the evictions. Whether or not Maud wanted to, she could not bring her son to Ireland. To a certain extent, she was able to rationalise this neglect through a conviction that her political work was of greater importance because its success would result in the happiness of so many more children. In later years she explained her emotions of the time in this unconsciously revealing sentence:

> To me Ireland was the all-protecting mother, who had to be released from the bondage of the foreigner, to be free and able to protect her children.[19]

Back in Donegal, Maud learned that she was becoming a legend – the woman of the Sidhe who rode into Donegal on a white horse surrounded by birds, to bring victory to the people. It was a lot to live up to in this, one of the poorest and most remote of counties. The Plan of Campaign was slowly running out of steam. By 1890, 84 of the 116 estates affected by the Plan had reached agreement with the landlord and the struggle continued on only 18 others. Because Colonel Olpherts owned almost the whole of the land around Falcarragh, a major difficulty was finding land on which to build the Land League huts. The only real hope lay in mobilising influential support against the barbarity of eviction and for that task Maud was uniquely suited. Not only was she beautiful and capable of attracting those who would normally be impervious to the plight of the destitute, but she also had contacts amongst those with direct access to power. Maud, however, was not interested in begging the English for reform of an iniquitous system; her political views were never complex, centring always upon the fundamental issue of removing the British presence that was the basic root cause of the problem. For that reason she detested the English sympathisers who packed into Falcarragh and Gweedore, finding it difficult to be civil to those 'sincere, good, worthy people' whom she sarcastically described as insisting that 'England must undo her wrongs and make you all love us'. Her scornful rejoinder was to hope this would mean clearing out of Ireland. On the one occasion that Maud managed to get out of bed earlier than the sightseers she found herself looking 'wonderingly at the big serviceable boots of the English ladies outside their bedroom doors'. She also remarked that the concerned ladies were anxious about her health, fussing over the unsuitability of her light shoes. Whatever the circumstance, Maud retained her fashionable clothes.

In one bizarre scene, as Maud and her co-workers visited a family threatened by eviction, she was astounded to see, unrolling himself from a fur rug, an elderly Liberal MP whom she discreetly referred to only as 'Sir John'. While in London she had informed him that she 'could never look at an Englishman without seeing prison-bars' and he had now followed her to renew his plea that she become his wife, gaining political influence by presiding over what would become a great Liberal salon in London. When he then handed over a large diamond pendant her amusement faded. She had been told that she was 'wasting her time on the bogs' and now she was to be bribed with jewels. Her political integrity insulted, Maud angrily handed the pendant to the woman of the house, saying that the 'kind gentleman' had brought it to help her and so that she could also shelter others. A furious Sir John, before returning to Dublin the following day, retrieved his bauble for the exact sum of money owed. A calculated meanness typical of the English they all agreed.

This farcical encounter helped to bolster Maud's image as a mythical goddess who could conjure diamonds from nowhere. It also emphasised the distance that now existed between Maud's background and the path she had chosen. It wasn't glamorous work, traipsing the wilds in winds so severe she found it almost impossible to breathe, accepting hospitality in small, smoky cabins whose ragged inhabitants often spoke no English and whose possessions were minimal. Her nights were spent in a tiny bedroom, sitting upright, fighting against suffocation and coughing up streaks of blood. The danger of arrest was also real. Several of the Irish Party MPs who supported the Campaign were serving gaol sentences and the Conservative government had determined to make prison conditions so severe that protest would soon end. But Maud's break with her past was irrevocable. It was not enough to beg for favours; Ireland could only be freed through her own efforts and that included the activities of the ordinary people, those of no property.

> If there be rags enough he will know her name
> And be well pleased remembering it, for in the old days,
> Though she had young men's praise and old men's blame,
> Among the poor both old and young gave her praise.

('Her Praise')

No sooner had one suitor been dispatched than news came of another. The mail car brought Maud a letter from Millevoye who was in Dunfanaghy hotel, where he had fallen ill while on his way to discover why Maud was in that 'wild country' neglecting their alliance. Maud was annoyed, not liking anyone, even a 'great friend' to follow her without consultation. Lucien, alone, sick and unable to communicate with the locals, obviously needed her and so she spent the next week nursing her lover, who had a narrow escape from pneumonia. But they quarrelled seriously as he dismissed her working in obscurity on such a 'side issue' instead of doing valuable propaganda work against the British Empire. Maud 'thought of the hopeless families sheltering in the bare mountains, of the joy of reinstating them in their houses' and could think of nothing else. Millevoye returned alone to France. Baby George, in Maud's account at least, was never mentioned. But Millevoye's uncharacteristic pursuit must have at least been partly connected to the fact that they were now parents, and Maud had been away for some time.

At the end of June 1890, Maud was persuaded by Tim Harrington to take a break from fighting evictions in order to campaign against the government at a by-election in Barrow-in-Furness. Her autobiography recounts how she made her first political speech, to an audience of 1,500. It was very emotional, recalling the scenes of destitution she had so recently left:

> I told of the old couple driven out of the house they had built fifty years ago; of the woman with her one-day-old baby left on the roadside, of the little children trying in vain to kindle a fire in the rain; of the desolation of the overcrowded workhouse and the separated families.[20]

It is a vivid picture and one can easily imagine Maud drawing it. But was she so pivotal to the election result, with Conservative newspapers 'trying to palliate the political significance of the defeat, [having] headlines about the election being won by the beauty of a woman', as Maud claimed of her success?

The Times appears to have ignored Maud, although the *Barrow Herald* for 1 July praised her as a 'lady orator' and 'enthusiast'.[21] In actual fact, the by-election had been caused by the resignation of Caine, the sitting MP, in protest at sections of a proposed local taxation bill which he believed would give undue benefit to the licensing trade. Caine stood for re-election as an Independent Liberal while another man was accepted as the Gladstonian Liberal candidate. Both were favoured by the temperance lobby, so neither had an advantage on that score: the crucial difference was that Duncan, the Gladstonian Liberal, was a home ruler and Caine was a liberal unionist who refused to make his views on Home Rule plain, even when heavily pressed during the election campaign. Caine and Wainwright, the Conservative candidate, were defeated by Duncan and it can certainly be said that the 'Irish Question' was a crucial factor (prominent Irish Party MPs spoke in support of Duncan), but in Maud's account the Liberals did not stand and the Irish Party demonstrated their independence of their erstwhile allies through supporting their own candidate.[22] The significance of this deliberate gloss on events is either an indication that Maud was rather naïve about political realities in her early years as an activist or alternatively, and far more likely as an explanation, that in her later years she was so concerned to demonstrate her consistency in opposing any alliances with British politicians that she was prepared to reinterpret events in order to achieve this.

Maud's work in Donegal came to an abrupt end when Pat O'Brien arrived in Falcarragh with news that a warrant was out for her arrest. She agreed to leave for France because in her state of health she 'knew that jail would be the end of everything and before I died I wanted to get the prisoners released, I wanted to see Millevoye and I wanted to begin the fight against the British Empire in international affairs'. It was an ambitious programme which coincidentally combined the personal with the political. As dramatic as ever, Maud depicted herself as a political exile, forced to recuperate in the south of France and unable to return to Ireland until the Conservative government was out of power. She was not to be in Donegal again until the War of Independence, two decades later, when she helped the White Cross to organise the feeding of school children.

Maud and Millevoye stayed in St Raphael until Maud felt herself strong enough to continue her work. She then returned to Paris. When the Conservative government lost the election, Pat O'Brien wrote to say that the warrant for her arrest was cancelled and Maud at last felt free to go back. She still retained her Paris flat, presumably as a home for George. Maud's own chronology, as recalled in *A Servant of the Queen*, is again inconsistent. Although the Liberals were not returned to power until 1892, Maud did not remain in exile for the next two years but was back in Ireland the following summer. A carelessness about dates was not the only reason for her doubtful chronology – 1891 was to be a very unhappy year for Maud, an unhappiness so profound and so unable to be spoken of publicly that its only expression lay symbolically with the death of Parnell in October – which was one of the few events of that year to be mentioned by her.

The sojourn in St Raphael had not been idyllic. General Boulanger was no longer the expected saviour of right-wing French people obsessed with the return of their lost territory of Alsace-Lorraine, but his followers were still plotting. A visit by Paul Déroulède, a leader of the League of Patriots, who was quite prepared to enter into an alliance with Britain if it would further his aims, made Maud realise that her alliance with Millevoye could easily be threatened by other political interests. Soon after that visit she decided she was cured and could return to Paris to resume her work. In her heart, she knew Millevoye was unworthy of her. He had already attempted to persuade her to become the mistress of a man who could help his political projects and she found herself repelled by the sexual act, but at the same time deeply in love. She couldn't refuse her lover, but she could lessen their intimacies by leaving Paris as frequently as possible. It was a cruel and ironic situation for a woman of such physical beauty and such an outwardly unconventional manner. Defying convention could be a very lonely affair.

In July, Willie Yeats heard that Maud was in Dublin. As he waited in her rooms in Nassau Street he found himself overcome with pity when she came through the door, her great height filling the frame.

This was not the vibrant, impulsive woman he remembered, 'she did not seem to have any beauty, her face was wasted, the form of her bones showing, and there was no life in her manner'. As they talked, Maud hinted at unhappiness and disillusionment. The 'old hard resonance' had disappeared, leaving a woman 'gentle and indolent' and Yeats found himself more in love than ever, particularly since now the object of devotion more accorded to his ideal of womanhood: she was in need of protection and peace.[23] But Willie was still in enough control of himself to continue with his own plans and the following day he left Dublin to stay with old friends in County Down. A letter from Maud a week later, hinting at her sadness and recounting a dream of their having been brother and sister sold into slavery during a past life, had the desired effect. Willie returned to Dublin at once and asked her to marry him. She replied she could not marry and would never marry, although she could not explain the reasons, but she needed his friendship. For the next few weeks their relationship assumed a pattern that would recur: when Maud required emotional support her dear friend, the deeply in love but unrequited Willie, would be there. It was a time of tranquillity for them both, and they were obviously happy together. They visited Maud's old nurse in Howth, whom Willie overheard whispering to her former charge to ask if they were engaged to be married. He read out his yet unfinished The Countess Cathleen and noticed how moved Maud became at the passage 'the joy of losing joy, of ceasing all resistance'.[24]

At that time Maud was obviously greatly reliant on Willie for emotional support. She seemed to have abandoned her old independence to the extent that poor Willie, who was always in debt, found that after their visit to Howth he had spent ten shillings, which seemed to him 'a very great sum'.[25] Yet normally Maud would always insist on paying her share – as Yeats assured John O'Leary when asking him for a loan of money before one of Maud's visits to London.[26] Fearing arrest if she undertook any political activity and appearing to lack the will to seek any other outlet for her energies, Maud was having time to think. The excitement and bustle of her normal routine left little time for reflection. In one of her rare moments of introspection, Maud admitted that at a difficult period in her life she 'redoubled work to avoid thought' and perhaps that was one of the reasons why she always appeared to crave action. She was very impatient with the introspection of Willie, declaring proudly that she 'never indulged in self-analysis'.[27] The poet, so intuitive concerning Maud's inner life, felt from their first meeting that she possessed 'a mind without peace'. Now the person behind that mind was being forced to assess her life and its direction.

Willie was not the only one to feel Maud's beauty was incompatible with 'private, intimate life'. For those to whom she appeared as a larger than life mythical creature, the possession of a messy and intricate personal life was simply not possible. How much she confided to her sister at this stage is unclear, but Kathleen was now married to Captain Pilcher, whom Maud disliked, and opportunities for confidences between the sisters were limited. In later years Maud wrote to Kathleen that she hadn't told of her troubles because she 'preferred to be envied rather than pitied'.[28] Maud herself wanted to live up to her image. Her loneliness must have been crippling.

The worst blow of all was yet to come. Maud was suddenly called back to France, telling Willie an improbable story of being summonsed by a secret political society she had joined and whom she could not disobey. In reality, little George was dying of meningitis and the call to return was from Millevoye. George died on 31 August, plunging Maud into a frenzy of the bitterest grief. She forgot how to speak French, her second language, and slept only when heavily dosed with chloroform, an addiction she eventually overcame after a hard struggle. Almost forgetting her self-imposed discretion, she wrote to Willie of the death of her 'adopted' child, an incoherent letter of wild sorrow, telling of death birds pecking at the nursery window. The little body was embalmed and a memorial chapel built but nothing could assuage either Maud's grief or her feelings of guilt and responsibility. For the rest of her life she was to wear black and on her deathbed she asked a friend to slip George's booties into her coffin before it was closed. Unknown to the other members of her family, she had carried them with her throughout the turbulent years she had yet to live.

Maud contemplated leaving Millevoye and in October she returned to Ireland, to the ever-faithful Willie, waiting for her at the pier at Kingstown harbour. By a cruel irony, the ship was also carrying home the body of Parnell, who had died in the arms of his wife Katharine on 6 October, and whose funeral was shortly to take place. National mourning and personal grief combined to produce a barely suppressed hysteria in Maud. As she and Willie breakfasted at her hotel, her extravagantly deep mourning was eyed with great disapproval; far too theatrical for the death of a politician was the obvious expression on people's faces, but Maud was oblivious, repeating over and over the details of the child's death, seeking comfort in speech and in Willie's belief in the occult. Alone, she went to Parnell's funeral (Willie hating such events), and as she stood by the graveside, in the rain and mud of Glasnevin, the shooting star that was witnessed by many, as the uncrowned king of Ireland was lowered into the ground, appeared to her as an omen, a sign of hope for her future. 'Life out of death, life out of death eternally', Maud wrote, seeming to prophesy a future for Irish nationalism despite the death of its leader, but she was really thinking of how to bring her dead son back to life.

Political activities were quite forgotten as Maud and Willie threw themselves into the study of the occult, conjuring up apparitions for themselves that told of past lives, developing cabalistic rituals to help explain why Maud's spirit was so troubled, why she always desired power and excitement, and initiating Maud into the Order of the Golden Dawn which was so dear to Willie's heart. At a meeting with the poet and mystic George Russell (AE), the talk came round to reincarnation and Maud asked how soon a child could be reborn, and if reborn, where. Russell's reply that it could be reborn into the same family affected her deeply, although Willie, with a pang of conscience, kept his doubts to himself.[29] Maud's encounter with prominent spiritualists in London, where she and Willie had travelled so that Maud could be properly initiated, had its comic aspect. She liked Madame Blavatsky but found the other Theosophists a 'nondescript gathering', while the Golden Dawn members seemed to her to be 'the very essence of British middle-class dullness', their cloaks and badges incongruous with their drab appearance. Although Maud passed four initiations and learned a number of Hebrew words, this was not what she was looking for. Discovering a Golden Dawn password to be identical to that of the Freemasons gave her the excuse she needed to resign. Maud was also realistic enough to know that all this was a diversion from her true interests and that she was in danger of frittering away her abilities, thereby achieving little. However, her belief in the supernatural remained with her throughout her life, and she and Willie often made attempts, of varying success, to meet each other on the astral plane.

Willie was also astute enough to realise that if he wanted to keep Maud by his side he would have to offer her something more than simply his own great desire of their living lives 'devoted to mystic truth'. He knew that Maud's life would not continue in this vein, that her old energy and zest would return, but he was also resolved that this time they would work together.

CHAPTER 3

IRELAND'S JOAN OF ARC

The rancour and bitterness that followed the Parnellite split was a disillusioning experience for many Irish people. It was a common feeling that politics was a distasteful business, best left to those who didn't mind harsh words and public enmities. Yeats believed that young people would now be more interested in 'some unpolitical form for national feeling' and he hoped that this could be developed into a cultural revival.[1] His ambitious plans included organising literary societies in London and Dublin, publishing Irish books, and founding circulating libraries in country towns so that the scattered rural population would have access to such works. His motivation, as he later admitted, included both patriotism and desire for a 'fair woman'. The woman in question was in London, staying with her sister Kathleen at Hans Place, where their cousin May had also made her home. May hinted to Willie that she and Maud had been discussing him as they read his love poems in the vellum-bound manuscript book which had been his gift to Maud.[2] Although Maud was about to be initiated into the Golden Dawn, Willie now confided to her his other ambition: his plans for a literary revival and her starring role as 'the fiery hand of the intellectual movement', working to found branches throughout Ireland.[3] Maud agreed to join the scheme, although one feels it was largely to please her friend, rather than from any heartfelt enthusiasm. Significantly, she failed to mention any of these discussions in her memoirs, while Willie dwelt at length upon his hopes; another example of their widely differing feelings and priorities.

At the beginning of November, Maud was due to go to Paris for a short period of around ten days, returning briefly to London before continuing on to Dublin. Willie was forced to remain in London, to try to make some money through his writing – a necessity completely neglected when Maud was around. When they were apart he spent half his time either writing to her, or writing about her to others. To AE he now begged 'Go and see her when she gets to Dublin and keep her from forgetting me and occultism'.[4] He urged John O'Leary to encourage her to work for the Young Ireland League because she needed 'some work of that kind in which she could lose herself'.[5]

Maud was later to admit to Willie that he had saved her from despair, but despite all his efforts, she did not immediately devote herself to his cherished project. Her old energy was slowly returning, as were her own political preoccupations. She wanted to work for the evicted tenants and those imprisoned as a result of their activities in the agrarian struggle. A friend in France, seeing Maud's unhappiness, had suggested that she organise a series of lectures on their plight, collecting funds for the evicted at the same time, so Maud returned to London to prepare those lectures.[6] Despite impressions to the contrary, her oratory was based on facts, not empty rhetoric.

She does not appear to have gone to Dublin as planned, because in the spring of 1892 she embarked on a lecture tour of France, beginning at Cercle des Luxembourg and continuing on to Valenciennes, Arras, Rouen, Bordeaux, Cognac, Périgueux and La Rochelle. Maud was on the threshold of widespread popular acclaim. The wall of silence that Britain had built up around Ireland was torn down as not only France, but also the rest of Europe, began to learn the truth about Ireland's struggle for independence. Millevoye's contacts were invaluable as in that year alone it was calculated 2,000 articles about Maud's speeches were published in the French press.[7] In Ireland, Willie was busy ensuring that the nationalist press also gave Maud maximum coverage. In looking back over this period, he realised that

> a mastery over popular feeling, abandoned by the members of Parliament through a quarrel that was to last for nine years, was about to pass into her hands. . . . Her oratory, by its emotional temper, was an appeal to herself and also to something uncontrollable, something that could never be co-ordinated.[8]

Standing in front of her audience Maud was the embodiment of the 'Celtic Druidess . . . her great black eyes full of flame'.[9] Her description of the Great Famine of 1847 left her audience in tears; it was no wonder that they felt provoked to violence against Britain:

> Ireland was heroic in her suffering. Whole families, when they had eaten their last crust and understood that they had to die, looked once upon the sun and then closed up the doors of their cabins with stones, that none might look on their death agony. . . . If you come to my country, every stone will repeat to you this tragic history. . . . I have been told it by women who have heard the last sigh of their children without being able to relieve their agony with one drop of milk. It has seemed to me at evening, on those mountains of Ireland, so full of savage majesty, when the winds sighed over the pits of the famine, where thousands of dead enrich the harvests of the future – it has

seemed to me that I heard an avenging voice calling down on our oppressors the execration of men and the justice of God.[10]

As if to make up for her previous indolence, Maud now threw herself into a frenzy of activity. She said of this period of her life that 'it was one of ceaseless activity and travelling. I rarely spent a month in the same place'.[11] When she began to campaign for those gaoled because of their fight for their land she learned of the existence of another group — the Treason-Felony prisoners. The law defining 'treason-felony' had been deliberately devised with the Irish in mind. It meant that those who might have been charged with sedition could instead be convicted as felons: not political prisoners but criminals. The Fenians in the 1860s had been convicted under the Act and the next wave of Irish prisoners, in the period 1881–1888, were imprisoned as a result of an ill-fated dynamite campaign. They were the forgotten men of Irish politics. Physical force was a discredited tactic; innocent people had been killed and the Irish Party refused to speak on their behalf, for fear of jeopardising Home Rule through association with them. But the prisoners were held in horrific conditions; many of their relatives could not afford to travel to England to visit them, and several were known to have gone insane as a result of their experiences.

The cause of the treason-felony prisoners was one which Maud was to be closely associated with. Willie Yeats used his political contacts to help her gain access to those working for the prisoners. They attended a meeting of the Amnesty Association, set up in 1892, whose chairman, Dr Mark Ryan, welcomed Maud's interest in the prisoners. He advised her to attempt to obtain a visit so that she could see the conditions for herself. With 'some help and a little diplomacy' (which included purloining Uncle William's crested notepaper and the use of 'Edith', one of her other names), Maud was granted a permit to visit eight of the prisoners in Portland gaol. No date was given (although the account in her memoirs is placed early in her career), but from all the evidence she presents, the visit must have taken place around 1893–4. The prison made a huge impression on her, one she never forgot, as she watched gangs of convicts chained like beasts to great carts of stones they had hacked out from the quarries. In typical Maud fashion, she described how the pity she felt for those gaunt, suspicious, desperate men, some of whom had had no outside contact in ten years, gave her a vision of the future:

A strange thing happened, which I have never been able to explain. Like one in a dream, I rose and told O'Callaghan, who had lost an eye in prison and who was clinging to the iron bars of the cage while the warder tried to prevent him telling the circumstances, to say no more, for I knew all he could tell me. I begged him to endure a little longer, and promised that he should be free in less than six months. I was still in the same dream when the next prisoner came in; I told him that he would be free in eighteen months, and to the next I said that he would be released in a year.[12]

The men, she said, were released in the order and in the time that she had foretold. No one can deny Maud's lifelong concern for the welfare of prisoners and her untiring devotion to their cause. In a revealing remark Willie Yeats said her visits to prisoners moved her deeply, they 'brought to light the woman in her', but there is no evidence that Maud secured their release in the manner described.[13] Mercy was only shown in three cases, where the prisoner's medical condition was so grave as to constitute a risk of dying in prison, while all the others served close to the full term. Those driven insane were kept in gaol despite evidence that they should be released. Dr Gallagher, an American, had been degenerating mentally and physically for many years and when he was released in 1896, after serving thirteen years, spent the rest of his life in an insane asylum. In 1898 the last prisoner, Tom Clarke, was released. He had served fifteen years.[14]

Maud's dramatics do her an injustice. She did not single-handedly secure the men's release but she did tour the length of England and Scotland, speaking on their behalf for the Amnesty Association and helping to build that organisation into a powerful lobby. Her correspondence on the issue sometimes took up to eight hours a day and she forced the issue of their continued incarceration into the public arena and undoubtedly embarrassed politicians. Who knows, she may have hastened the date of their release. In 1899 Matthew McNamara, in presenting the final report of the Amnesty Association, paid tribute to Maud, whom he described as an 'ardent and zealous advocate in the cause of Irish freedom' who had 'turned her untiring energy and literary ability toward the efforts made for the release of her countrymen'. Maud's intervention was certainly instrumental in enabling the Association to develop a much higher profile than had previously been the case.[15] Another tribute to her work came from John Daly, one of the treason-felony prisoners. On his release he was elected Mayor of Limerick and he ensured that the freedom of the city was conferred on his comrade, Tom Clarke, and on Maud, because of her work for their release. Tom later married John Daly's niece Kathleen and, ironically, Kathleen was later a cell mate of Maud's in Holloway prison.

In June 1892 Maud kept her promise to Willie, crossing to Dublin to attend a meeting of the Rotunda which was intended to explain to the existing Dublin societies and to possible new sympathisers, the aims and purposes of the National Literary Society. Dr Sigerson,

Count Plunkett, John O'Leary, Willie and Maud were amongst the speakers. She also arranged for William Ledwidge, a popular Irish singer, to perform at a concert she organised in aid of the society. Maud became one of the vice-presidents of the National Literary Society, a lengthy list which included Katharine Tynan as the only other woman. A subcommittee of five, including Yeats and O'Leary, was established 'to consult with Miss Gonne as to the best means of promoting her scheme of Reading Rooms and libraries'.[16] Strictly speaking, this idea had not originated with Maud as Willie had discussed similar plans with her over six months previously, but perhaps he wanted her to give public voice to the plans, hoping that if she were closely associated with them, her interest in the venture would be maintained. From the outset, Willie realised that her beauty and eloquence would have an electrifying effect in the dull little country towns and, a very practical consideration, she was one of the few who possessed sufficient money to be able to travel freely around Ireland. The proliferation of committees continued, as a library subcommittee with Willie as the secretary, O'Leary, Maud and Mary Hayden amongst its members, was appointed to consider the feasibility of establishing libraries throughout the country. Willie diligently went ahead with the task he was most interested in: the selecting of books that would educate the spirit and nurture a specifically Gaelic intellect. But he had to work without Maud, who returned to France in the autumn, still restlessly pursuing several different interests.

She was reunited with Millevoye, spending some time in Royat for her health's sake and then undertaking a series of lectures, mainly in Paris, on behalf of the evicted tenants. While in Royat Maud wrote frequently to Willie, who reported hopefully to O'Leary that she was writing 'in a more cordial spirit than she has done for a long time'.[17] He was eagerly awaiting her return to Ireland and the start of the long-promised lecture tour on behalf of the libraries scheme, but Maud's letters continued to postpone the arrival date. Her doctor would not hear of her return for the anniversary of Parnell's death, she informed O'Leary, placating both him and Willie by her questions on the progress of the scheme and by her assurances that she was busy writing to all her friends for donations of books.[18] She was not too ill to return to Paris at the beginning of November to initiate another of her schemes, this time attempting to promote the sale of Donegal tweed by persuading French fashion houses to purchase it. How successful this was is uncertain, although it showed enterprise and demonstrated how close to her thoughts the Donegal tenants still were. In the meantime, Yeats was fighting his battle over good literature versus patriotic rhetoric and Maud was not there to support him. One suspects that Millevoye was one of the reasons. He had praised her lecture tour as achieving far more for their alliance than anything she did in the obscurity of Ireland and he must have been applying the same pressures once again. Maud had to extricate herself from her French life if she was to return to fulfil her promises.

In early January Willie send Maud a fairly punishing schedule of proposed meetings that she was to speak at between 20 January and 25 February.[19] However, the *Cork Examiner* of 24 January reported that Maud had been unable to leave Paris, owing to illness. Maud later lectured at Loughrea and New Ross, but the other meetings were cancelled. Three of the seven libraries that had been planned did materialise in the wake of her appearance: three consignments containing one hundred volumes were sent to Loughrea, New Ross and Listowel and at the end of 1893 fifty books were sent to the Arklow reading room with other grants being made to societies in Ballygarret and Westport. Willie's report as secretary of the library subcommittee was greeted with disapproval, the Society feeling that the lack of proper records and absence of any minute book demonstrated a lack of order in the conduct of affairs. Willie himself attributed his troubles to some 'obscure young men' who overturned his projects and appropriated his books.[20] He retired, hurt and angry, and the project ended in disarray. To make matters worse, Maud refused to back him over the question of literary merit, happily confessing to a liking for patriotic sentiments regardless of their worth otherwise. Whether it furthered the national cause was her criterion, and over this they were always to differ. While Willie accused her of a lack of discrimination, she countered by declaring him to be a snob. They had a violent quarrel, accentuated by Willie's sexual frustrations and his perception that Maud did not understand the extent of his disappointment on the failure of his literary plans because she had never taken them as seriously as he had wished.

The quarrel with Maud was followed by her serious illness as a cold developed into congestion of the lungs. Dr Sigerson, who was attending her, would not admit Willie, with whom he had also quarrelled over the library scheme, to her bedside. The distraught poet was forced to rely for information on a most unsavoury woman, one of Maud's 'objects of charity', who had offered her services as nurse. This disreputable character, for unknown reasons, then proceeded to invent tales that further widened the breach between the pair. Willie had arranged to meet her at night, to hear news of Maud's condition. He was told he would never see his friend again as the woman invented a wild tale of Maud possessing numerous lovers who were forcing her to rush back to France in order to be present at a duel that was to be fought between them. She was undoubtedly deranged, venting her hatred for Maud by this fever of the imagination. One terrifying moment experienced by the sick woman was when she woke late one night to find those 'vague, moist' eyes looming over her face. She refused to go to the other side of the room when begged to, saying that Maud might die at any moment and she was waiting for the moment of death. Finally, May Gonne arrived to take charge of her cousin. Maud was obviously desperately keen to leave Dublin and all its unpleasant memories. She refused to listen to Dr Sigerson's protests and had herself carried to the train, too ill to walk. But the nurse had some success with her cruel rumours; one did the rounds, eventually finding its way to Willie: he had been Maud's lover, there had been an 'illegal operation' and he had been present at the operation.[21] Maud's unconventional lifestyle had obviously offended the conservative-minded inhabitants of the predominantly Catholic city. Who cared whether the tale was really true? It was comforting to believe that the free and easy had to face retribution for their sins.

Yeats was completely crushed, his dreams shattered. He went to Sligo, to the solace of that familiar landscape, where he wrote 'Into the Twilight' to renew his courage. Nature, the service of Ireland, and esoteric faith remain:

> Though hope fall from thee or love decay
> Burning in fires of a slanderous tongue.

Penniless, he decided to return to his father's house in London. He did not return to Irish political life until 1897.

Maud was now in France, seeking comfort with Millevoye but discovering that her lover was in despair, his political life in ruins as he and one hundred other deputies, including Déroulède, had been forced to resign in the wake of tales of corruption and graft over the building of the Panama Canal. French society was hardly more congenial than the Irish one she had so recently left, as anti-Semitism became rife and accusations of spying, based on forged documents, redounded against the Millevoye faction who had hoped to discredit Clemenceau, leader of the Radicals and arch-enemy of the reactionaries. Maud discovered plots, supposedly originating from Clemenceau, which were designed to break up her relationship with her lover. But nothing improves a relationship so much as opposition and the belief that one is needed by the beloved. Once Maud's health improved, personal considerations preoccupied her, particularly the possibility of achieving the reincarnation of her son George. She and Millevoye resumed their physical relationship, he acquiescing in Maud's fantasy. On one macabre occasion they made love in the vault of the memorial chapel; when Maud did conceive, she cherished the hope that conception had taken place at that time.[22]

Maud's absence from Ireland, after the collapse of the libraries venture and her illness, was a lengthy one. Apart from a lecture in Limerick in September of that year she does not appear to have been in Ireland again — at least not for political purposes — for another four years. Willie, however, did not stay away from her for that length of time. In February 1894 he made his first journey to Paris. He described the visit in his memoirs:

Maud Gonne was of course my chief interest; she had not left France for a long time now and was, I was told, ill again. I saw her, and our relations, which were friendly enough, had not our old intimacy. I remember going with her to call upon some friend and noting that she mounted the stairs with difficulty.[23]

The reason for Maud's prolonged stay in Paris, for her lack of the 'old intimacy', for her being 'ill' and mounting the stairs with difficulty, was that she was three months pregnant. Her daughter Iseult was born on 6 August 1894.[24] The effort of concealment, especially from someone who knew her so well, must have cost her a great deal. Willie remained in Paris until the end of the month, as the play he wanted to review, *Axel* by Villiers, had its opening night postponed three times. He and Maud attended the play together, she quietly translating and disagreeing with Willie's approval of its sentiments.

Maud met the Amnesty Association in London that March, but it was her last engagement until after her confinement. It was too risky to show herself in a more advanced state of pregnancy. In preparation for the child's birth and the increase in household staff this would necessitate, she moved to a spacious apartment on the Avenue d'Eylau. Millevoye, in response to encouragement from Maud, took over the editorship of the newspaper *La Patrie* and as her lover's political fortunes improved, she found herself with an unrivalled opportunity for propaganda. She could freely expound her views on Britain's suppression of Ireland's struggle for nationhood, confident that any article written by her would be published. Chris Healy, a journalist from Liverpool who was in Paris at this time, recording his impressions of famous figures he met, devoted a dozen pages of his subsequent book to Maud. From this evidence there is no doubt that Maud was extremely important in creating a strongly anti-British attitude amongst the many important people she associated with:

> Not only has she guided the pens of MM Millevoye and Drumont, the editors of *La Patrie* and *La Libre Parole,* but in many cases the articles denunciatory of Great Britain which have enlivened the columns of those papers have been written wholly by her, although they have appeared above the name of some member of the staff. . . .
>
> At her handsome apartment in the Avenue d'Eylau are to be seen deputies, journalists and irreconcilables – men who have great power in the moulding of French public opinion . . . it would be ill to under-estimate her ability. She is shrewd, witty, and has the rare ability of uniting opponents to act against a common enemy.[25]

Maud was enthralled by her baby daughter and reluctant to leave her, afraid of what might happen if she was apart from her child. In *A Servant of the Queen* she insisted, in one of the rare dates she recorded, that she made her first visit to America in 1894. The true date was October 1897. The only explanation for this deliberate error is that it was a clumsy attempt to conceal the date of Iseult's birth. The furthest she actually ventured after the birth was a trip to England in July 1895 – when Iseult was almost a year old – to speak in Newcastle against John Morley, Gladstone's Chief Secretary for Ireland, who had ignored her pleas for the release of the treason-felony prisoners. He was one of the casualties in the resounding defeat the Liberals were to suffer. For the next ten years the Conservatives and Liberal Unionists ruled unchallenged.

In December 1896 Yeats returned to Paris, to Maud, 'the old lure', even though he had, for the first time in his life, established a sexual relationship with a woman. It would last a year, until Olivia Shakespear realised that Maud still had first place in her lover's heart. One of his reasons for returning to Paris was to continue the development of their dream for a 'Castle of the Heroes', where the finest men and women of Ireland would come for spiritual inspiration and teaching. Many years later, Maud described their fantasy:

> The land of Ireland, we both felt, was powerfully alive and invisibly peopled, and whenever we grew despondent over the weakness of the national movement, we went to it for comfort. If only we could make contact with the hidden forces of the land it would give us strength for the freeing of Ireland. Most of our talk centred round this and it led us both into strange places . . . .[26]

Their preoccupation was preparing the rituals for the order. Although Maud saw its effects primarily in political terms, working for the separation of Ireland from Britain in the same way as the Masonic lodges worked for union, she was also deeply involved with the mystical aspects of the project. She and Willie took hashish to heighten their perceptions, recording their fantasies in a special notebook. While Willie thought that this collaboration would so unite their minds that Maud would eventually become his, she again broadened the scope of their activities into a more overtly political arena, persuading Yeats to help her found a Paris branch of the Young Ireland Society, called *L'Association Irlandaise*. Millevoye attended some meetings, and when Maud launched her newspaper *L'Irlande Libre* on 1 May 1897, he wrote an editorial in *La Patrie* welcoming its existence. For over a year he contributed articles to her paper, but their relationship was slowly declining.

Maud's prolonged absence from Ireland led to the removal of her name from the National Literary Society of which she had been a founder member a few short years previously. The *Shan Van Vocht,* a political and literary journal edited in Belfast by Alice Milligan and Anna Johnson, was indignant on Maud's behalf. As an editorial angrily remarked, Maud, 'though merely a woman's name, would have served to connect the society in the eyes of the Irish race with what some of us hold to be the National movement'.[27] It was high time Maud returned to Ireland.

1897 was the year of Queen Victoria's Jubilee. It was also the year that Irish nationalists began to organise 1798 Centenary Commemoration Committees, to ensure that the anniversary of the United Irishmen's Rising – the closest Ireland had yet come to establishing the Republic – would be suitably remembered throughout the world. On 4 March a meeting was held in Dublin, with John O'Leary in the chair, to select a committee to organise events for the forthcoming centenary.[28] It was a large body of two or three hundred members, many of whom welcomed this opportunity to break away from the bitter political atmosphere which had followed the Parnellite split. Branches were soon established throughout the country as well as in Europe, America, South Africa and Australia – an indication of the extent of the Irish diaspora. The main aim of the Dublin branch was the erection of a memorial to Wolfe Tone, leader of the United Irishmen, and Yeats became president of a subgroup of the committee, the Wolfe Tone Memorial Association. He was also made president of the '98 Centennial Association of Great Britain and France.

Political life was suddenly alive with possibilities, but the old ugliness and suspicions remained. In Belfast, Alice Milligan and Anna Johnson were leading figures in an effort to unite the warring factions. An Irishwomen's Centenary Union was formed, ostensibly for the whole of Ireland, but strongest in the north, where sectarianism made it prudent for some men to take a less prominent role in the celebrations, for fear of offending Protestant customers or clients. In such cases, the women often stepped into the breach, their activities – decorating the graves of patriots and organising exhibitions – less public than the planned meetings and demonstrations. The *Shan Van Vocht* announced that the aim of the women was to 'give [the men] safe guidance out of the hurly-burly of the political faction fight into which they have wandered from the straight path'.[29] Maud was not associated with this organisation, probably because she was out of the country during its formation, but it was also a bit low-key for one of her temperament. She did, however, find herself affected by another factional dispute as soon as she involved herself in the centenary movement.

Maud decided that as her contribution to events, she would go to America to raise funds for the memorial to Wolfe Tone. She thought it would be a simple matter of obtaining authorisation from the planning committee and was furious to find herself refused that permission. Returning from Dublin in April, she headed straight to Yeats in his London flat. He offered to intervene and called a meeting in his apartment at Woburn Buildings. The necessary resolution in Maud's favour was passed. Yeats now learned that the British and Irish groups contained two violently opposing factions, a result of a dispute within Clan na Gael, the secret Fenian organisation which controlled almost everything in Irish-American politics. The Clan had been riddled with internal intrigue since 1883, with John Devoy, who was to become the most important figure in Irish-American politics until the 1920s, accusing his opponents, a group of three known as the Triangle, of offences ranging from disloyalty to embezzlement. The culmination of years of bitterness occurred in 1889 when one of Devoy's friends, a Dr Cronin, was murdered in Chicago and Devoy accused Alexander Sullivan, a Chicago lawyer and one of the Triangle, of the murder. It was a miserable, unproductive period in Irish-American political life. The O'Leary group in Dublin were on one side, and Yeats and his associates were supposed to be on the other. Yeats decided that if he allowed his name to go forward for the presidency of the English committee, he could save the movement from collapsing into these different groupings. He had a more grandiose scheme as well, devised partly from his ever-present fear that if the Irish problem was not solved there would be another attempt at insurrection in which Maud would naturally take part and be either killed or maimed as a consequence. To prevent some 'wild Fenian movement' Yeats tried to interest those involved in the centenary celebrations in a scheme which would have as its aim the gathering together of all the differing groups into a 'Convention' which would sit permanently and devise policy, attending Westminster only as a delegation directed by the Convention. It would be a step on the path to a total withdrawal from Westminster, a peaceful strategy for establishing total independence. He thought Maud was in agreement and was disconcerted to overhear her irreverently referring to his scheme, suggesting that it would be preferable either to withdraw from Westminster entirely, or else send to England eighty ragged and drunken Dublin beggars or eighty pugilists, 'to be paid by results'.[30]

Ireland, not France, was where excitement lay. Iseult was nearly three, no longer a baby, and Maud could afford to have an extended absence from her daughter. She returned to Ireland in June, in time for Victoria's Jubilee. In London the Labour leader Keir Hardie had asked her to help in organising anti-Jubilee demonstrations. Maud's poor opinion of the fighting ability of the English, formed as a result of her sight of their melting away before the police batons in Trafalgar Square, led her to reply that the English had first better learn to do a little fighting without Irish help. Ireland could secure worldwide attention for its protests in Dublin, if everyone took part, and was not diverted into aiding the English efforts. In Dublin, Maud was to meet someone as physically brave as herself, who combined a flair for the dramatic gesture with a powerful intellect and penetrating analysis of society. He was James Connolly, at this time organiser for the Irish Socialist Republican Party. By 1914 Connolly would be Acting General Secretary of the Irish Transport and General Workers Union and founder of the armed workers movement, the Irish Citizen Army. But Connolly was always far more than simply an organiser and activist; as a socialist theoretician whose influence is acknowledged internationally, his insistence upon the interdependence of the national and socialist struggles continues to be of crucial importance today. As Commandant-General of the Irish Republican Army during the 1916 Rising he was to die facing a British firing squad. 'The bravest man I knew', was Maud's estimate of his qualities.

It had been arranged that a Convention of the '98 Centenary Committee would be held at the City Hall on Jubilee Day, as a symbolic gesture of contempt for the Jubilee celebrations. Some of the '98 Centenary branches were organising their own events; in Limerick the recently released John Daly suggested the flying of black flags as a symbol of defiance, and Connolly and his small Irish Socialist Republican Party took up this suggestion, developing it into an imaginative programme of resistance. Maud lent him Pat O'Brien's slides of battering rams and eviction scenes which she used in her lectures, and she arranged for the use of a window in the National Club in Rutland Square where a lantern could be set up to throw the picture onto a huge screen opposite. Connolly arranged with council workers to interrupt the power supply at the appropriate time, so that the festive lights would not compete with the slides, and Maud made black flags embroidered with facts about famines and evictions that had occurred during Victoria's reign.[31] Connolly also asked Maud to speak at a meeting of his socialist party. Thinking it would be a small group of the faithful in a small hut, she agreed. When Maud and Yeats arrived in Dublin, they discovered the streets covered with posters announcing a socialist meeting to be held in Dame Street, with Maud as the principal speaker. It's difficult to know whether Maud had the greater objections to so close an identification with socialism, or whether the prospect of speaking at an open-air meeting, something she had never done, terrified her. Whatever the overriding reason, she immediately wrote to Connolly, refusing to speak. Willie Yeats retained a vivid impression of Connolly's despair when he came to call on Maud. If she refused to appear, his credibility as an organiser was ruined as no one would believe him again. Maud remained adamant, but Willie said that he 'softened her heart' after Connolly left.[32] She went to his home, where she met his wife and four children, shocked by her first encounter with the grim reality of life in a Dublin tenement, where whole families lived packed together in one room of a crumbling, stinking building.

The next day there was a great crowd in Dame Street and Maud, standing on a chair, told the people how she was refused permission to decorate the graves of some of the United Irishmen when she went to St Michan's Church, the custodian explaining that it was on account of the Queen's Jubilee. Joining the throng below her, Willie was enthralled by the power of her presence:

> She said then, speaking slowly in a low voice that yet seemed to go through the whole crowd, 'Must the graves of our dead go undecorated because Victoria has her Jubilee?' and the whole crowd went wild.[33]

In trying to analyse the mystery of Maud's influence, Yeats came to the conclusion that some portion of her power came because she could still,

> even when pushing an abstract principle to what seemed to me an absurdity, keep her own mind free, and so when men and women did her bidding they did it not only because she was beautiful, but because that beauty suggested joy and freedom.[34]

This was not simply the biased evidence of someone hopelessly in love. Even when she was an old woman, a taken-for-granted feature of Dublin street life, many testified to the continued magic of her presence.

While the Centenary Committee met that evening, sounds from the workers' band that Connolly had organised could be heard outside. Maud suggested the suspension of the meeting so that the delegates could witness the parade outside. Her black flags were hidden in the porter's lodge, wrapped in a huge paper parcel. The delegates went outside, where they saw Connolly heading a procession which included a rickety handcart carrying a coffin inscribed as the 'British Empire'. Maud and Willie joined in, along with many of the '98 delegates, the black flags distributed to good effect, and to the strains of the Dead March, the procession moved off down Dame Street. As soon as the police realised what was happening, they advanced with batons raised. Reinforcements arrived from Dublin Castle. The spectators began to be dispersed by baton charges and the fighting intensified. By the time Connolly reached O'Connell Bridge he realised it was impossible to continue and in a flash of inspiration he ordered the coffin to be thrown into the Liffey, the whole crowd taking up the chorus 'Here goes the coffin of the British Empire. To Hell with the British Empire!'[35] Connolly was arrested and spent the night in the Bridewell. Maud and Willie continued along O'Connell Street to see how the magic lantern show was doing. Maud was in her element, striding along the darkened streets with a 'joyous face', and as they watched the crowd stone the windows of those houses containing Jubilee decorations she had 'a look of exaltation' as she walked, 'her laughing head thrown back'. Willie stopped worrying if he should try to prevent the stone throwing and gave himself up to the excitement of the moment, to the 'joyous irresponsibility and sense of power' that Maud was so transparently experiencing.[36]

The night was to end in tragedy as one old woman was batoned to death and two hundred people were treated for their injuries. The accounts by Maud and Willie of what happened to themselves during the rest of that evening are conflicting. Maud said that she had to insist on being let out of the locked door of the National Club, where she and Willie had ended up, as he did not want her to rejoin the crowd once it was learned that someone had been killed.[37] Willie, on the other hand, said that Maud was very angry when he made them lock the door and keep her in. He refused to let her out unless she explained what she meant to do. She did not get out and later she was supposed to have told him that he had made her 'do the only cowardly thing of her life'. Despite the great discrepancy in the accounts, what does remain is Maud's encouragement of direct action and her personal bravery in wanting to be in the thick of the crowd, whether or not she actually managed to get there late on Jubilee night.

Maud also had a very practical side to her. The next morning she went to the Bridewell, sent in a breakfast for Connolly and spoke to him before he went to court. She then went to tell his wife what had happened, came back to court to pay Connolly's fine herself and to arrange bail for the others who had been arrested. She later got Tim Harrington to agree to defend them. Maud also sent Connolly a note of congratulation which he treasured so much that he preserved it amongst his papers, where it was found after his execution:

Bravo! all my congratulations to you! You were right and I was wrong about this evening. You may have the satisfaction of knowing that you saved Dublin from the humiliation of an English jubilee without a public meeting of protestation. You were the only man who had the courage to . . . carry through in spite of all discouragement – even from friends![38]

The sentiments say much about Maud and her views on how to conduct a political campaign. The fact that Connolly thought it worthwhile to keep the paper says a great deal about the deep regard he felt for her.

This was a period of hectic activity as nationalists sought to capitalise on the moment. During a six month period beginning in April, Maud spoke several times in Paris, four times in Dublin, and at least once in London, York, Glasgow, Manchester and Cork. But she was also careful of her health, and she and May spent three weeks in

Aix-les-Bains after the Jubilee excitement, as Maud was tired and suffering from a bad attack of rheumatism. In typical fashion she recounted how, with the aid of a fortune teller, she won a lot of money at the gambling tables; it turned out to be enough for the legal expenses of those arrested during the riots.[39]

In the autumn Willie joined her on a lecture tour of Scotland and the Midlands and during the long train journeys they spent much time discussing political and mystical affairs. From Manchester he wrote to his new friend and patron, Lady Gregory:

> After the meeting this morning Miss Gonne and myself went to the picture gallery to see a Rossetti that is there. She is very kind and friendly, but whether more than that I cannot tell. I have been explaining the Celtic movement and she is enthusiastic over it in its more mystical development.[40]

It was not all leisure and art galleries. Yeats explained that his letter was not all it could be because he had just chaired a very noisy meeting for three hours and was 'very done up', while another meeting was scheduled for that evening. He was finding the 'infinite triviality of politics' exceptionally trying, but it is more than likely that his companion preferred the noise and bustle to the proposed tranquillity of the Celtic vision they had been discussing.

Soon after this tour, on 17 October 1897, Maud set sail for America. She was to find herself, unwittingly, in the midst of the Clan na Gael feud. She was labelled a British spy and John Devoy gave orders that her appearances in New York be boycotted. The visit, in other words, was not the unqualified success Maud later described, but she managed a gruelling schedule of meetings that encompassed New York, Washington, New England, Ohio, Chicago and Colorado. Throughout, she tried to reconcile the warring factions, urging the various leaders she spoke with to stop wasting the strength of the organisation on 'dead men's quarrels' and to get on with the work of fighting the British Empire. James Egan, recently released from Portland gaol, accompanied her to speak of the horrors he had experienced. At the end of the visit Maud found herself with £1000, to be divided up between the Amnesty Association and the Wolfe Tone memorial fund. On 27 December, she was given a final reception at the Cooper Institute in New York City. The warmth of the tributes she received was reflected in the sentiments in her parting gift, an embossed and framed resolution of gratitude from the Irish-American women of Brooklyn, who thanked 'Ireland's Joan of Arc' for abandoning 'a charming home ... devoted friends ... high social position' in order to 'disseminate the doctrine of union and independence among the scattered children of Erin'.[41] She was a heroine to the nationalist-minded women of America, even if the male leadership continued to treat her with some suspicion.

Maud was back in England during the first week of January. She spoke at a meeting of the Centenary Association and soon afterwards she and Willie went off to the west of Ireland, to get into contact with the mystical forces in the land. What this involved was unspecified, although the pair often used to lie with their ears to the ground, listening to what they insisted was the music of the fairies, later on trying to persuade musical friends to reproduce the sounds for them. Yeats wrote to AE that Maud had seen a vision of 'a little temple of the elements' which she proposed to build when the '98 events were over, making it the centre of their mystical and literary movements. The constantly impoverished poet then added a plaintive postscript, asking how much he would need to live on for a couple of weeks in the country.[42] Maud's income allowed her to take brief holidays when she pleased, but her proud companion was continually counting the pennies in his pocket, confiding his worries to everyone except the woman he loved.

They saw much more than mystical spirits during their two weeks in the west. Drought in the growing season had been followed by torrential downpours in the autumn. Potato blight was rampant in the western seaboard, while the waterlogged land meant a shortage of fuel as the turf could not be dried. Connolly had already been to Kerry and when he and Maud met together in Dublin, they decided that, in the absence of any organisation, they would attempt to mobilise the peasantry into resistance so that the passive acceptance of famine which had occurred in 1847 might not happen again. They drafted a leaflet, *The Rights of Life and the Rights of Property,* which was supplemented by quotations from the writings of popes and saints, dug up by Connolly in an effort to allay the scruples of the deeply religious Irish peasantry. Their message was simple:

> The very highest authorities on the doctrine of the church agree that no *human* law can stand between starving people and their right to food, including the right to take that food whenever they find it, openly or secretly, with or without the owner's permission.

Maud gave Connolly £25 from the money collected in America, to pay for the costs of printing and for travel. She then left for Mayo, where she had arranged to carry out organising work for the '98 celebrations. Connolly was to forward copies of the leaflet to her before leaving for Kerry.[43]

Her first stop was Castlebar, where she joined James Daly in inspecting the graves of the French soldiers killed in 1898 at the battle known as the 'Races' of Castlebar: General Humbert and his French soldiers, together with the unarmed Irish, had routed the English, who fled so fast that they gave the battle its name. Daly presented her with an old French coin and a bullet from one of the graves which she later had made into a brooch. The local centenary committee intended erecting crosses to mark the graves, this to be done before August when the French delegation was arriving for the laying of the foundation stone for the Ballina memorial.

On 12 March Maud arrived in Ballina. It was quite an occasion for a small market town. As she stepped down from the train a young boy, holding in one hand a banner of green and gold bearing the words 'Who fears to speak of '98?' and an elaborate bunch of flowers in the other, presented the bouquet to the visitor, who kissed his cheek. The horse was drawn from her wagonette and 'willing hands' pulled it to where Maud was staying. Despite the distress in the countryside, the atmosphere was carnival-like:

> the band proceeding and playing, and the crowd cheering, Miss Gonne all smiles, and greatly appreciating the attention she received. In the evening ... at eight o'clock a procession was formed, a number of men carrying lighted torches, lighted tar barrels, and the band playing. ...

The reporter for the *Ballina Herald,* who compiled lengthy reports on her visit, was clearly taken with Maud. At the evening meeting her 'kind and sympathetic disposition ... sweet voice, clear enunciation and graceful action' were 'pleasing beyond description'. When she concluded her lecture by appealing to the patriotism of her audience

> the effect was almost electrical. Having seen and heard Miss Gonne, one is not surprised at the influence she wields, whether in private circles, going about on errands of charity, or on the public platform.[44]

Her host, Thomas Kelly, was an old friend from Land League days. He was also a commercial traveller and he told Maud that on his return from Ballycastle he had seen ten new unfinished graves; the people were too weak to do the work of burying their dead properly. The next day, Maud took the mail car to Ballycastle. The proprietoress of the hotel told her that a man had died of hunger the day before and the doctor had, as usual, signed 'heart failure' on the death certificate. If starvation was admitted, the local authorities would face prosecution for not providing relief, and the relief funds were running out. That evening she addressed a big meeting at the hotel and distributed the leaflets she and Connolly had prepared. The following day she was in Belderrig, the heart of the famine.

Sitting up all night in a cold bedroom above the general store, huddled in her old fur cloak, Maud wrote articles for the papers and a begging letter to America, appealing for funds to feed the children and nurse the sick. The next morning she and some of the local women were out visiting the sick, cooking oatmeal and condensed milk – the only food available – on an open fire. The villagers were far too weak to think of organising themselves in the way Maud's leaflet suggested. Her suggestion that they steal the landlord's sheep from the mountains shocked them and although they welcomed her promise that she would organise for a fish-curing plant so that they could preserve herrings when they had good catches, the immediate problem of stopping the famine remained. A proper system of relief was vital, the one in existence – paying heads of households sixpence a day to work on the roads – being completely inadequate. As the people had been forced to eat their seed potatoes, a reoccurrence of famine the following year was inevitable unless the authorities organised the immediate free distribution of seed potatoes, paying relief rates to those who planted them. The local parish priest, to Maud's surprise, welcomed her presence and congratulated her newspaper article for cogently summarising the situation.

Together, Maud and the priest drew up a list of demands, including the raising of relief rates to one shilling a day. Local officials, including representatives of the relief works and the Congested Districts Board were due to meet officials from Dublin Castle to discuss the situation. Thousands of starving, ragged people crowded into Belmullet on the day of the meeting; a quiet, anxious crowd, waiting to hear what would be the result of the meeting between Maud and the local priest and the group of officials. Maud described the sneering smiles which greeted her reading of the list of demands. In response, she threatened that the people would take matters into their own hands, with bloodshed an inevitable result. As she bluffed them, they could all hear, through the open window,

> the confused murmur of that great throng and the strange soft sound of thousands of bare feet beating on the hard earth.[45]

The eeriness of that description in *A Servant of the Queen* has an undeniably authentic ring to it. Her threat worked, the demands were granted and she left Mayo in order to use her influence and charms in Dublin, to secure the erection of a fish-curing plant in Belderrig. She returned to help with feeding the school children and nursing the sick. Her devotion to the people was never forgotten. Sean MacBride, many years later, was to recall the overwhelming hospitality he would receive from the people of Mayo, when they discovered that he was the son of Maud Gonne. Maud's final reflection was that she had helped to save many lives – and talking in the British House of Commons would never have achieved that.

In April, worn out, she returned to her Paris flat where she resorted to her usual routine of recuperation after an excessively active time: she stayed in bed for two weeks, reading novels. According to Nancy Cardozo, fairly frivolous authors as well as such heavyweights as Balzac and Hugo were included in her eclectic reading matter. She also, if only because of Willie Yeats's influence, kept fairly up to date on the Irish literary scene. The old lung trouble had returned, a result of the damp and cold she had been exposed to in Mayo. Willie followed her over to Paris and wrote worriedly to Lady Gregory that Maud looked ill and tired. But in May she was well enough to attend a meeting of the Paris '98 Centenary Committee and to speak about the centenary at Amiens. She seems to have been the main contact between the French and the Irish during this period of building up support for the forthcoming ceremonies.

Her hectic schedule continued. Back in Dublin in June she was speaking at a demonstration when the horse drawing her car fell. Maud was thrown out, breaking her arm in the process. The following day a messenger informed Willie of the accident and he rushed round to offer his services. As he wrote to Lady Gregory, who must have been getting weary of all the concern shown to Maud, she was not the pale invalid he had expected to see, but was 'cheerful and talkative'.[46] Nevertheless, Willie intended staying on for a few days in case he could be of use in helping with her correspondence or with any other task. While Maud was in need of help, unable to stay in a hotel because of her broken arm, she stayed with Sarah Purser, a well-known portrait artist, who had painted a sugary portrait of Maud at twenty-one. Maud always disliked it, and Yeats thought it vulgar, remarking that people found it difficult to believe that so witty a woman could be a bad painter. Sarah's wit was often at Maud's expense. Her attitude towards the younger woman was ambivalent, summed up in one of her best-known remarks, made to the love-sick Willie: 'Maud Gonne talks politics in Paris, and literature to you, and at the Horse Show she would talk of a clinking brood mare.'[47] Despite this, at that stage in her life, Sarah was one of the few women in Dublin that Maud could describe as a friend. Her concerns were primarily political and few other women had yet entered that arena. When she had fallen ill in Dublin previously, she had been forced to ask her cousin May to come to her aid. She was in less dire straits on this occasion, but her closest women friends were still in Paris and London, not Dublin.

Maud's sarcastic reflection that talking in the House of Commons would not have prevented famine had been prompted by the gradual take-over of the centenary movement by the parliamentarians. What had started out as an effort to revive the nationalist spirit had ended in less idealistic fashion as the different factions of the parliamentary party jostled for advantage. Internal dissent began to drain the committee's work of its previous enthusiasm and arguments on whether all funds should go to one central memorial to Wolfe Tone in Dublin, or whether local committees should have their own monuments, threatened to bring all the hard work of the past year to a disillusioning end. Maud supported the local committees because their existence provided greater opportunities for spreading nationalist ideas around the country and Willie accused her of encouraging bad art. She quite agreed that Irish artistic taste was influenced by cheap Italian plaster statues, but retorted how could it be otherwise in a country which did not allow art students to use nude models. She would have preferred the monuments to have taken the form either of great rocks with names inscribed, or of Celtic crosses, but her main concern was to encourage local initiative and that was what pleased her most about the events of '98.[48] She disliked the overladen symbolism cluttering up the Ballina monument, but the memorial to the French unveiled by her son Sean in Kilcummin in 1987 – almost one hundred years later – did accord with her desire for greater simplicity. It would have given her enormous pleasure to think that her view would eventually be accepted. The question of art versus the people was a well-worn debate between her and Willie. For Maud, the people and the furtherance of the national idea was always the determining factor. As Willie became increasingly preoccupied by élitist notions of leadership, of rule by an aristocracy, Maud remained essentially democratic in her willingness to allow ordinary people their right to determine events.

She enjoyed the ceremonies in Castlebar and Ballina. Avril de St Croix was one of the small French contingent to arrive eventually that summer and it must have been a satisfying experience to have her old friend witness the reception accorded to her by the Mayo people. The *Connaught Telegraph* reported that 'not on any occasion for many years past has such a vast assemblage of people been seen in Ballina' and *United Ireland* said that Maud Gonne had 'roused the dormant spirit of a military race, and a wild defiant cheer ran through Mayo town'.[49] But the previous week had seen the culmination of all the year's work in Dublin, at the laying of the foundation stone for the Wolfe Tone Memorial. For Maud, this was a less triumphant occasion. She refused to stand on the platform, in protest at the presence of some of those parliamentarians who had previously been hostile to the '98 movement. She was not asked to speak. Yeats was one of the speakers, and Maud stood with the crowd below to listen. She does not mention what he later claimed to be the crowd's response to his speech. Thinking of the vast procession of people who had just passed through Dublin he announced, 'The people themselves made this movement'. But a cry rose from the great crowd, 'No, no, it was Maud Gonne that made it.'[50] Did this happen? Yeats had no reason to invent it, but why did Maud not refer to it. If she had heard, she showed an uncharacteristic reticence.

Maud left the proceedings early, feeling dispirited and depressed as she walked down Grafton Street.[51] Willie Yeats might have generously given her credit in his reminiscences, but for all that, she had not been invited to speak at the largest gathering to have been organised by the nationalists in many years. And surely, her work had merited her that. In all the jostling for position and rank, it was easy to elbow aside one who was still, for all her commitment, a freelance, without the backing of any organisation other than a united front that had ended up containing more factions than she had ever anticipated.

CHAPTER 4

A DAUGHTER OF ERIN

Maud had come a long way from the impetuous, naïve young woman whose one ambition was to work for Irish freedom. A testing political apprenticeship had been served, from which she had emerged – in the eyes of many – as 'Ireland's Joan of Arc'. Other women were still largely invisible, but over the next few years the revival of nationalist fortunes would help to provide the impetus for what Maud had always wanted: an organisation specifically for Irish women.

Her private life, however, was not so straightforward. 'Ireland's Joan of Arc' was also, as the gossips would describe it, involved in a sinful relationship with a foreigner. Only a few close French friends and her immediate family were aware of the situation, as a carefully maintained secrecy surrounded her personal affairs. The deceit and pretence this involved placed an enormous strain upon Maud, particularly when her relationship began to fail and she found herself unable to gain relief by confiding in friends, fearful that scandal would ruin her political career. The stresses and strains of her double life had been evident before, but the tensions were increasing. Finally, she broke down and told Willie Yeats the full story.[1]

In late November 1898 Maud and Willie were in Dublin, as usual staying in different hotels – to save her reputation, Willie insisted, to Maud's wry amusement. One morning Willie woke up dreaming that Maud had kissed him and when he joined her for breakfast, she enquired if he had had a dream. She was silent when he told her, but just before he returned to his hotel that night, Maud confessed that she had dreamed the counterpart of his dream: a great spirit had put their hands together and told her they were married. When she finished her account, for the first time 'with the bodily mouth', she kissed him. The following day Maud was upset, sitting gloomily over the fire, apologising to Willie for having spoken to him in that manner and raising hopes that could not be fulfilled. Bit by bit, she confessed the story of her life, things he had heard 'all twisted awry by scandal, and disbelieved'.

Maud began by confessing a fantastical alliance she felt she had contracted with the devil when, as a young girl, she had longed to have control over her life. Although a common adolescent experience, in Maud's case her father was dead within a fortnight, leaving her stricken with remorse. Life was seen as a melodrama: she believed the devil now had her soul in exchange for her freedom to live her life as she chose. When she came of age she did what she most wanted – she settled in Paris and became Millevoye's mistress. With many halts and incoherencies, Maud explained the reality of her relationship with Millevoye, and the fact that they had lived apart since the birth of Iseult. Their lives were, however, still connected as she persuaded herself that only her influence kept him faithful to their political ideal. The burden of guilt she had carried around with her – and which had never left her despite all the frenetic activity – was now partly dissolved in this stumbling, tearful confession.

With great difficulty Maud admitted to feeling a 'horror and terror of physical love'. It was not an admission that Willie expected to hear, but he resolved to treat her as a sister, determined that if she came to him it must not be the result of a 'temporary passionate impulse'. Later on, as he lay awake at night reflecting on his behaviour, it seemed to him that he had acted 'not from a high scruple, but from a dread of moral responsibility'. Maud's complexes and phobias were, in other words, too much for him to cope with. Far better to continue the fantasy world by which lovers divided in the flesh could become one in their dreams. From this time until 1903, Maud and Willie pursued a 'mystical marriage' with vigour, renewing it in 1908 when they were reconciled following Maud's marriage and divorce. It was a spiritual eroticism which struggled to find expression amidst the stifling conventions of the time. It certainly had its bizarre side but it was also an honourable attempt to develop an outlet for sexual energies which could incorporate their very different needs without impinging upon individual freedom.

Maud went back to Paris, to be followed over by Willie, and the process of confession continued. Willie gave no more details of what Maud confided in him, but he found it a devastating experience. On 4 February he wrote to Lady Gregory 'If you knew all . . . you would understand why this love has been so bitter a thing to me, and why things I have known lately have made it, in a certain sense, the bitterer, and the harder.'[2] The following week he wrote her another letter:

> I have had rather a depressing time here. During the last months, and most of all while I have been here she has told the story of her life, telling gradually, in more detail, all except a few things which I can see are too painful for her to talk of and about which I do not ask her.[3]

Lady Gregory told him not to leave Maud's side until she agreed to marry him, but he replied that he was exhausted and could do no more. His outburst must have been caused partly by the humiliating realisation that at certain stages in Maud's life (for example, early in her second pregnancy), when he thought they were getting closer to each other, she was secretly pursuing her clandestine existence. And now, despite everything, she still continued her involvement with French politicians and intriguers, her 'life of hatred . . . her deepest hell' as Willie described it, imploring her to give herself to the 'divine love' they had spent so much time talking of. But despite everything, her relationship with Millevoye did not come to a final end for another two years.

Often, when Maud was at her lowest ebb, Willie tried to persuade himself and his friends that she would finally relent and agree to marry him, but the reality was very different. Maud had enormous personal resilience and strength of character. She also had the unwavering conviction that the political path she had taken was the only choice she could ever have made. It was far more important to her than any lover, as this undated fragment of a letter from her to Willie indicates:

> All I want of you is not to build up an imaginary wall of effort between yourself and life – for the rest the gods will arrange – for you are one of those they have chosen to do their work. As for the possible danger which you speak of for me, I am under the great shield of Lugh. The day I am no longer protected, if that day comes, my work for Ireland will be over. I should not need *and could not accept* protection from any one, though I fully realise and understand the generous and unselfish thoughts which were in your heart and I love you for them. . . . I am in my whirlwind, but in the midst of that whirlwind is dead quiet calm which is peace too.
>
> Always your friend, Maud Gonne.[4]

A brief political *rapprochement* with Millevoye occurred in the autumn of 1899, when the outbreak of the Boer War gave the French right some cause for alliance with other factions in opposition to Britain's attempt to maintain its dominance in southern Africa. Maud had no quarrel with the overblown chauvinism propounded by her erstwhile lover and the two once again shared a political platform, but the heart of resistance to Britain was in Ireland, from which British troops were being hastily shipped out in order to fight against the Boers, and where a recruiting drive to augment numbers had to be vigorously contested. It was back to Dublin and to the thick of the struggle for Maud. It was a golden opportunity to attack British imperialism and the old adage 'England's difficulty is Ireland's opportunity' might, as many nationalists hoped, finally become a reality.

The *United Irishman,* a new separatist paper, had been established in Dublin by Arthur Griffith, an austere, reserved young man who had recently returned from South Africa, where his great friend John

MacBride was engaged in organising an Irish brigade to fight on behalf of the Boers. Griffith was soon to fall under Maud's spell, nicknaming her 'Queen'. His conservative nationalism, which at this time still conceded the possibility of a king, lords and commons for Ireland, was very different from the socialism of a man like Connolly, but Maud's eclectic brand of nationalism made alliances with whomsoever would be useful to Ireland, cheerfully overlooking ideological differences. Griffith's publication was invaluable as a means of publicising Maud's activities: during the first ten months of the weekly's existence almost every other issue contained an item by Maud. She no longer had to rely on La Patrie and the declining support of Millevoye.

At the beginning of October an enormous crowd of 20,000 flocked to the Custom House in Dublin to hear a panel of speakers, Maud included, denounce the war and send messages of support to the Boers. Griffith's report of the meeting described the unyoking of the horses pulling Maud's brake. After it was pulled around the streets the people, 'having given ringing cheers for Miss Gonne and the Transvaal, quietly dispersed'.[5] The following week, on 10 October, an Irish Transvaal Committee was formed at a meeting held in the offices of the Celtic Literary Society. Maud took the chair, calling for a vote of congratulations to Major MacBride on his work and it was agreed that a flag be sent out to the Irish Brigade.[6] After Maud presided at the second meeting of the Irish Transvaal Committee, Willie Yeats wrote to his sister Lily that she was 'working with extraordinary energy' to discourage Irishmen from joining the British army and in encouraging recruitment for the Irish Brigade.[7] She certainly threw herself into this new initiative with all her old zest, delighted to be working for a cause that was capable of mobilising so many. An ambulance fund was started by the committee and Maud immediately pledged £5, the highest donation. In November she and Griffith found half the population of Cork turned out to greet them when they arrived to speak at a meeting. Once again the horses were removed and the people pulled Maud's carriage through the streets.

The most publicised protest organised by the Irish Transvaal Committee took place shortly before Christmas. The old team of Maud Gonne and James Connolly was reunited in protest against the conferring by Trinity College of an honorary degree upon the British colonial secretary, Joseph Chamberlain. The police banned the rally and threatened all the speakers with arrest. Maud found herself woken at one o'clock in the morning by a police inspector who insisted on reading the banning notice to her as she sat up in bed. She characteristically refused to make his task any easier by receiving him in her living room. Several speakers did fail to turn up, but John O'Leary, Connolly, Maud and Pat O'Brien (a substitute for Michael Davitt who was unable to attend), all decided to go ahead. As they drove towards Beresford Place the police managed to haul down the driver but Connolly, who had deliberately taken the box seat in the front, immediately seized the reins and drove through the cordon, scattering police and people alike. As they rushed to Beresford Place, the brake swaying dangerously, Sean O'Casey stood watching them:

> ... a long car, benched on both sides, drawn by two frightened hearse horses. A stout, short, stocky man, whose face was hidden by a wide-awake hat, was driving them. Several other men, pale-faced and tight-lipped, sat on the seats, facing each other; and with them was a young woman with long lovely yellow hair, smiling happily, like a child out on her first excursion.[8]

John O'Leary hastily managed to read out the resolution of support before mounted police steered them into the yard of the Store Street police station. No one wanted the embarrassment of arresting an MP and they were allowed to leave. As they neared Dublin Castle, still full of elation after their mad chase around Dublin, Connolly turned to Maud and half-jokingly whispered 'There are only two sentries at the gates. . . . Shall I drive in and seize the Castle?' She took the suggestion seriously, but felt that unarmed people could not succeed. Regretfully, they drove past, but Maud's memoirs added forebodingly 'I had plans for arming which I hoped would materialise.'[9]

Maud's activities included much more than straightforward propaganda. That was the public face – she also had more illicit tasks to perform against the British Empire. Her trips to Paris now included obtaining French passports for Irishmen who had volunteered to fight in the Irish Brigade, and she arranged for the sending of the ambulance from Irish sympathisers to the Transvaal. She also tried to interest the Transvaal representative in Brussels in a lunatic scheme whereby bombs disguised as lumps of coal were to be placed in the holds of British troopships sailing for South Africa. Maud's rationale was that although there would be great loss of life the end result would be to halt Irish enlistment to the British army and therefore ultimately save Irish lives. The horrified Dr Leyds exclaimed that this was not a recognised method of warfare, while Maud chillingly replied that 'whether you kill your enemies on land or at sea, it does not seem to me to make any difference'. Dr Leyds later summed her up as an 'indiscreet karakter'. For her part, she found him a 'polished diplomat', and not the man of action she had hoped for.[10]

The mad bombing plot had other repercussions, as the money the IRB had advanced for the scheme was appropriated by an unidentifiable Irishman and rumours of informers and dirty tricks by the British secret service threatened to discredit the valuable work of the solidarity movements. Maud was disillusioned with secret societies, which lost their glamour for her, although her enthusiasm for violent measures was not noticeably curbed. When the culprit was discovered,

Maud argued against shooting him as she did not believe in asking people to do something she was not prepared to do herself. Another tour of America had already been lined up, and this fortunately extricated her from an awkward situation.

The purpose of this visit was to arouse American sentiment in favour of the Boers and to isolate Britain from the international community. In America the question of imperialist expansionism was the subject of intense debate, while the cause of peace was more popular than it had ever been. Maud, however, was not advocating pacifism. On the contrary. Her first speech, in the vast auditorium of the Academy of Music in New York City, was an exhilarating and colourful occasion. The speaker's desk was decorated with the Stars and Stripes, and the flags of the South African Republic, the Orange Free State and Ireland were draped from the proscenium boxes. As Maud walked out onto the stage she discovered five hundred extra chairs had been placed upon it to accommodate the demand for seats. It was an emotional evening, the walls reverberating to the sounds of hisses and cheers as the audience responded to her denunciation of British conduct in the Transvaal and description of the heroism of those fighting for the Boers. Given the reality of Boer treatment of the original inhabitants of southern Africa, it's interesting to realise that Maud did not attempt to laud their behaviour, blithely stating that 'it matters not to the Irish people whether the republics are right or wrong. The fact that they are fighting England makes us their friend'. But she shared the almost universal disregard of native inhabitants of colonised countries, whose rights to existence were negligible in comparison with that of the white settlers: 'England's methods of warfare have not changed since she turned loose the red savages armed with scalping knife and tomahawk to make savage war on the American colonists.' Racist attitudes were widespread, even amongst revolutionary nationalists. While referring to the escapades of the Irish Transvaal Committee, succeeding in holding their meeting despite being forbidden to do so, Maud declared, to the crowd's roar of delight, 'we spoke all the same, and more than that, we flaunted the Transvaal flag right in front of Dublin Castle!' Her belief was that, because of the Boer War, only 6,000 troops remained in Ireland and Britain did not dare to provoke the Irish. It was obvious what she hoped would be the outcome of this particular war, as her ringing conclusion affirmed:

> To Ireland I say that freedom is never won without the sacrifice of blood. Our chance is coming. The end of the British empire is at hand. Your motherland calls you. She has been the land of sorrow long enough.

The event was not all blood and thunder. In the fashion of many Irish evenings, the speeches were followed by songs and recitations. The well-known singer Chauncy Olcott, who had written 'My Wild Irish Rose', was discovered to be in the audience. He delighted the crowd by coming up to the stage and singing for them.[11]

Maud again visited cities containing large numbers of Irish emigrants, an enthusiastic reception greeting all her appearances. It was not a major tour, but she did help to mobilise larger numbers in support of the Boers and she also came back with enough money to keep the *United Irishman* afloat.

On 8 March Maud sailed to France; as soon as she landed, she fell ill with a bad bout of enteritis which kept her out of public affairs for almost a month. It could hardly have occurred at a more inconvenient time, and Maud fretted to be well and on her feet again, ready to confront her most hated adversary, Queen Victoria – the Famine Queen.

The work of the Transvaal Committee was having an effect: Irish enlistment was virtually at a standstill and some means of reviving pro-British sentiment was vital. The government decided that the Queen should visit her Irish subjects, ignoring all the warnings and predictions against such a measure. Yeats wrote an open letter to the *Daily Express*, 'Whoever stands by the roadway cheering for Queen Victoria cheers for the Empire, dishonours Ireland, and condones a crime.'[12] Many agreed with him. Despite workers having a day off in her honour and those in Guinness's brewery discovering an extra shilling in their pay packets, Victoria's entry into Dublin, on 4 April, was less than triumphant. Silent people stared at her carriage. A counter-demonstration by the Transvaal Committee was quickly broken up by the police. Maud's frustration on her inability to be physically present was channelled into one of her most famous articles, published initially in *L'Irlande Libre* and then translated as 'The Famine Queen' for the 7 April issue of the *United Irishman*. It was a sustained and powerful polemic, the conclusion of which repeated her determination to fight against the recruiting of Irishmen:

... Taking the Shamrock in her withered hand, she dares to ask Ireland for soldiers – for soldiers to fight for the exterminators of their race! And the reply of Ireland comes sadly but proudly, not through the lips of the miserable little politicians who are touched by the English canker, but through the lips of the Irish people:

Queen, return to your own land; you will find no more Irishmen ready to wear the red shame of your livery. In the past they have done so from ignorance, and because it is hard to die of hunger when one is young and strong and the sun shines, but they shall do so no longer. See! Your recruiting agents return alone and unsuccessful from my green hills and plains, because once more hope has revived, and it will be in the ranks of your enemies that my children will find employment and honour.

To her infinite satisfaction, the authorities ordered the seizure of all copies of the paper, so Maud's article – the reason for their action – instantly achieved the notoriety they had wished to avoid. Within a few days Maud was in Dublin, arriving to find that Arthur Griffith was in gaol as a result of horsewhipping the editor of the society journal *Figaro* for publishing an article claiming Maud to be in the pay of the British government because her father's army pension was supposedly paid into her estate. It was an indication of Griffith's deep devotion to Maud that the taciturn young journalist could be provoked to such an uncharacteristic act in defence of her reputation. The outcome of the successful libel case she won against the *Figaro* was yet more publicity for the 'Famine Queen' article. Maud sat in the crowded courtroom, resplendent in a new hat she had bought for the occasion, enjoying the experience of the lawyer reading out her article to the jury in a vain attempt to influence them against her. Colles, the editor, later admitted that Dublin Castle had footed the bill for his defence.[13]

One of the ploys used by officials to bear out their claim that the majority of Irish people continued to support the monarchy was the staging in Phoenix Park of a free treat for 5,000 children, rounded up from the city's schools. An article in the *United Irishman* complained that nationalists had never made any effort to organise an event for children, even such a simple one as an outing to a monument. It was a remark that struck a chord.

After twelve o'clock Mass on Easter Sunday, a small group of fifteen women met in the rooms of the Celtic Literary Society. Maud, although still feeling fragile after her illness, was amongst them. Their primary purpose was to raise a subscription for a 'nice strong blackthorn with a silver ring, bearing an Irish subscription', to compensate Griffith for the loss of his stick, a South African sjambok he had treasured as a memento of his time there and which had been broken on Colles. It was an informal little group which also discussed hair and the latest fashions (black and khaki because of the Boer War) and then someone mentioned the comment about giving a treat to children who refused to go to the park when Victoria was over. They all looked at each other and unanimously exclaimed 'Let us do it'.[14]

Events moved quickly after that. At long last Maud had found kindred souls who 'resented being excluded, as women, from National organisations'. It was what she had longed for over the years and she was determined not to let the impetus wane. An article in the following week's edition of the *United Irishman* announced the formation of a committee, with Maud as president, to organise an excursion for the children who had refused to attend the Queen's breakfast. The Patriotic Children's Treat Committee, as it was soon termed, conceived their venture on a lavish scale, hoping to reach the majority of the 30,000 children they calculated would be eligible. As enthusiasm mounted, the numbers of women attending the weekly planning meetings increased: fifty-nine were present by the 19 May meeting, with Anna Johnson travelling down from Belfast to take part. Generous donations began to pour in, including one thousand oranges from one benefactor, twenty tons of sweets from another and forty thousand buns from a variety of bakers, including John Daly of Limerick – Maud's old friend from her treason-felony campaigning days. As the chosen day drew near, two members of the committee spent two hours each afternoon in the offices of the Celtic Literary Society, enrolling the names of the children. By 30 June, 25,000 names had been registered. Clonturk Park was the final venue chosen, one of the few places suitable for the large numbers envisaged and for the final four days before the event, over one hundred women and men packed and made up food in a shop in Talbot Street lent for that purpose.

Arthur Griffith enthused that 'Dublin never witnessed anything so marvellous as the procession through its streets last Sunday of the thirty thousand school children who refused to be bribed into parading before the Queen of England.' It was a colourful, joyful scene as lorries piled high with casks of ginger beer and thousands of paper bags full of sandwiches, buns and sweets moved through the Dublin streets at the head of a gigantic procession of children, all carrying green branches to symbolise the rebirth of the nationalist spirit. Many held up cards proclaiming 'Irish Patriotic Children's Treat – no Flunkeyism here'. Maud and Maire Quinn accompanied the procession in an open carriage while men from the Celtic Literary Society and the Gaelic Athletic Association acted as marshals. After all the games had finished, the children listened to speeches. Maud was the only woman with sufficient self-confidence and experience to take a place on one of the four platforms which had been erected. She urged the boys never to disgrace themselves by joining the English army or police and urged the girls to work to further the national ideal. Her spirits were high as she surveyed the masses of young faces looking up and told them of her hope that Ireland would be free by the time they were grown up, so that they could put their energies into building a free nation rather than the 'arid task of breaking down an old tyranny'. Forty years later, she was still meeting women and men who would come up to her in the street and say 'I was one of the patriotic children at your party when Queen Victoria was over.'

The Patriotic Children's Treat Committee had organised the largest peaceful demonstration that anyone could remember and letters of congratulation poured in. On behalf of the builders' labourers, Thomas Timmins wrote 'there is no name that will ever shine out with greater prominence in the history of our country than that of our beloved lady, Miss Maud Gonne'. Yeats mused gloomily to himself 'How many of these children will carry bomb or rifle when a little under or a little over thirty?' As many realised, the treat was more significant than a simple children's event.

When the committee met to sort out their accounts, they realised that this could not be the end of all their hard work and new-found talents. A permanent organisation must be created, so that they could have a more clearly defined role in the revitalised nationalist movement. After some discussion it was agreed that they would form a National Women's Committee, but as many members would be away during the summer they decided to postpone launching the new organisation until the autumn. In the meantime, as Franco-Irish celebrations were to be held in Paris that July, Jenny Wyse-Power and Maire Quinn were delegated to represent the committee. Maud, naturally, was already planning to attend, but she also had other more personal affairs to see to that summer.

Apart from their attendance at public demonstrations, Maud and Millevoye only came into direct contact with each other on one occasion during this period, and that was at an opera. Maud had been sent complimentary tickets for a performance of *La Valkyrie,* to give to the Irish delegation. They had, unfortunately, already left and, regretting the absence of Arthur Griffith and Maire Quinn, whom she felt would have loved it, she invited Millevoye and her old friend Avril de St Croix in their place. That evening, Maud discovered Millevoye had a new protégée, a singer whom Avril acidly described as a 'café-chantant'. Avril had tried to warn her, whispering that Maud was away from Paris too much, but it was another few weeks before she finally understood, not only that her relationship with her lover had come to an end, but that their political alliance was also finished.[15]

Maud's belief that she was still necessary to Millevoye in order to keep him faithful to their ideals, sprang more from her imagination than from any desire on his part. Her discovery that the singer had written an article for *La Patrie,* calling for the liberation of Alsace-Lorraine and pointing to Germany, not England, as the enemy of France, finally convinced her that the relationship was over. Millevoye had long been scathing about Maud's 'absurd Irish revolutionists' and she now realised that his political concerns had never included Ireland but were solely involved with the fate of right-wing movements within France. Although her account of the ending of their affair was highly romanticised – the erstwhile lovers facing each other in 'a flowery meadow, surrounded by snow-capped mountains at the foot of Mont Blanc' – the pain of that moment when she felt her heart turn to stone is almost tangible, despite the gloss and the passing of time. They only met again on a few occasions, when Millevoye renewed his sporadic contact with their daughter Iseult. He was to die in 1918, while Maud was in Holloway prison.

Maud had another concern that summer: to spend time with Iseult and also with her half-sister Eileen, who had recently joined her household. 'Bow', the faithful old nurse had died, and so she brought Eileen, now 'a bright girl of sixteen' to Paris, to learn French until her mother, still in Russia, decided on her future. An old French widow, Madame de Bourbonne, presided over the Gonne household. But by the autumn Maud was back in the fray, speaking at pro-Boer meetings in Britain and relishing the riots they provoked. She also – at last – had the thrill of presiding over the very first meeting of a unique new organisation: Inghinidhe na hEireann. At the beginning of October the inaugural meeting of Inghinidhe na hEireann – Daughters of Erin – took place.

Maud was elected president, Annie Egan, Jenny Wyse-Power, Anna Johnson and Alice Furlong were joint vice-presidents. Maire Quinn, Dora Hackett and Elizabeth Morgan were the secretaries and Sarah White and Margaret Quinn the treasurers. They were a mixture of older women, the wives or widows of well-known nationalists, and young independent working women. Many were the sisters or girl-friends of members of the Celtic Literary Society. St Brigid was to be their patron, and they pledged themselves to an ambitious list of objectives:

The re-establishment of the complete independence of Ireland.

To encourage the study of Gaelic, of Irish Literature, History, Music and Art, especially among the young, by organising the teaching of classes for the above subjects.

To support and popularise Irish manufacture.

To discourage the reading and circulation of low English litera-ture, the singing of English songs, the attending of vulgar English entertainments at the theatres and music hall, and to combat in every way English influence, which is doing so much injury to the artistic taste and refinement of the Irish people.

To form a fund called the National Purposes Fund, for the furtherance of the above objects.[16]

The women also pledged themselves to 'mutual help and support' and, to protect themselves from possible victimisation in employment, all adopted Gaelic names. They must have enjoyed deciding on their *nom de plumes*. Maud took the name 'Maeve', after the warrior queen of the west. Maud's influence, particularly her eclectic mixture of beliefs in mythology and religion, was evident in the fact that the central branch of the Inghinidhe was under the patronage of Brigid 'in her dual character of Goddess and Saint'. At their first ceilidh, Maud gave an address on 'the Goddess Brigid' (to redress the balance Maire Killeen was to talk on the Saint Brigid on a future occasion), starting her talk with the appellation 'my sisters and friends'. It was obviously a moving occasion for Maud; not the adulation and anonymity of the mass meeting, but the warmth and intimacy of a social evening with friends. She told them how honoured she was to be chosen by her sisters to inaugurate their work and it was no mere platitude. Not since the disbandment of the Ladies' Land League had Irishwomen possessed their own organisation, and Maud shared their determination to prove women's capabilities and to claim women's rightful place within the heart of the nationalist revival.

One of the most lasting achievements of the Inghinidhe was their dedicated work in providing free classes in Irish, history, music, dance and drama for the children of Dublin. An impressive array of talent could be called on. Maud gave classes in drama when she was in Dublin and Ella Young, who taught history by retelling the myths and legends, gave a lively account of the enthusiasm felt by pupils and teachers alike:

> In a room perched at the head of a rickety staircase and overlooking a narrow street, I have about eighty denizens of untamed Dublin: newsboys, children who have played in street alleys all their lives, young patriot girls and boys who can scarcely write their own names. Outside there is a continuous din of street cries and rumbling carts. It is almost impossible to shout against it if the windows are open, and more impossible to speak in the smother of dust if the windows are shut. Everyone is standing, closely packed – no room for chairs![17]

The only accommodation they could afford was an empty loft in Strand Street, which had to be reached by climbing up a ladder, while their equipment was primitive or non-existent. Maire Perolz taught history and Irish by the light of a lantern, lightheartedly exclaiming that this made it all the more fun, while dancing teachers often had to lilt an accompaniment as they had no musical instruments or people to play them.[18] Nevertheless, their pupils started winning prizes at the Gaelic League Feis, and they could hardly cope with the demand for classes. In contrast with the stern educational theories of the day, the children were motivated by their own desire to learn and by the promise of future treats: hundreds of children attended a Christmas treat, and prize-winners had the joy of being taken on outings and excursions to places of historic interest.

All of this was in keeping with Maud's own theories of education, which she had come across on the Continent, and her interest in legends and mythology was shared by many of the membership. While these activities benefited the children who came, and proved to be of enduring worth to the nationalist movement – developing as they did both a more literate younger generation and a host of politically seasoned women activists – the personal effects upon Maud were equally considerable. For the first time in her life she had the company of a group of women who shared her commitment to Ireland and whose friendship provided her with some of her happiest memories. Ella Young loved the ancient gods and the ceremonies of the Celts. She, Maud and Helena Moloney were amongst those who would sail out to Ireland's Eye where, amidst the seagulls, they would light the Bealtaine fire of the old Gaelic festival, which also served to boil their tea kettle. Ella would then, wrote Maud, 'at the last ... kindle from it a tiny fire in which she burnt herbs she had gathered from different parts of Ireland ... which sent up a sweet scent like incense'.[19] The women would sit round the fire, telling of strange, inexplicable incidents, revelling in the companionship and the contrast with their daily lives. Maud missed Ella greatly when, disillusioned with the Free State, she left Ireland in 1926 in order to teach Celtic mythology at the University of California. She had been a friend blessed with a gift for making life colourful.

Inghinidhe na hEireann continued with its programme of activities. To raise funds for their classes they began to organise entertainments, the most popular of which were 'tableaux vivants' (living pictures), illustrating legends and scenes from the nationalist past. Male actors were recruited from the Celtic Literary Society and as confidence in their abilities grew, their performances became more ambitious. It was part of the Inghinidhe's intention to provide an alternative to the despised and unedifying diet of cheap music hall that was standard fare, and budding playwrights began to present their material for consideration. Alice Milligan, Maud's old ally from the *Shan Van Vocht*, wrote two plays that were produced in August 1901. In one of them, *The Deliverance of Red Hugh*, Maud read the legend of Red Hugh as the play opened. Ella Young described her as the curtain rose, sitting

in an ancient carved chair, with an illuminated parchment book on her knee. She had a splendid robe of brocaded white poplin with wide sleeves, and two little pages in medieval dress of black velvet held tall wax candles on either side of her. The stage was strewn with green rushes and branchlets of blossomed heather.

Maud Gonne has a sun-radiance about her. The quality of her beauty dulled the candle-flames.[20]

Cultural events were not their only concern. Maud had no intention of allowing this new organisation to dissipate its potential by becoming simply an equivalent of the Gaelic League or any other of the groups concerned with reviving the ancient culture of the Gaels. For too long she had been, as she said of herself, a 'freelance' within the nationalist movement, her presence accepted because of her personal power and charisma, while other women continued to be excluded.

Discussions relating to the federation of the various literary, political and athletic societies had been going on throughout 1900, and in September of that year delegates from several different groups met in the rooms of the Celtic Literary Society and agreed to the formation of Cumann na nGaedheal. Its first annual convention was held in November, with Willie Rooney presiding. John O'Leary, as so often before, was honoured with the presidency, while the Irish hero of the Boer War, Major MacBride, was elected vice-president *in absentia*. Maud became an honorary secretary. As Sydney Gifford, a very active member of Inghinidhe na hEireann and (using the name 'John Brennan') well-known journalist later affirmed, the affiliation of Inghinidhe na hEireann with Cumann na nGaedheal was highly significant, because at last Irishwomen had won the right to membership of political and cultural societies on equal terms with men.[21] And this was due to Maud, who had been involved throughout the discussion stages and who had insisted that women must play an equal role with men.

Just before that inaugural meeting Maud had been in Paris with Griffith, on behalf of the Irish Transvaal Committee. The British forces had almost won their brutal encounter with the Boers, herding the civilian population into concentration camps and using a scorched earth policy to wipe out further resistance. President Kruger was in Paris, still trying to raise support for the Boer cause and the Irish delegation was there to meet him. They were also there to greet their own Irish hero. Most of the foreign volunteers had left Africa as the war was now a guerrilla one, where only those with local knowledge and an ability to speak the language could be of use. The Irish Brigade disbanded and John MacBride wrote to his old friend Griffith to say that he was on his way home. He could not go to Ireland, as he would face arrest for treason, so France was to be his place of exile. During Maud's last American tour she had praised John MacBride for having 'saved Ireland's honour' by organising the Irish Brigade in the Transvaal. She was finally to meet the man himself as she and Griffith, together with members of the Paris Young Ireland Society, went to the Gare de Lyon to ensure that he was given a hero's welcome.

A wiry, soldierly-looking man with red hair and skin burnt brick-red by the African sun stepped down off the train, touched to find so many old friends there to greet him. Griffith was staying in Maud's apartment, where MacBride was to join them for dinner. They ended up talking through the night, Maud furiously smoking one cigarette after another, listening excitedly to someone who had actually engaged the British forces in battle. She was thrilled to hear of Irishmen fighting England and delighted to hear tales of guns and soldiers captured by the Irish Brigade, exclaiming how good it was at last to see the situation reversed. Wanting to impress her new friend, Maud told of trying to stop recruitment to the British army and with a laugh

MacBride replied that many Irishmen deserted to join the Irish Brigade.[22]. As she listened, Maud was more convinced than ever that action was what counted. She had worshipped her soldier father, and worked closely with writers, philosophers and men of action, but no one had ever reached the heroic proportions of John MacBride, whom some have described as a 'fighting machine'. Her relationship with Millevoye irrevocably over and marriage to Willie Yeats never on the cards, Maud was ripe for a new liaison, one that would combine the most important of all her beliefs and causes.

MacBride's most immediate preoccupation was what to do now, an unemployed hero, since Ireland was out of the question for him. Griffith and Maud persuaded him to undertake a lecture tour of America, combining their resources to write a suitable lecture for him to deliver, as he had confessed his inability to compile one himself. On 9 December, MacBride arrived in America. But it was a painful ordeal for one more used to open spaces and action than crowded halls and words. Finally, in desperation, he wrote to Maud, begging her to join him, adding that 'he could not get things going unless [she] came'.[23] On 10 February Maud joined MacBride.

Ireland's Joan of Arc and the hero of the Irish Brigade made a formidable combination, although their reception was not over-whelmingly triumphant: the high point of solidarity with the Boers had passed and such fervour could not be automatically rekindled simply because Major MacBride was present to give his account in person. Besides, as one journalist complained, 'We hope that with a little practice, the Major will be able to tell the story off-hand, for having to read it takes away very much from its interest.'[24] Over the next months he did succeed in learning his speech, his letters to his mother showing his increased self-confidence and his growing admir-ation for Maud, 'Miss Gonne astonishes me the way in which she can stand the knocking about. For a woman it is wonderful.'[25] Although Maud was criticised for some of her speeches in which she attacked the United Irish League by name, as well as constitutionalists gener-ally, she was also at pains to tell of the constructive work carried out by nationalists at home. She described the formation of Cumann na nGaedheal, urging the Irish women of America to give it their moral and financial support and praising them for the enthusiasm they had so far shown. She also gave particular emphasis to the anti-recruiting success of the women of the Transvaal Committee and Inghinidhe na hEireann. It must have been a very satisfying experience to be able to highlight the specific contribution of women, rather than simply describing the political situation.

Maud continued to be the star attraction of the double act which was gradually travelling across America. When they reached Boston she received a telegram from Griffith, telling of the premature death of his best friend, Willie Rooney. Although in complete agreement that

Rooney's loss to the movement was irreparable, Maud replied in a
surprisingly unsympathetic vein, saying that the only consolation she
had ever found for sorrow was in redoubled work. The warm,
generous friend could disappear when involved in a new venture, and
for that moment, her American tour was uppermost in her mind. But
when they reached Philadelphia there was a broken-hearted letter
from Griffith, giving details of the circumstances surrounding
Rooney's death from overwork. Griffith spent a week in hospital
himself at this time, so close was he to a complete breakdown, and
another letter reached Maud in St Louis, begging her not to stay away
too long. She had been absent for almost four months and she finally
decided that it was indeed time to leave. MacBride had to be reassured
that he was now capable of continuing alone, and then they went their
separate ways. Maud's verdict on the tour was that it hadn't accomplished much, apart from raising some money to keep the *United
Irishman* going.[26] Her memoirs claim that John MacBride proposed
to her during this time, her reply a declaration that marriage was not
in her thoughts as long as there was a war on – and, of course, there
was always an Irish war on.

Maud's return was to France, not Ireland. Griffith might be in need
of her, but she had Iseult to see first. It had been a long time since she
had seen her little daughter, whom she had placed in a convent in
Laval while she was away. There was little of the maternal role in
Maud: her attitude was more reminiscent of an indulgent godmother
who could happily shower gifts on a child, confident that she would
not be around to deal with the consequences. This time, Maud had
smuggled out from America a baby alligator as her present for the
little seven year old. When she arrived in London and told Kathleen's
children of Iseult's pet, they were desperately envious of their cousin,
but were diverted by the dachshund puppy Maud had bought for
May, as well as by the French scent and bonbons she had hidden in her
bag for the rest of the family. The children regarded their Auntie
Maud as 'attractive and mysterious', as she came and went in their
lives with little explanation and less ceremony. The family were all
gathered in London to attend May Gonne's marriage to Bertie Clay,
an English civil servant stationed in India and home on leave. Despite
the Gonne curse against happy marriages, apparently the result of an
ancestor who had stolen church lands, Maud hoped that marriage
would prove 'a great adventure' for May; the monotonous existence
of her cousins, living dull, uneventful lives in a beautiful house,
disturbed her greatly. Their youth was passing, and they might as well
be dead; unlike Maud, who at the age of thirty-five had packed in
more than most could manage in a whole lifetime.

The family was still at dinner when Willie Yeats arrived. It was the
famous occasion when, looking critically at Maud who looked tired
and who still wore her dark travelling clothes, he contrasted that sight

with her sister Kathleen, whom Maud lovingly thought looked 'more than ever like a tall lily, with her pale gold hair and white evening dress'. Willie complimented Kathleen on her gown and told her she looked beautiful. Kathleen's remark that it was 'hard work being beautiful' he later turned into the poem 'Adam's Curse', which Maud found so redolent of memories that she reproduced it in her autobiography.[27] Maud was always careless of her appearance, her beauty no more than a weapon to be used in the cause of Irish freedom. Her niece Thora remembered her mother sitting in front of a mirror, painstakingly crimping her hair, while Maud dashed into the room, quickly sticking in a pin to hold up her mass of curls before rushing off again.

The next day, Maud and Willie went to see the Lia Fail, Ireland's Stone of Destiny, on which kings used to be crowned, and which was stolen by the English. Maud and Willie used to visit it regularly in Westminster Abbey, dreaming of its return to their Castle of the Heroes. Willie returned to his perpetual question – why didn't Maud marry him and live a peaceful life amongst artists and writers? Her reply was revealing in many ways, admitting as it did both the sorrows of her life and her determination not to indulge in introspection:

... you make beautiful poetry out of what you call your unhappiness and you are happy in that. Marriage would be such a dull affair. Poets should never marry. The world should thank me for not marrying you. I will tell you one thing, our friendship has meant a great deal to me; it has helped me often when I needed help, needed it perhaps more than you or anyone ever knew, for I never talk or even think of these things.[28]

Maud believed her past sufferings, and the conviction that she could never again suffer as much, had strengthened her and given her a great calm. Once again she dismissed Willie's appeal, declaring her only interest to be in her political work. In many ways Maud was right in what she claimed. Her life had reached some kind of stability. Her political work was flourishing, and now that her affair with Millevoye had ended she planned to spend more time in Ireland and was preparing to move into a house in Coulson Avenue with George and Violet Russell for neighbours. She had also found a new romantic interest, who conveniently could not return to Ireland, so she would still be free to live her own life. The new century offered the promise of a contentment notably lacking in the turbulent years that had gone before.

CHAPTER 5

MARRIAGE

Inghinidhe na hEireann was going from strength to strength. Familiar scenes of enthusiasm followed Maud as she travelled around, publicising the new group. She helped to establish branches in Ballina, Cork and Limerick and, during the second year of the group's existence, they were instrumental in staging what was to become one of the most significant plays in the nationalist repertoire: *Cathleen ni Houlihan*.

The Inghinidhe actresses were being coached by two talented brothers, Frank and William Fay, whom Maud had persuaded to take an interest in her group. Willie Yeats, watching them at work, was impressed. He had recently finished *Cathleen ni Houlihan* and badly wanted the woman who had inspired it to take the title role. Maud had refused to act in his *Countess Cathleen*, arguing that she could not divert her energies from her political work. This time her participation in the play was his condition for giving it to Inghinidhe na hEireann. The Fay brothers were to act as producers. From Paris, Maud wrote excitedly to Willie:

> delighted to hear that you have given Cathleen ni Houlihan to Fay. Did you write him that I would act the part of Cathleen? Have you got another copy that you could let me have, as I would like to learn the words here and then go over them with you in London. . . . They must begin rehearsing it without me – as they are very slow and take a great time rehearsing a play and I would not be in Dublin long enough to do all that with them. I have a lot of work here, a lecture on the 4th, one the 14th and one the 20th Feb. and another on the 4th March beside a lot of other work.[1]

Still the same Maud, busily attending to her numerous interests and resorting to fairly autocratic behaviour to ensure no time was wasted with unnecessary preparations. That could be left to others. One of Maud's greatest assets was her ability to spot potential talent, which the charm of her presence had little difficulty in converting into reliable and willing assistance. It was one of the explanations for her successful pursuit of so many ventures. This time, it was support for the beleaguered Boers that ensured Maud's continued stay in Paris during the first rehearsals of *Cathleen*. But Major MacBride was also back in Paris, although she didn't mention this to Willie.

Maud was worried about MacBride's future, marooned in France with little ability to speak the language, and felt he should have stayed in America where he had many more openings. She was keen to advertise his existence, in the hope that some positive offer might be the result, so before one of the largest of the public meetings she was due to address, Maud informed the organisers that Major MacBride would share the platform with her. Despite intensive coaching on her part, his French was so bad the audience thought he was speaking Dutch.[2] But anti-British feeling was sufficiently strong in Paris to guarantee a standing ovation regardless. However, her other commitments were looming and, as promised, March saw her in Dublin rehearsing her part.

Cathleen ni Houlihan was everything that Maud had wanted from Willie's genius. Set at the time of the French landing during the '98 Rising, the simple one-act play concerned a peasant cottage visited by an old woman with a long cloak: Ireland herself. The musical lilt of the Irish speech rhythms had a simplicity that appealed to the sophisticated and uneducated alike:

OLD WOMAN: It is a hard service they take that help me. Many that are red-cheeked now will be pale-cheeked; many that have been free to walk the hills and the bogs and the rushes will be sent to walk hard streets in far countries; many a good plan will be broken; many that have gathered money will not stay to spend it; many a child will be born and there will be no father at its christening to give it a name. They that had red cheeks will have pale cheeks for my sake; and for all that they will think they are well paid.

She goes out. Her voice is heard outside singing.

They shall be remembered for ever;
They shall be alive for ever;
They shall be speaking for ever;
The people shall hear them for ever.

On 2 April 1902, in the tiny St Theresa's Hall, the Irish National Theatre Company, as the group now termed itself, gave the first performance of *Cathleen ni Houlihan*, together with AE's play *Deirdre*, in which Maire Quinn, Helen Laird and Maire nic Shiubhlaigh acted. In front of the footlights, the banner of the Inghinidhe – a golden sunburst on a blue background – was displayed in all its glory, and the

packed theatre of 'gleaming shirt fronts mingled with the less resplendent garb of the Dublin worker' waited in eager anticipation. Many had
come to honour the memory of Willie Rooney, in whose memory
Yeats had dedicated his play. Maire nic Shiubhlaigh, who was later to
model her performance on Maud's interpretation, described the
sensation caused as the leading lady strode through the hushed
auditorium, typically ignoring the painstaking rehearsals of the Fays,
her dramatic entrance in blatant disregard of theatrical tradition. All
who witnessed the performance which followed were in agreement as
to its power. When Maud flung off the cloak of the old woman and
drew herself up to her full height to become 'a young girl with the
walk of a queen', she became the very image of a free nation. As Maire
nic Shiubhlaigh wrote:

> Watching her, one could readily understand the reputation she
> enjoyed as the most beautiful woman in Ireland, the inspiration
> of the whole revolutionary movement. She was the most ex-
> quisitely-fashioned creature I have ever seen. Her beauty was
> *startling*. . . . In her, the youth of the country saw all that was
> magnificent in Ireland. She was the very personification of the
> figure she portrayed on the stage.[3]

The begrudgers said that Maud did not act the part so much as live
it, but her performance was all Yeats had hoped for. He wrote
delightedly to Lady Gregory that Maud had played the part 'magnificently and with weird power'.[4] By the third and final night, crowds
were being turned away from the theatre. The small group had lacked
the resources to book the hall for more than three nights but in that
short time the play entered the realms of mythology. After the 1916
Rising Yeats asked himself 'Did that play of mine/Send out certain
men the English shot?' and Maud was always to regret that he never
again produced such an emotive masterpiece. To many people – and
maybe also to herself – she was Cathleen ni Houlihan for ever more. It
was perhaps no coincidence that her favourite poem of Yeats's was
'Red Hanrahan's Song About Ireland', with its refrain 'But we have
hidden in our hearts the flame out of the eyes/Of Cathleen, the
daughter of Houlihan.'

A further result of this theatrical triumph was the consolidation of
the Irish National Theatre, which moved into a hall in Camden Street.
Yeats became president of the new organisation, while Maud joined
Lady Gregory, AE and Douglas Hyde on the board of directors. The
first tentative stage in the creation of a truly national theatre had been
achieved.

The winter of 1902 saw Maud back in Paris, where her friendship
with John MacBride was flourishing. He had secured a position as

secretary to the correspondent of the *American Sun* and Laffan's Bureau at a salary of £2 a week. It wasn't an enormous amount of money, but it enabled him to live, and although Maud suspected his employer of pro-British tendencies, she was relieved that MacBride had some means of supporting himself, however small. As a woman with an adequate income and a generous nature, she found the male insistence on maintaining traditional codes of behaviour to be a source of continual irritation. She found herself having to use all her powers of diplomacy to avoid offending the penniless young Irishmen she came into contact with in Paris, whom she felt were 'morbidly sensitive' about their lack of money. Maud would have to pretend to prefer walking, even when desperately tired, to save them the cost of the cab they would have insisted paying for, and MacBride was at least as sensitive as all the others. He was also extremely conventional in his attitudes. On one occasion, trying to prevent him from spending unnecessarily, Maud suggested they have tea in his room. He was shocked at the suggestion, but she gaily told him 'he must get rid of the English idea that a bedroom was a less proper place than a sitting room, for he was full of queer conventions'.[5] He did manage to put aside his scruples on this issue and the pair spent the winter discussing 'fantastic plans' in MacBride's little attic and in Maud's more comfortable drawing room. These were not romantic discussions about a happy future life; the couple's courtship revolved around the spinning of elaborate plots to win Irish freedom. Maud's hopes for French assistance had disappeared with the ending of her affair with Millevoye, but her old optimism was being rekindled as she developed her new alliance. MacBride was an Irishman, and there was no possibility that he would ever be diverted from the struggle as Millevoye had been. MacBride had many clandestine contacts within the revolutionary movement and the mysterious hints he occasionally uttered served to convince Maud of his importance – to her personally as well as to Ireland. One day he announced that he was making plans to meet secretly with some American contacts that he felt would prove of great use in the future. Spain was to be the rendezvous point.

Spain was also an ideal place for a honeymoon, and Maud agreed to become the wife of John MacBride. She was thirty-six, he was thirty-five. Letters Maud wrote to her sister Kathleen throw much light on all the pressures she was experiencing at this stage in her life.[6] They reveal a woman far removed from the popular image of Cathleen ni Houlihan:

> Little sister, neither you or anyone on earth quite knows the hard life I have led, for I never told of my troubles and I have preferred to be envied rather than pitied. Now I see the chance, without injuring my work, of having a little happiness and peace in my personal life and I am taking it.

Most importantly of all, Maud was concerned for the future welfare of Iseult, whom she still referred to publicly as her niece. 'Marriage I always consider abominable but for the sake of Iseult, I make that sacrifice to convention.' She revealed her need for what she termed 'companionship', feeling that with Iseult growing up and soon to enter society she could only get such companionship within marriage. Her relationship with Millevoye was over and all her energies were concentrated upon Irish affairs. Defying convention and studiously ignoring the gossips had been possible in France, but it had certain repercussions in Ireland, one of the most crucial of which was that it was impossible for Maud, as an unmarried woman, to bring Iseult over to her little house in Coulson Avenue, without provoking much unwelcome speculation. She had once proudly stated 'they may say what they like about me, but not to me', but no one could remain indifferent for ever. Marriage would provide the necessary respectability. Throughout, one receives no indication of a woman deeply in love, 'I am sorry you don't like the idea of my marriage – but overall I think it is the best thing I can do. I am getting old and oh so tired.'

Maud made it plain that she regarded her relationship with MacBride to be a political alliance as well as a personal one. She explained to Kathleen that they were both interested in the same work and 'the Irish movement is a people's movement'. All of that was fairly incomprehensible to someone married to an army officer and uninterested in politics. Kathleen remained unconvinced and very concerned for her sister's happiness. She wondered if Maud would not be happier with Willie, but Maud replied:

As for Willie Yeats I love him dearly as a friend, but I could not for one moment imagine marrying him. I think I will be happy with John. Our lives are exactly the same and he is so fond and thoughtful that it makes life very easy when he is there and besides we have a vitality and joy in life which I used to have once, but which the hard life I have had wore out of me; with him I seem to get it back again a little.

She again made it plain that she expected marriage to MacBride would not alter her lifestyle in any way; she would be 'just as independent and live my life as I always have and go on with my work in the same way'. Marriage to Willie, with all his ideas on art and life, would never allow for that. Kathleen seems to have persevered with her objections. Her own unhappy marriage obviously gave her greater cause to be concerned for her sister's future. But Maud rebuked her for listening to 'tales of very prejudiced people', when Kathleen repeated unsavoury rumours concerning MacBride (probably about his drinking). Ironically, she concluded by stating that they were both strong enough to separate, but that she did not anticipate this. She admitted 'marriage is a hideous risk' and then she went ahead with her plans.

Kathleen was not the only person to have forebodings. Everyone who knew them seems to have tried to prevent the marriage. Arthur Griffith pleaded with Maud:

> Queen, forgive me. John MacBride, after Willie Rooney, is the best friend I ever had; you are the only woman friend I have. I only think of both your happiness. For your own sakes and for the sake of Ireland to whom you both belong, don't get married. I know you both, you so unconventional – a law to yourself; John so full of conventions. You will not be happy for long.[7]

The widowed Mrs MacBride wrote from her home in the west of Ireland to tell her son that Maud would not make him happy, and his older brother Joseph warned 'She is accustomed to money and you have none; she is used to going her own way and listens to no one. . . . These are not good qualities for a wife.'[8] When Maud visited Iseult in her convent, to explain about the forthcoming wedding, that 'strangely wise child' (as Maud later described her daughter), wept and clung to her mother, begging her not to marry, saying she hated him. The nuns had to drag her away, while Maud felt close to tears herself. Even the long-dead Tommy warned her against the marriage. Maud was convinced, as she lay exhausted in her desolate flat the night before the wedding, possessions packed and waiting for the removers, fireplace full of burnt papers, that she heard her father's voice say 'Lambkin, don't do it. You must not get married.' At that moment, her fiancé called to take her to dinner. The two of them showed each other their letters of caution and then, with her characteristic laugh and disregard for the opinions of others, Maud shrugged and declared 'a short life and a merry one'. She was a person who thrived on opposition, it challenged her, but sometimes she saw only the challenge and not the good sense contained within. She and John MacBride were married on 21 February 1903.

A few days before the marriage, Maud became a Roman Catholic. Her autobiography tells of her conversion in a chapter entitled 'The Inevitability of the Church', where she describes her meeting with the Boulangist priest Canon Dissard, who predicted that she would eventually convert. He was to be the one to receive her formally into the Church, although she gives no date for this, and neither does she mention her marriage as a reason. But in a letter to Kathleen, Maud admitted that it was because of John MacBride that she had put aside her doubts, although she was hardly the most orthodox of believers:

> I want to look at truth from the same side as the man I am going to marry . . . and whether I call the great spirit-force Archangels, whether I call them the Sidhe or the gods matters little.

Typically, there was a political bonus in this move, as she explained to Willie Yeats, 'I have often longed to denounce the priests and could not because I was a Protestant, but now I can.'[9] The Protestant Church was also the church of the oppressor; through this act Maud drew even closer to the people of her adopted country. But it was not something she wished to publicise and the event itself was private, with Maud refusing to give any information to the newspapers. She took the name of Honoria, the name of MacBride's mother, who was one of her sponsors. Despite her eclectic views on religion, in 1910 she deepened her identification with the Church by becoming a member of the Third (secular) Order of St Francis, lover of animals and a saint whose teachings strongly attracted her.

At her parish church of St Honore d'Eylau in Paris, Father Van Hecke, former chaplain to the Transvaal Brigade, performed the wedding ceremony. The bride wore 'a costume of electric blue', the best man carried the green flag of the Irish Brigade and the bridesmaid the blue flag presented to the Brigade by the Inghinidhe. For some reason Maud Collins, the wife of MacBride's best man, was Maud's bridesmaid. None of her own close friends were asked to act in that capacity. Had she wanted their presence or had she decided to confine the occasion to her new family? She did insist on having as quiet a ceremony as possible, although the Inghinidhe had not forgotten their president – they sent over the wedding-breakfast table decoration of shamrocks and violets. Maud was not the conventional bride, smiling sweetly while the men gave the speeches and offered the toasts – it was she who gave the final toast at this wedding: 'To the complete independence of Ireland'.[10]

In Maud's old age she confided to a friend that she and MacBride had heard that the King and Queen of England were going to visit Spain, and the two concocted a plot to assassinate the King. MacBride was to do the actual deed but he needed a cover, which the honeymoon trip would provide. Maud was totally unabashed in telling this tale, which was heavily censored by her family before she was permitted to include any reference to Spain in her autobiography. It sounds like an adventurous fiction, but some may feel that this offers a plausible explanation for what finally precipitated Maud into marriage. Their wedding trip was to Spain at any event, but there is no evidence of any assassination attempt. Records show that the King visited Portugal on 2 April and Gibraltar on 8 April, so it might simply have been that their intelligence was inaccurate, leading them to be in the wrong place at the wrong time.[11]

Maud's chief memory was of the cold. She froze in the Spanish winter and felt she had never been so cold in her whole life. It was not an auspicious start to married life. After a week they travelled to Normandy, where they spent the rest of their honeymoon in a small country inn. From there, Maud replied to the letters of congratulation.

On 28 February she wrote to Lady Gregory, describing the complications involved in marriage to a Boer War veteran:

> ... I was married at the English Consulate, as well as at my parish church, so I think it is quite legal.
>
> We had heard that there was a possibility of the English trying to arrest Major MacBride at the consulate – but I do not think it would have been really possible, as even if the consulate is English territory, which is doubtful, they could not have imprisoned him there for long, and once outside he would have been free. No such attempt was made. The Consul was rather rude and began asking irrelevant questions, but when Major MacBride refused to answer, and told him it was no business of his, he went through the ceremony without further trouble.
>
> Once more, let me thank you for your kind wishes, and with kind regards, I remain, dear Lady Gregory, very sincerely yours, Maud Gonne.
>
> I am looking forward eagerly to the appearance of your new book on Finn, your Cuchulain is one of my husband's and my favourite books.[12]

The insistence on maintaining her own name was notable. The polite postscript concerning the liking of herself and her husband for the work of Lady Gregory looks like the afterthought of someone anxious to think of something pleasant and personal to say to someone with whom one has never been on close terms. Maud also knew that her letter would be relayed to Willie Yeats and, for that reason also, would have wished to present as cordial an image as possible. She says nothing about the marriage or honeymoon, but Lady Gregory was not a friend to confide in. At this stage Maud had not been in contact with Willie for some time. Her courage failed her when it came to letting him know of her plans to marry: she could not have faced his anguish, or have given a satisfactory explanation for her decision. She sent him a telegram which he received just as he was about to give a lecture:

> Some may have blamed you that you took away
> The verses that could move them on the day
> When, the ears being deafened, the sight of the eyes blind
> With lightning, you went from me
>
> ('Reconciliation')

Afterwards, he remembered nothing of his talk as he wandered alone through the Dublin streets, devastated by the shock of this betrayal. Two poems written in 1905, 'O Do not Love Too Long' and

'Never Give All The Heart', are explicit statements of his bitter feelings:

> I loved long and long,
> And grew to be out of fashion
> Like an old song,

and:

> He that made this knows all the cost,
> For he gave all his heart and lost.

The honeymoon was not a long one. Irreconcilable differences between Maud and her husband soon began to manifest themselves. She began to realise the extent of his drinking and some claim that she refused to share her bed after the first few months of marriage. What is beyond doubt is that in May, Maud was in London making her peace with Willie and telling him of her unhappiness, confessing that she had 'married in a sudden impulse of anger'. As usual, Lady Gregory was soon informed of Maud's situation. She replied in sympathetic vein:

> It is very sad your friend should have taken such a step for what seems so slight a motive. It shows how hard it is for any of us to escape from our surroundings. What did it matter to her what Paris people thought... and yet there is an imperceptible influence closing round one all the time – a net to catch the feet.[13]

Her oblique references would seem to indicate that one of the factors which had influenced Maud was conventional opinion – not only in Ireland, but in France also – which viewed her lifestyle with increasing suspicion, making it difficult for her to continue as before. The journalist, Chris Healy, reported that Maud was totally out of favour in upper-class French circles. The Princess Karageorgevitch had icily informed him 'We used to receive Mlle. Gonne at one time, but we do not know her now.' Had the ending of her affair with Millevoye removed the protection created by his patronage?[14]

In later years Maud was to claim that she cut her honeymoon short in order to mobilise public opinion against the visit to Dublin of the new monarch – King Edward VII. Rumours of an impending royal visit had been circulating in Ireland for a year. Inghinidhe na hEireann had circulated leaflets to women voters in the local government election of January 1902, urging them to vote against anyone who had participated in welcoming Queen Victoria. They were the first group to organise any protest and although it was a year before the King actually arrived, Maud's organisation had demonstrated its determination to mobilise a greater resistance than that offered to his mother. Nationalists were stronger and more confident of their ability to muster support than they had been three years previously. As soon as news of the impending visit was made public, the playwright Edward Martyn wrote a letter of protest, 'It is for Nationalist Ireland to ... tell the government with one voice that if they bring the King here under any other guise than as a restorer of our stolen constitution they will regret their rashness.' Tim Harrington, the man who had advised Maud to work for the Donegal peasants, was now the Lord Mayor of Dublin, and she felt sure that he would resist pressure to welcome the King. But on 9 May, Arthur Griffith published inside information which claimed that an address of welcome would be placed on the agenda of Dublin Corporation while Harrington arranged to be conveniently out of the city. Maud's account of hearing this news from Yeats depicts her travelling over from London, wondering how to prevent this capitulation and eventually having the brainwave that Harrington, who was billed to chair a meeting of the Irish Parliamentary Party (as she saw from large posters stuck around the city), must be publicly challenged to repudiate the rumour. As soon as she arrived in Ireland she sent out a dozen telegrams: 'Without fail be at my cottage, Rathgar, three o'clock tomorrow afternoon. Meet Griffith, Martyn, Moore and others for most important conference. Maud Gonne.'[15]

The delegation decided to call itself the 'People's Protection Committee', and Edward Martyn was chosen to ask the crucial question. Maire Quinn, after welcoming Maud back with a big hug, rushed off to round up members of the Inghinidhe and Cumann na nGaedheal, who would take up 'strategic positions' in case of trouble. Maud thought it was all going to be 'great fun'. On 18 May she led the small delegation onto the stage to confront the Irish Party. Martyn was too nervous to hold the prepared statement without trembling, so Maud whisked it out of his hands, and in her most commanding voice asked Harrington if he was going to welcome the English King. Harrington refused to answer the question, the audience began to take sides and violence was the predictable result. To Maud's eternal annoyance, Seamus MacManus carried her off the stage to safety while angry Irish Party stalwarts rushed the platform and members of Inghinidhe na hEireann and Cumann na nGaedheal left their seats to protect the delegation. As MacManus and Maud left the Rotunda they met ambulances hurrying to collect the casualties.

It was an exciting night. The *Irish Times* declared the delegation to have been responsible for 'one of the most sensational incidents in the recent history of Irish politics' and AE wrote to Yeats that Maud had 'rudely shocked last night in the most gorgeous row Dublin has had since Jubilee time. The Rotunda meeting was a free fight and two MPs are incapacitated'. Maud's happy reflection was that Harrington had been removed from his difficult situation as no one could now suggest asking him to leave Dublin. Once again, Maud's memoirs might have claimed much credit for herself, but contemporary accounts confirm the importance of her role. Her intention had been to mobilise public opinion and this was undoubtedly achieved.

As a result of the publicity generated by the 'Battle of the Rotunda', a series of meetings was launched to protest against any address of welcome being voted by Dublin Corporation. By July, when the Corporation finally met to vote on the question, the address was voted against by a majority of three. As the nationalists left the crowded council chambers where they had assembled to watch over the count, Maud was cheered with 'almost delirious enthusiasm' as she and Jenny Wyse-Power left the building. For the first time since the Norman invasion, Dublin refused recognition to a British monarch.[16]

Soon after the Rotunda protest, Maud returned to France and her family. She and her husband, together with Iseult and Eileen, were about to have a summer holiday together. Great-Aunt Augusta had died, leaving her a legacy with which she was able to buy a house on the Normandy coast. It was one of the few occasions on which she had sufficient capital for such a purchase. The Gonne trust provided an income, but its assets could not be touched, which is why Maud often resorted to selling off her jewels. Early in June she wrote to Kathleen, describing the place near Colleville that was to become almost a second home to her:

> I am down by the sea with John and the children an economy treat for the summer months. The more I see of this place the more I love it. It is so wild and so country. The garden goes down to the sea and the fields full of wild flowers come down to the garden, and there is no one but ourselves. We go about most of the day in bathing dresses and shrimping and fishing take up a lot of time. I paint and am teaching what little painting I know to the children but it is a case of the blind leading the blind. However, we daub away very contentedly amid our singing birds and barking dogs. I may have to go over to Ireland again shortly but only for a very short time.[17]

The 'short time' mentioned was for the actual visit of the King on 21 July. As their contribution to the protests surrounding his visit, Inghinidhe na hEireann posted up copies of the Coronation Oath, which repudiated the basic doctrines of the Roman Catholic religion and linked the monarchy with the Church of England. Although lacking the money to pay for the 10,000 copies they had printed – Maud the optimist declared St Brigid would provide – they went ahead regardless. But Maud, returning home to Coulson Avenue after the postering session, felt dissatisfied with the tameness of the gesture.

She wanted something more defiant as an expression of her personal opposition to the King, although this time assassination was not on the agenda. Pope Leo XIII had just died, but the profusion of Union Jacks around the city meant that there could be no mourning for the pontiff. On impulse, yet realising the reaction it would provoke, Maud hung out a black petticoat on a broom handle before going to bed. The next morning her unionist neighbours spotted the makeshift flag amidst the sea of Union Jacks festooning the street and the police were summonsed to remove it. What became known as 'The Battle of Coulson Avenue' began. Maud immediately put up another petticoat and she, along with Maire Quinn, 'a fine strong lump of an agricultural girl', and her housekeeper 'Mrs Fitz', defended the house against the efforts of the police and irate neighbours to pull it down. While Maud harangued the police, Maire threw a bottle at a neighbour perched on Maud's roof. He fell off, suffering a bumped head and possible broken arm. Maire's fiancé, Dudley Digges, had put a notice on the door of Inghinidhe's office, telling all members to go to Coulson Avenue, while Griffith sent athletes from Cumann na nGaedheal. Once the reinforcements arrived, the police decided they were outnumbered and withdrew. Maud's black flag for the Pope stayed defiantly aloft for the rest of the King's visit. The visit itself proved to be so uneventful that the bored journalists, deprived of newsworthy stories, gave Maud's antics more publicity than the event would otherwise have merited.[18]

Maud and her lieutenant, Maire, later travelled to Belfast in order to take part in a nationalist rally on the Falls Road. Inghinidhe na hEireann also organised another of their Children's Treats, which this time took place on the same day as that arranged for loyalist children in Phoenix Park. It was on a much less lavish scale than their previous triumph, having been hurriedly organised within a week. Despite the pouring rain they claimed that 15,000 children attended, as opposed to 9,000 in Phoenix Park. But they had not attempted to mobilise much support, and admitted that they had not collected enough money to cover expenses, which had to be covered from Inghinidhe's own funds.[19] Maud's return to Dublin at this time was the likely reason for their sudden decision to provide for the children. In all her political activities, she always remembered children's needs, while many of the younger women members of Inghinidhe na hEireann were by now far more interested in other forms of political activity, working alongside the male members of Cumann na nGaedheal.

Inghinidhe na hEireann, despite the prolonged absences of its president, was by now a fully integrated component of the national movement. Maud was a vice-president of Cumann na nGaedheal and at its fourth convention, held in November 1903, Maire Quinn and Mary Macken became two of the secretaries of the organisation. While her protégées' political careers flourished, the vicissitudes of

Maud's personal life entailed her growing isolation from the mainstream of the steadily reviving nationalist movement.

The last public event Maud took part in during that crowded year of 1903 was a continuation of her old dispute with Willie Yeats over art versus propaganda. The occasion was the first night of Synge's first play, *In the Shadow of the Glen,* a starkly realistic depiction of a young wife trapped in a loveless marriage to a peasant farmer, who escapes by running away with a tramp. Maire nic Shiubhlaigh played Nora and Willie Fay was the tramp. In the middle of the performance, Maud walked out of the hall, to be followed by Maire Quinn and Dudley Digges. The next day reviews unanimously damned the play. Most nationalists disliked it for its impugning of the virtue of Irishwomen, but Maud's objections were on political rather than moralistic grounds. It would have been untypically hypocritical of her to pretend that Ireland possessed no Noras, frustrated and bored with life, disliking their husbands, so she discreetly avoided that issue:

> It is for the many, for the people that Irish writers must write, and if the Irish people do not understand or care for an Irish play, I should feel very doubtful of its right to rank as national literature, though all the critics in England were loud in its praise and though I myself might see beauty in it.[20]

The Irish National Theatre was dissolved as a result of the bitter differences of opinion amongst its members. When a new company was formed, Maud was not on the board of directors. Although she and Willie made their peace yet again, her public gesture of disapproval was a blow that took time to forgive. As Yeats went off to a lecture tour of America, thankful he had some means of escape from the controversy, Maud returned to Paris and her marriage. She was five months pregnant.

While in Colleville Maud had asked Kathleen for the address of a Mrs Gunn, who was presumably a midwife since Maud explained 'I may need her services in six or seven months. I think she would be a greater comfort than a French nurse.'[21] It was a rather wistful comment, as if Maud would have liked to return to the familiarity of the English-speaking world. But with her husband an exile, that was not possible. On 26 January 1904, Maud's son was born. His name was registered as 'Jean Seagan MacBride', the more modern form 'Sean' not used until many years later. At long last, almost thirteen years after the death of George, Maud had another son. Despite everything that might happen in the future, her life had a source of happiness that nothing could dispel. It was as if she had been reprieved from those desperate feelings of guilt she had struggled to overcome for so long. Friends have testified to the joyful chaos of her home in France, baby Sean at its heart, as Ella Young witnessed:

Thomas Gonne. Reproduced by F. Czira. (Courtesy of Anna MacBride White)

Kathleen Gonne. (*Courtesy of Anna MacBride White*)

May Gonne. (*Courtesy of Anna MacBride White*)

Portrait of Maud by Sarah Purser, painted shortly after she began her political career. Note the presence of 'chaperone', the pet monkey. 'Sweet one and twenty' was Maud's unenthusiastic comment on this attempt to capture her likeness. (*National Gallery of Ireland*)

Maud and the faithful Dagda. A studio portrait taken around 1889. (*National Library of Ireland*)

Lucien Millevoye in his study, 1902. The dog in his lap suggests that he shared Maud's love of dogs. (*Roger-Viollet*)

Maud speaking to a crowd, probably in Ballina, at the unveiling of a monument commemorating the United Irishmen's Rising of 1798. Her friend Madame de Sainte-Croix is possibly the owner of the large hat, standing behind Maud. (*Courtesy of the MacBride family*)

Sketch of the Humbert Monument in Ballina. Maud disliked its overly elaborate details, but defended it as coming from the heart of the people. (*Courtesy of Mary Hiney Loftus*)

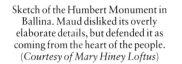

A simple plaque laid by Maud at Kilcummin, Co. Mayo, scene of General Humbert's landing in 1798. (*Photo by Paddy Hillyard*)

"I CAME HERE TODAY TO
STAND ON THIS HISTORIC
SPOT IN ORDER TO
COMMEMORATE THE LANDING
OF MY COUNTRYMEN HERE
ONE HUNDRED YEARS AGO"
MAUD GONNE MacBRIDE
22ND AUG 1898.

A modern memorial to the French forces, erected beside the wall containing Maud's plaque, and unveiled by Sean MacBride in 1987. Its simplicity would have appealed to his mother. (*Photo by Paddy Hillyard*)

A scene from the first production of Cathleen ni Houlihan, with Maud (on right) in the title role. Dublin, 1902. (*Raymond Mander and Joe Mitchenson Theatre Collection*)

Maud, her husband Major John MacBride and their infant Sean, the flag of the Irish Brigade in the foreground. Paris, 1904. (*Courtesy of the MacBride family*)

Maud and baby Sean. (*Courtesy of the MacBride family*)

Maud, Sean and Iseult Gonne. (*Courtesy of the MacBride family*)

There are many dogs, large and small: Great Danes, Toy Pomeranians, haughty court-bred Pekinese, and one Persian cat. There is a parrot that curses in Spanish, and a comrade that yells in a language of its own. There are many servants. Everyone speaks French. The centre of delight in the household is Maud Gonne's son ... a golden-haired boy.[22]

The love and pride Maud had felt for her other children could not be publicly expressed because she was not married to their father. This made Sean's arrival even more important. The scrapbook devoted to his birth was beautifully painted by Maud with intricate Celtic decorations. The frontispiece declared it to belong to 'Seagan Gonne MacBride – belonging to and of Ireland.' All the memorabilia relating to his arrival was scrupulously inserted, including two unused theatre tickets for the night before he was born. Congratulations on his birth came from all over the world, many with salutations to 'the future President of Ireland'. Maud's friend Barry O'Delaney sent a telegram to the Pope, announcing 'the King of Ireland had been born'. Clearly, with such illustrious parentage, much was expected of the offspring.[23]

Sean's scrapbook declared that he 'first breathed Irish air on 8 April 1904'. Maud took her son to Ireland to be baptised, even though MacBride was unable to travel over with her. His mother and other relatives came up to Dublin from their home in Westport, and the police busied themselves tailing all the guests, detailing who bought a single ticket only, who left their luggage in the station, who went off drinking, and other fairly useless information. They obviously suspected that even a family christening, given the characters involved, could become an occasion for sedition. John O'Leary was their choice as godfather – which almost prevented the ceremony from taking place at all, given his reputation as a Fenian and agnostic. Maud eventually discovered a young priest in the Church of the Three Patrons who was willing to do the honours. All this was dutifully filed in the police report, which then gave the wrong location for the church. It was a satisfying amount of attention for the infant son of Maud Gonne and John MacBride.[24]

Maud would have preferred to remain in Ireland, but could not. She left the five-months-old baby that June, in order to attend the annual Wolfe Tone ceremonies in London, but in October she did what she had been longing to do: she brought Iseult over to Dublin with her. She found it much easier to explain the ten year old's presence now she was a married woman. At AE's house she met for the first time a man who was to be her correspondent and friend for the next twenty years – the wealthy Irish-American lawyer, patron of the arts and sponsor of many penniless nationalists – John Quinn. In Dublin, Maud maintained the same charming façade she had always presented, parrying questions concerning her husband's welfare. In reality, the marriage was in the final throes of disintegration. The irreconcilable differences between wife and husband could no longer be overlooked. MacBride was humiliated by Maud's comparative wealth, jealous of her past and suspicious of her friends. His solace was drink, which led to violence. He might hesitate before striking Maud, but she also had Eileen and Iseult to consider. On 25 February 1905, Maud filed for divorce. The charges included drunkenness and an assault on the cook, but the most serious of charges was that in the summer of 1903, while Maud was absent, he had adulterous relations with a young girl living under her protection.[25]

The legal issues were complex. Maud's parents were English while she had lived in Paris for most of the past fifteen years. John MacBride had been born in Ireland but had forfeited his British citizenship when he became an honorary citizen of the Boer republic, which no longer existed. Ireland had no provision for divorce, only legal separation. The hearing was being conducted in Paris, under French law. On 9 August, almost six months after the first filing of charges, the court passed judgement. A legal separation was granted; Maud would have custody while MacBride could visit his son every Monday from three to five in the afternoon at his mother's residence, in the presence of a third party. A divorce was not granted because of the complications of international law. Maud appealed to have the visitation rights reduced, the greatest source of contention being a clause in the judgement stating that Sean could spend each August with his father, once he reached the age of six.[26] Maud was terrified that the MacBride family would refuse to return her son to her, and certain that Irish law would support them against her. She won her appeal, but by then the weekly visits had ceased. MacBride had become completely demoralised with his life in Paris and had taken a chance on returning to Ireland. Although he was under constant police surveillance, they made no attempt to arrest him. Maud's revenge was to speak only French to Sean – to prevent any real communication between father and son on the few occasions they were together. Her fears remained for many years. Her niece Thora stated that she kept a large dog in her apartment, to protect Sean and Iseult, and she slept with a gun under her pillow. She would not take Sean to Ireland, or go there herself, except for short visits.

Eileen Wilson, despite the circumstances of her birth and the alleged assault upon her by MacBride, was not destined to become the kind of victim beloved by Victorian melodrama. In August 1904, Maud's eighteen-year-old half-sister married the man she had been corresponding with during the past year. He was Joseph MacBride, John MacBride's elder brother. After their London wedding the couple went to live in the family home at Westport. Despite the difference in their ages and the awkwardness of the Gonne–MacBride divorce, it was a happy marriage. Eileen and Joseph had five children and in later years, when the embarrassment of John MacBride's presence was no longer a factor, the two families renewed contact. Despite taking different sides over the Treaty, the various MacBride cousins continued to meet and sometimes to holiday together.[27]

One ironic fact, not known then and only revealed in 1989, was that John MacBride had had an affair with a Malayan woman while in South Africa. An illegitimate son, Robert, was the outcome. Although MacBride appears not to have acknowledged the relationship, the death penalty imposed upon his great-grandson, 26-year-old Robert, for his involvement in a car bombing, has recently forced the family to publicise the liaison in an attempt to pressurise the Irish government to intercede on his behalf. Derek McBride (different spelling), Robert's father, is currently serving a twelve year gaol sentence for his part in ANC activities.[28] Major John MacBride might not have had much to leave his family, but he undoubtedly contributed to the flair for military activity which has been exhibited by so many of his descendants – in Ireland as well as in Africa. But was he the prudish, awkward young man that Maud described in her memoirs, who was gently scoffed at by the worldly-wise woman for his hesitancy in visiting her apartment? That image had certainly put her at her ease. After the turmoil of her relationship with Millevoye and the anguish of Yeats's unrequited passion, what Maud valued in the unsophisticated soldier were his qualities as a political rather than sexual companion. If she had later discovered the truth about his past, it is inconceivable that she would not have used the information in her bitter divorce as further proof that MacBride was unfit to have custody of their son.

Her various family problems curtailed Maud's political activities for a considerable time. Newspapers in England, Ireland, France and America all reported the murky details of the divorce petition and the proceedings were dragged on by MacBride suing the *Irish Independent* for libel. That trial took place in December 1906, with MacBride eventually winning a derisory technical victory: to call him a drunk was not libellous, since evidence supported the accusation; to accuse him of cruelty and infidelity was libellous as those charges had not been proven. He was awarded an insulting £1 damages. The unwelcome additional publicity made it difficult for Maud to continue her normal role as propagandist on Ireland's behalf, since her personal notoriety attracted the curious. Court proceedings preoccupied her during 1905 and in the following year she gave only a very few lectures to groups in France. She also signed an anti-English editorial in Millevoye's paper *La Patrie* on 4 May. Had her difficulties softened his heart towards her?

One whose heart was most definitely softened with pity was the faithful Willie. Maud went to London to seek comfort from the one person who had always unstintingly offered her his support. Although she had told him that she would fight alone, knowing she had brought her problems on herself through her rash decision to marry in the face of well-founded opposition, she was soon relying on him for help. Willie travelled back to Paris with her and was soon writing in anguish to Lady Gregory, 'Dear friend, I turn to you in every trouble. I cannot bear the burden of this terrible case alone – I know nothing about lawyers and so on. When you know the story you will feel that if she were the uttermost stranger, or one's bitterest enemy, one would have, even to the putting aside of all else, to help her.'[29]

Friends did rally round. Her cousin May suggested that John Quinn, as an influential lawyer, could be of assistance. Lady Gregory went to London to confer with lawyers. Even Maud's priest wrote a letter in support of her action in petitioning for divorce. But John MacBride had friends too: John O'Leary, an old drinking companion as well as fellow member of the IRB, took his side against Maud, and there were others. In October 1906 Maud returned to Dublin for the first time since the divorce. Her determination to appear in public was typically courageous and defiant. The occasion was the opening night of Lady Gregory's play *The Gaol Gate*. As she and Willie entered the theatre together, someone in the crowd recognised the tall, black-clad figure at the poet's side. There was a shout of 'Up John MacBride' and a hissing that spread around the auditorium. Mary Colum, then a young schoolgirl, found herself, quite by chance, sitting near the woman she regarded as a living legend, whom she had never before seen:

> Her height would have drawn attention anywhere, but it was her beauty that produced the most startling effect. It was startling in its greatness, its dignity, its strangeness. Supreme beauty is so rare that its first effect is a kind of shock.[30]

Maud showed none of the emotion she must have been feeling as she smilingly turned to face her attackers. A counter-hissing in her support now began, drowning out the others. The crowd was silenced, and the curtain went up. Willie was enraged as he stood beside her. He greatly admired her courage and her determination to have no bitterness against her detractors, but he could never share her consistent love for the ordinary people of Ireland. He recalled his indignation in a later poem, where he makes his 'Phoenix' say:

> The drunkards, pilferers of public funds,
> All the dishonest crowd I had driven away,
> When my luck changed and they dared meet my face,
> Crawled from obscurity, and set upon me
> Those that I had served and some that I had fed;
> Yet never have I, now nor at any time,
> Complained of the people.

Ten weary and frustrating years of exile were to follow, and in all that time Maud maintained her concern for the people. Despite her family commitments she managed to sustain her contacts in Ireland, as well as embarking on one of the most constructive of her many ventures: the feeding of school children.

CHAPTER 6

EXILE

Maud's prolonged absences from Ireland did not lessen her interest in the activities of Inghinidhe na hEireann. Maire Quinn and Dudley Digges, now married, had emigrated to America shortly after the protests over Synge's play and Helena Moloney, a new recruit to the nationalist cause, took over as secretary. Helena assumed the Celtic name 'Emer' (in mythology she had been the wife of the legendary hero of Ulster, Cu Chulainn) for her Inghinidhe work, and for the rest of her life was affectionately known by that name within Maud's family circle. She had joined the group shortly after hearing Maud speak at a public meeting at the time of Edward VII's visit. The effect of Maud in full flow was electrifying and under that influence Helena went to the Inghinidhe offices where she saw Dudley Digges's note urging all members to go to Coulson Avenue. Intrigued, she made her way there, promptly joining in the defence of Maud's black petticoat. It was, she said, her 'baptism of fire', and she signed up more formally the following week.[1] Since that time, Helena had proved herself to be a loyal and hardworking lieutenant, diligently writing weekly reports to her president and sometimes coming over to Paris so that the two could develop their ideas at greater length. Despite Helena's briefings, when Maud began to gather together information on the group for a series of radio broadcasts in 1950, she retrospectively found herself amazed by the extent of the work which had been undertaken by the women of Inghinidhe na hEireann.[2]

Much of Maud's day now was taken up with the care of her family and a domestic routine was developed for possibly the first time, as she was no longer the same whirlwind of activity, rushing in and out of people's lives, constantly travelling from one place to another. She worked hard on her painting, illustrating three of Ella Young's books of poetry and legends with her own reworkings of Celtic design, as well as submitting some of her paintings to an art exhibition.[3] She also painted portraits, which she apparently sold on a commercial basis. A sketch of Iseult and a watercolour of baby Sean reveal an appealing delicacy of touch; her execution was hesitant but she succeeded in capturing the inner spirit of her subjects. A series of correspondence with a wide range of people was initiated, in all of which her longing for Ireland was apparent. The latest Irish plays and books were read avidly and discussed, a substitute for the activity she would so much have preferred. But she was temperamentally unsuited to domestic life in a Paris suburb, regardless of her skill as a cook or her creativeness as an artist. Life had to hold more than that. There were various political occasions organised by the Irish community in France, and to those Maud brought Sean as soon as he was old enough. When the St Patrick Society held its annual celebration, Maud dressed the three-year-old boy in a white suit, put her membership cross around his neck and sent him round the members, distributing the shamrock that had been sent over from Ireland by the Inghinidhe. It was one of his first memories.[4] When Maud was busy organising meals for the Dublin school children four years later, little Sean proved to be very useful. At another meeting of the St Patrick Society he went amongst its members with his collecting card, again wearing his mother's cross of the Knights of Saint Patrick and his collecting card was almost filled within minutes. Maud's exile wasn't lonely, her lament was simply that she was away from Ireland at a period when freedom seemed a real possibility. After one visit she wrote to John Quinn that she had enjoyed her time in Ireland, where 'everything seemed much more beautiful and much more alive than in France'.[5] More nationalist groups were organising and, with a reunited Irish Party urging Home Rule upon the Liberals as a condition for their continued support, an air of optimism began to pervade political life. Maud shared the general confidence that Home Rule, at least as a first step, would come to Ireland within the next decade. Maud's circle of acquaintances and associates in Paris was almost as wide as in Ireland. It included people like Madame Cama, the Indian nationalist leader, who was also in exile in Paris. They were close friends: on her behalf Maud enlisted John Quinn's support in preventing a Hindu nationalist named Har Dyal from being extradited to England from America[6] and Sean sometimes stayed with Madame Cama when his mother was away.

One person who spent an increasing amount of time in Paris was Willie Yeats. He went over to see Maud in June 1908, and in place of actual marriage she offered to renew their 'spiritual marriage'. Willie recorded his agreement in a journal, at the same time giving an indication of Maud's state of mind, 'She believes that this bond is to be recreated and to be the means of spiritual illumination between us. It is to be the bond of the spirit only and she lives from now on, she said . . . for that and for her children.'[7] To cement this reconciliation Maud presented him with a notebook bound with white calf, in which he was to keep a record of their astral unions. Willie pasted into this book two letters from Maud, recording occasions when she did achieve a vision of union, once that July and again in October. He was only once successful, usually having only confused dreams which caused a return of the sexual frustration and nerve strain that had tormented him during the 1890s.

Maud was now forty-two years of age. She had had a lover and a husband and was the mother of two children. Her life was, at least for the time being, fairly uneventful, and Willie's continued adoration after the scandal of her divorce obviously meant a great deal to her. Her feelings might have been less intense if she had been back in Ireland, with all the stimulus and friendship available there, but in Paris it was as if the past years had not occurred. Maud was writing warmly to Willie almost as soon as he had left for London:

> Friend of mine
> It was sad you had to leave Paris so soon – there is so much I wanted to talk to you about & so much we had not time for – Next time you come you must arrange to have a little more time to spare.
>   I was so tired last night when I got home I could not do much, but several times I felt your thought with me quite distinctly. . . . I think a most wonderful thing has happened – the most wonderful I have met with in life. If we are only strong enough to hold the doors open I think we shall obtain knowledge & life we have never dreamed of . . . .[8]

On 26 July Maud wrote again and when Willie received the letter three days later he recorded in his notebook that he had made evocation 'on the night of 25'. Through coincidence or otherwise, the pair had simultaneously succeeded in communing at the same time. Willie had concentrated on the red and green globes of Mars and Venus, their zodiacal signs, seeing cascades of roses and apple blossoms and experiencing 'a great union' with Maud. The following morning he noted that he felt unusually well and 'for the first time in weeks physical desire was arrested'.[9] Maud had written to tell of the 'wonderful experience' she had had on the night of the 25th, when she had sent her astral body to his rooms in Woburn Buildings:

> Last night all my household had retired at a quarter to 11 and I thought I would go to you astrally. It was not working hours for you & I thought by going to you I might even be able to leave with you some of my vitality & energy which would make working less of a toil next day. . . . We went somewhere in space I dont know where – I was conscious of starlight & of hearing the sea below us. You had taken the form I think of a great serpent, but I am not quite sure. I only saw your face distinctly & as I looked into your eyes (as I did the day in Paris you asked me what I was thinking of) & your lips touched mine. We melted into one another till we formed only *one being, a being greater*

than ourselves who felt all & knew all with double intensity – the clock striking 11 broke the spell & as we separated it felt as if life was being drawn away from me through my chest with almost physical pain. . . . Then I went upstairs to bed & I dreamed of you confused dreams of ordinary life. We were in Italy together. . . . We were quite happy & we talked of this wonderful spiritual vision I have described – you said it would tend to increase physical desire – This troubles me a little – for there was nothing physical in that union – Material union is but a pale shadow compared to it . . . .[10]

There is no doubt here that Maud both craved an intense emotional union with Willie and that she drew away from any suggestion that their friendship might develop along more conventionally intimate lines. In October, when the white notebook was in her possession, she described a vision she had of themselves as Maeve and Aileel:

I saw Aileel's love for me lighting the years like a lamp of extraordinary holiness, and voices said, 'You did not understand so we took it from you and kept it safe in the heart of the hills for it belongs to Ireland. When you were purified by suffering so you could understand we gave it back to you. See you guard it for from it great beauty may be born.'[11]

It was Maud's way of saying that she understood the importance of Willie's poetry and that she accepted the central role she played as his muse, the subject of so much of his verse. When he visited her in Paris that December, what one critic has termed his 'nobly extravagant' 'No Second Troy' was the result:

What could have made her peaceful with a mind
That nobleness made simple as a fire,
With beauty like a tightened bow, a kind
That is not natural in an age like this,
Being high and solitary and most stern?
Why, what could she have done, being what she is?
Was there another Troy for her to burn?

Although in many ways Maud and Willie were closer than ever before, this was not just a more fruitful repetition of their previous 'spiritual marriage'. For one thing, Willie was no longer an inexperienced virgin. He had had several mistresses and was pursuing a sexual relationship with Mabel Dickinson, a medical masseuse, while all this continued. He also maintained his time-consuming and troublesome association with the Abbey Theatre, despite Maud's continuous urgings for him to concentrate on his poetry, which she felt was of far greater value to Ireland than his theatre management. In other words, on many matters they continued to disagree sharply and to follow separate lives. There was another important difference between them, which had not existed before: Maud's Catholicism, which meant that she could not regard herself as free to remarry, even if she won a divorce, because of the Church's prohibition.

Many scholars have pondered over the vital question as to whether or not Maud and Willie ever consummated their love affair. The consensus of opinion seems to be that, as Curtis Bradford has phrased it, Yeats 'temporarily forced his relations with Maud Gonne into a more normal pattern'.[12] This probably occurred around May or June 1909, when Maud visited Willie in London and their pursuit of the occult was most intense. Richard Ellman, the foremost authority on Yeats, verified this when he repeated the answer given to him by Georgie Yeats, the poet's wife, 'I wouldn't have brought it up myself, but since you have discovered it, I can confirm that Yeats and Maud Gonne did have a brief affair at that time.'[13] But such happiness was shortlived. Willie wrote with agitation in the astral union manuscript book:

We are divided by her religious ideas, a Catholicism which has grown on her – she will not divorce her husband and marry because of her church. Since she said this, she has not been further from me but is always very near. She too seems to love more than of old. In addition to this the old dread of physical love has awakened in her.

This dread has probably spoiled all her life, checking natural and instinctive selection and leaving fantastic duties free to take its place . . . and all the while she grows nobler under the touch of sorrow and denial. What end will it all have? I fear for her and for myself. She has all myself. I was never more deeply in love, but my desires must go elsewhere if I would escape their poison. I am in continual terror of some entanglement parting us, and all the while I know that she made me and I her. She is my innocence and I her wisdom. Of old she was a phoenix and I feared her, but now she is my child more than my sweetheart. . . . Always since I was a boy I have questioned dreams for her sake – and she herself always a dream . . . the phoenix . . . when she is reborn in all her power to torture and delight, to waste and to ennoble. She would be cruel if she were not a child who can always say, "You will not suffer because I will pray."[14]

By the end of 1909 he began to accept Maud's refusal to love him in the way he wished. His desires did go elsewhere, and their platonic affair resumed. But the split of carnal from spiritual love was so painful that only very gradually was he able to recover sufficiently to begin to look for a more conventional emotional life. Maud's distaste for the sexual act, a result no doubt of the puritan morality of the period, was a common feeling amongst women of her social class. Revealingly, she had once told Yeats that she believed only procreation could justify intercourse.[15] He, on the contrary, seems to have been fortunate enough to have established relationships with women who were often more experienced than himself, and who enjoyed physical intimacy. For whatever reason, Maud preferred to channel her passions into a less threatening, but equally stimulating spiritual plane. And, despite all the hardships she had suffered, both in her personal and public lives, Maud remained content to carry on her work, whether or not she received praise and recognition:

> Yet she, singing upon her road,
> Half lion, half child, is at peace.

('Against Unworthy Praise')

Maud had always valued the printed word, recognising its power to spread a message far beyond the few who might attend a political meeting. She had urged Millevoye to take over the editorship of *La Patrie* and she had set up *L'Irlande Libre*. She no longer had any association with Millevoye and her own publication had been discontinued. Griffith's new paper was named *Sinn Fein*, to reflect the organisation that had been set up in 1907 as a further development of the national council first established during the protests over Edward VII's visit. It was not what the radical members of Inghinidhe na hEireann wanted in a paper. Helena Moloney said they wanted 'a women's paper, advocating militancy, separatism and feminism'.[16] Whether she or Maud first broached the idea of starting their own journal is unknown, but Helena, with the enthusiastic backing of the absent Maud, called a meeting in the autumn of 1908 to see if there was enough interest in the venture. For some women, it was their first contact with the group. Sydney Gifford came along, full of awe, expecting to see heroines resembling those portrayed in magazine articles which sentimentally extolled the virtues of the women of past nationalist rebellions. What she found was a group of women, plainly dressed in Donegal tweed, discussing finance in a business-like manner. Ella Young was amongst the group, which also included another newcomer – the Countess Constance Markievicz, who burst into the room in her ball gown, having come direct from a function at Dublin Castle. It was one of the last she was to attend. Her spontaneous offer to donate the diamond ornament she was wearing to help pay for the journal was bluntly refused by the group, understandably suspicious of someone who might be a spy. All were enthusiastic about the venture, and a committee was formed to raise money for what was going to be a monthly journal, price 1d, contributors donating their work free. Helena was confirmed as editor.[17]

The first issue of Bean na hEireann (Woman of Ireland), appeared in November 1908. Helena worked almost without editorial assistance, but the journal received generous support from people like Griffith, Katharine Tynan (who wrote a serial for it), Roger Casement, AE, Plunkett, Pearse, and many of the other poets who would one day lead the Easter Rising. The contents were of a consistently high calibre; James Stephens, for example, gave some of his best poetry, and Maud's friendship with him and many of the other writers must have played a part in obtaining such contributions. Stephens and his wife were living in Paris at this time. Madeleine ffrench-Mullen, later a co-founder with Dr Kathleen Lynn of St Ultan's children's hospital (both also became members of the Irish Citizen Army), edited a children's column and Constance Markievicz contributed another regular feature, 'The Woman with the Garden', where practical gardening advice was intertwined with humorous parodies of nationalist propaganda, 'A good nationalist should look upon slugs in the garden much in the same way as she looks on the English in Ireland.' Helena wrote the Labour Notes, and the task of collecting that information led to her growing involvement with the small but developing labour movement. When James Connolly returned from America in 1910 she became a staunch supporter of the Transport Union, where he joined Jim Larkin as organiser. Helena's own politics determined a great deal of the editorial content of Bean na hEireann, although Maud would not have disagreed with most of the sentiments expressed. On occasions, however, differing perspectives were clearly seen, when Maud would correct the youthful, uncompromising attitudes of Helena. For Maud, a purist position was untenable if it meant the continued suffering of the young or the vulnerable. An editorial declared their battle cry to be 'Freedom for Our Nation and the complete removal of all disabilities to our sex.' They reserved the right to criticise all existing groups in their determination to construct for women a movement 'on Sinn Fein lines': fostering a spirit of self-reliance through encouraging women to participate in nationalist life at all levels.

Bean na hEireann gave Maud a new platform for her ideas which she was soon to put to constructive use, but before that there was a more immediate crisis to deal with. The start of 1910 was catastrophic for Paris. The rivers Yonne, Marne and Seine simultaneously overflowed their banks, causing the worst floods in 170 years. Maud was not the sort of person to stand aside in an emergency and she threw herself into the task of relief, working to feed, clothe and nurse those left homeless. She wrote to John Quinn after a day that had started before dawn and had still not ended at midnight, describing the distress she had witnessed, 'It is all a horrid nightmare. Beautiful Paris is a wrecked city.'[18] The children were sent away to the house in Normandy, as it was feared an epidemic would follow the flood. Iseult, in her quaint English, wrote a thank you note to Quinn for books he had sent her and Sean, describing the flood scenes with all the excitement of any child, 'The Seine's inundation is most interesting, but I regret that we are much too high up for it having a chance to come in our house; the idea of having a little black boat to walk about in the room is most exciting.'[19]

Perhaps Maud's work with the Paris relief committee provided some of the inspiration for the school meals campaign? That April, *Bean na hEireann* contained an editorial on a proposed scheme to feed children which could only have been written by her. The gentle, yet firm rebuke to Helena (A Worker) is quintessential Maud:

> During the coming winter Inghinidhe na hEireann intend to inaugurate a scheme by which a certain number of poor school children will be supplied with free food. We trust other societies will come in and help with this work. It is the intention of the Inghinidhe to try to get the municipal authorities to undertake it eventually. We thoroughly agree with 'A Worker' as to the ineffectiveness of charity in coping with the evil results of bad social conditions, but the stigma of charity ought not to be applied to a scheme like this. Surely little children who have to work hard with their brains at school, have as much right to a meal, as a thirsty citizen who drinks from the public fountain.[20]

Maud spent half of the summer of 1910 in the west of Ireland, her children with her. Although they stayed in Mulrany, not Westport, they were not far from the MacBride family home. For some reason, she didn't fear MacBride attempting to kidnap her son although, as she once explained to John Quinn, 'MacBride and the English law makes it impossible for me to have him in Ireland until he is old enough to defy both.'[21] Maud was fond of her mother-in-law, the rift was with her husband, not the rest of his family, and perhaps for Sean's sake she wanted contact with the family to be maintained? John MacBride did not appear on the scene on this occasion.

In October, leaving her children behind her in France, Maud returned to Ireland alone. In another letter to Quinn she said she was leaving for Ireland the next day, 'not to rest this time. I was terribly troubled this summer at the way the children in Ireland have to work in the schools when many of them are always starving. I believe it is that which is filling our lunatic asylums.'[22] Dublin had the highest infant mortality rate in the United Kingdom. The levels of poverty were appalling, many children went to school without breakfast and the schools provided no food for the children who attended. Medical authorities condemned the effects of 'long hungry school hours on their childish systems', yet nothing was done. A School Meals Act had been passed in England in 1906, enabling local authorities to provide a meal for school children, but the Act was not extended to Ireland, despite the overwhelming need. As Maud had emphasised, they did not want charity, simply the basic right of food for starving children. Their aim was to campaign for similar legislation for Irish children. For this, a small group of dedicated women, gathered together by Maud, were to work tirelessly over the next few years.

Sydney Gifford, in common with other members of Inghinidhe na hEireann, had yet to meet her president, who had already begun her life as an exile by the time the younger woman joined the organisation. The normally down-to-earth Sydney resorted to hyperbole when it came to describing her impressions of Maud. 'I won't attempt to describe her beauty to you, except to say that I had never then and have never since seen anything to compare with it. She was like a goddess, a creature from another planet, and when she spoke you thought she must speak in oracles.'[23] But, despite the glory of her appearance, Sydney discovered on their first meeting that the goddess sitting across the committee table was able to talk in a most practical manner about her plan to provide a hot meal for the poor children of Dublin. On this occasion Maud was able to tell the group that Canon Kavanagh of St Audoen's had asked her to start the work in the schools of his parish.

An important ally of the women was James Connolly, Maud's old associate. He was anxious to get trade union backing for the venture and so, on 10 November, Maud and Connolly attended a meeting of the executive committee of the Irish Trades Council, to urge support in obtaining passage of the amendment to the School Meals Act. The eventual outcome was a meeting on 12 December at the Mansion House, the Lord Mayor's residence, where arrangements were made for a deputation to go to London to present the matter to the Home Secretary.[24] The two women most closely involved in this were Maud and the militant suffragist, Hanna Sheehy-Skeffington, founder of the Irish Women's Franchise League, who was to become a close friend of Maud's from this time on. Other members of the committee were Constance Markievicz, Helena Moloney, Helen Laird, Madeleine ffrench-Mullen, Kathleen Clarke and Muriel, Grace and Sydney Gifford. Everyone who was free in the daytime took turns at the work, ladling out stew and washing greasy dishes and spoons in the open playground in all sorts of weather.

Many of the church-controlled schools were suspicious of this campaign. Maud took Sean to Italy in the summer of 1911 and whilst there tried to enlist the help of nuns to influence the Irish bishops on the matter, so that the 'secret opposition which we are meeting from some of the clergy in Ireland who seem to think it dangerous and subversive to feed starving school children' could be prevented.[25] In the meantime, Maud's contacts again proved invaluable. Canon Kavanagh was an old friend, one of the speakers at the Children's Treat of a decade ago. Before the end of 1910, 250 children at St Audoen's were being served with a hot lunch every day. On 31 December, Maud wrote to John Quinn from her home in Paris:

> I worked very hard in Ireland and succeeded in getting one school canteen started in one of the poorest parts of Dublin and enough money to ensure the feeding of 250 children for a year so I feel I can take a holiday with my own family with a clear conscience. I shall leave to go back in February to organise a second school canteen and above all to shake up our MPs to get a law passed enabling the school children to get fed in all our schools in Ireland.
>
> It is horrible to think that Ireland is the only country where education is compulsory where nothing is done to provide food for the bodies as well as the minds of the children. I am sure this school day starvation is the real cause of the overcrowding of lunatic asylums.
>
> The number of deaths from consumption in Ireland – the more I looked into the question – the more shocking I found this neglect of the children. It is one of the most vital national questions. If we are to get free and keep free, we must keep up the strength of the race . . . .[26]

John Quinn was always a generous supporter of Maud's activities. She was preparing to return to Ireland in February 1911 when she received a long letter from him, offering to contribute £25 to her project with a similar amount in three months' time. She was more than grateful for the donation, explaining how urgent was the need for more money as:

> We are just starting dinners at a new and very big school at Ringsend, a terribly poor district of Dublin, and it is always a little nervous work. The ensuring of sufficient money to keep the dinners going till we get the free meal act extended. Getting the children used to dinners and then stopping would be worse than never having begun at all.[27]

Maud reported that Iseult and Sean were angry at her for leaving them again so soon, but 'the hungry school children have got on my nerves so I must go'. *En route,* Maud spent a few days in London, trying unsuccessfully to win support from the Irish MPs. She later discovered that the school managers, fearful the legislation would entail public control of the schools, had been approaching the MPs secretly to urge them not to support the Bill. In an impassioned article entitled 'Responsibility', which was published in the *Irish Review* that December, Maud wrote that this 'small uninfluential body to which I belong, composed mostly of working women, are attempting in desperation to do what the state ought to do'. They had written to, or interviewed, all the Irish MPs with the object of getting the Free School Meal For School Children Act introduced to Ireland, 'but our MPs remain uninterested, and some tell us we must wait for Home Rule. In the meantime the children are starving.' She bitterly remarked 'Revolutions have been made for less valid causes and I do not think we can entirely shift the responsibility for our supine indifference.'[28] This was Maud at her most constructive and compassionate.

Teachers in the schools where the children were being fed reported that the rate of illness had decreased and there was much more life and noise in the playground, now the children had the strength to play. When Maud returned in October, after a five months' absence, she said she found a 'really marked improvement in the appearance of the children'. But she was torn between the needs of these children and the demands of her own two, as she commented in a letter to Quinn, 'I have been in Dublin for the last three weeks and am beginning to want to get back to Paris and the children, but I can't stir till the second school is in good working order – and in the meantime it is very pleasant seeing all my old friends. I love Dublin. People are so keen on things here.'[29]

In November 1912 Maud presided at a packed meeting in the Mansion House, where a resolution was passed stating that pending the extension of the Act, the Dublin Corporation should make a grant to meet the immediate needs of the children. The meeting also called on all Irish MPs to get the Act extended without waiting for Home Rule. Predictably, this was ignored, and the Corporation was advised by its lawyers that it would be illegal to strike a rate without the appropriate legislation from Westminster. Hanna Sheehy-Skeffington then drafted a bill, which Maud presented to Stephen Gwynn, MP. In September 1914, the Act was finally extended to Ireland. The following month the Dublin Trades Council passed a vote of thanks to the women's committee for all the work it had accomplished. The Council also sponsored a conference of all organisations interested in the proper application of the Act, but by then Maud was once again in France, marooned there by the start of the First World War. Dublin Corporation eventually appointed an all-male committee to oversee the distribution of school meals. None of the women who had been so crucially involved in the issue were invited to serve.[30]

During this period Maud had been dividing her time between Dublin and Paris with increasing irregularity as Sean, who seems to have been prone to every childhood ailment in existence, contracted a number of potentially dangerous illnesses. At the beginning of 1912 he suffered appendicitis, and after the anxiety of the operation Maud herself fell ill. In frustration she told Quinn that as soon as she felt recovered and could get her cousin to look after Sean, she would return to Dublin 'to push on' with the school canteens. She felt that in her absence the campaign only 'marked time' rather than advanced.[31] In 1913, after nursing Sean through measles, Maud's lungs again gave way and she contracted pneumonia. She was forced to recuperate at a sanatorium near Lourdes, 'a place no one would come to except they were nuns', an extremely bored Maud wrote to Willie.[32] She was longing to return to Ireland, where a massive labour dispute had begun, and she fretted about the fate of her school canteens. But she was unable to travel until October. Undoubtedly the effort she was putting into the feeding of the children had an effect on her health. Never strong, her resistance was weakened so that the strain of nursing her son became the final straw.

However, her absence from Ireland in the summer of 1912 was, in the circumstances, probably fortuitous – whether or not Maud herself ever realised this. A mass meeting of women from all the suffrage groups and other political organisations containing women was being organised for 1 June, with the intention of applying pressure on the government to include women's suffrage within the terms of the proposed Home Rule Bill. Knowing that the government would hardly enfranchise Irish women when they refused to give the vote to women in Britain, suffragists hoped that sympathetic Irish Party MPs might be persuaded into proposing an amendment to the Bill, specifically in order to include Irish women. The organisers of the mass meeting, the first of its kind ever held in Ireland, hoped that by its size, dignity and determination, their demand would be heard. They were careful in choosing who would be on the platform. The name of Maud Gonne might be acceptable in campaigning for the poor, but it appears that it was not acceptable to those influential men that the suffragists hoped to win over, as Mrs Oldham (the wife of the man who had first introduced Maud to the Contemporary Club) vehemently explained to Hanna Sheehy-Skeffington, in a letter full of underlinings emphasising her point:

> I consider Maud Gonne's name would *not* curry much favour with the constitutional audience and aims of the meeting, lots of nationalists have that opinion of her, either as freak or humbug or not responsible, according to their personal views. Certainly she would not carry any *weight* or *influence*, nothing like Mrs Wyse-Power, if you could get her as representing the daughters of Erin. I think the *public impression* is the thing to consider first at this meeting and I ask you again to use your influence . . . .[33]

Was it Maud's political views she objected to, or was it her status as a separated woman who had been involved in a scandalous divorce hearing? I suspect the latter. Whether Maud was ever aware of how controversial her presence would have been on this occasion is unknown, as she was not around for the planning discussions. Although Hanna Sheehy-Skeffington was never a woman to submit meekly to prejudice, in this case, because of Maud's illness, she was spared any necessity for intervening. Her organisation's journal, *The Irish Citizen,* reported the following message of support received from 'Madame Maud Gonne' in Paris:

I am very glad you are calling a meeting for the 1st of June to demand at least the same franchise as was offered to us in the Council Bill of 1907. It is a question of the most vital import-ance, not only to women, but to Ireland. The many social and economic problems which the Irish Parliament will have to face will need women's practical brains as well as men's to solve. I am a little consoled for my enforced absence by knowing that Inghinidhe na hEireann are doing all they can for the women's cause, which in this case is Ireland's cause also.[34]

The 'constitutional audience' might object to her presence, but she remained, defiantly, Maud Gonne and not a more abject, tamed, Mrs MacBride, separated from her drunken husband. That might have been acceptable. Maud was never a suffragist, being far too much of a nationalist ever to consider giving absolute priority to women's demands, but she wanted the franchise for women in a free Ireland and, in the meantime, the suffrage movement was challenging the government and therefore had her full support. She sent another message to the July 1913 mass meeting organised by the suffragists, this time on the proposed introduction to Ireland of the 'Cat and Mouse' Act, whereby hunger striking suffragists could be released and rearrested indefinitely, a government mechanism to defeat the hunger striking tactic:

The English Government is making itself as ridiculous and odious in dealing with the franchise question as it has always made itself in attempting to govern Ireland. Injustice and oppres-sion can only be maintained by arbitrary, tyrannical and crim-inal methods of government.[35]

By the time of this meeting, Inghinidhe na hEireann had, to all intents and purposes, ceased to exist. Helena Moloney's energies were more involved with the Socialist Party of Ireland and *Bean na hEireann* stopped publication in February 1911. Independently-minded women now had *The Irish Citizen* to read, a lively journal which covered an enormous variety of topics of interest to women, and the physical force tradition in Irish nationalism had its own publication, *Irish Freedom,* which first appeared in November 1910. The lack of Maud's guiding presence obviously had an effect, but times were changing in Ireland, and different organisations were needed to face those challenges.

In July 1911 there was yet another royal visit to Ireland – this time it was George V who came to enthuse loyalty in his unwilling subjects. A Nationalist Women's Committee, presided over by Jenny Wyse-Power, was one of the organisations formed in opposition to the visit, but Inghinidhe as an organisation was not included. However, Helena Moloney and Constance Markievicz joined forces with Connolly's Socialist Party of Ireland – as Maud had done ten years earlier – and the women initiated more dramatic gestures of defiance. Constance burnt the Union Jack at a public meeting and Helena threw stones at pictures of the King and Queen. After refusing to pay a fine of 40s, she was sentenced to one month's imprisonment, a sentence she was released from by Anna Parnell secretly paying her fine. Two men did go to prison, the police baulking at arresting a countess, even though she was the flag burner, and at a demonstration to celebrate the release of James McArdle, Helena succeeded in having herself rearrested for denouncing the character of the King. Constance was also arrested for coming to her friend's defence. What was about to develop into a test case for freedom of speech in Ireland was dropped by the government wisely finding a judge to dismiss the charges against the women.[36] Huge coverage was devoted to the affair, but Helena, still young and inexperienced, was worried because some of her friends thought her conduct 'reprehensible and rowdy'. A telegram of congratulations from Maud – 'Splendid. You have kept up the reputation of Ingheana [*sic*] na hEireann' – arrived and Helena later remarked 'I cannot describe how elated I felt when I received that. My heart was lifted up. This is just another example for that instinctive capacity for doing the right thing which Maud Gonne possesses.'[37]

Constance Markievicz had become a staunch supporter of James Connolly in a way that Maud, for all her admiration of the labour leader, could never be. The Countess had adopted socialism as her guiding force and, increasingly, it was her figure which came to symbolise the new militant spirit. Maud was associated with 'Romantic Ireland', but that was dead and gone. Constance, with her Citizen Army uniform of breeches, plumed hat and revolver, was an indication of what was to come.

The 1913 Lock-Out was one of the epic battles in the war between labour and capital. For almost a year Dublin employers locked-out members of the Transport and General Workers Union in an attempt to destroy what, under the charismatic leadership of Jim Larkin, was threatening to become a powerful force in the land. More than 20,000 women and men were out of work and nearly one-third of Dublin's population was affected. It was misery on a vast scale and the remnants of Inghinidhe na hEireann, together with members of various suffrage groups and trade unionists, rolled up their sleeves and set to work in the soup kitchens of Liberty Hall, headquarters of the union. The school feeding campaign was suspended as all children in the city were being fed during the emergency. Maud was unable to take part in this operation, but she wrote an article for the union's paper, *The Irish Worker*, entitled 'The Real Criminals', in which she proclaimed:

> because the workers have shown that poor and down-trodden as they are, their souls are not enslaved and they are worthy of Ireland, the employers have declared they will starve them into submission, and that their women and children shall die of hunger on the streets. In a free country employers of labour would never have dared to propose such a thing, for they would have been treated as the criminals they are.[38]

To Quinn she confided her opinion that Larkin was 'a *painful* necessity, but a *necessity* and has done great good in many ways'. She admired his magnetic influence upon crowds, but shrewdly gave her opinion that she feared he was 'too vain and too jealous and too untruthful to make a really *great* leader'.[39] Connolly would have concurred. She was in Dublin during October and November, and while there busied herself in ensuring that children were being fed. As she found out more about the appalling hardships inflicted on the Dublin working class, every meagre possession they owned left in the pawn shop to eke out the small amount of strike pay which was all the union could afford, Maud tried to work out some means of helping people to redeem their goods. Sean's illness called her away and she told Quinn that although she wanted to have Christmas with her son, she hoped to return to Dublin before the New Year. She was back at the beginning of 1914. The Lock-Out was over, the workers starved into submission, and it was a sullen, dejected Dublin that Maud returned to. She and a few others helped to get clothes and bedding out of the pawn shops; it was a delicate matter, performed privately. Maud found it deeply upsetting, as she told Quinn when writing to thank him for another of his generous donations:

> It was terrible the misery it brought us into contact with – whole families living in one room without a stick of furniture or bedding was no uncommon thing to find. And they are so brave and so uncomplaining and so loyal to leaders who seem to me to have made every blunder it was possible to make. The employers are triumphing horridly. They are asking conditions they would not have dared to ask before the strike. . . . It is all miserable.
>
> My only hope is in Home Rule. I feel that bad as that bill is, it will cheer us all up a bit, put us in a better position to get more . . . .

The Volunteer Movement is going ahead well all over the country. Men of all classes are taking part in it. It is very encouraging.[40]

The Volunteer movement mentioned by Maud was the nationalists' response to the Ulster Volunteers which had been set up in 1912 by unionists determined to fight against Home Rule. Events in Ireland were rapidly moving to crisis point as the country divided north and south and two armed groups faced each other, both determined to fight. Irish women were longing to play their part in this drama and, after much pressure, it was agreed by the Irish Volunteers that there would be a women's auxiliary organisation – the Cumann na mBan (Irishwomen's Council). Inghinidhe na hEireann became one branch of the group. Elizabeth Coxhead's assessment was that the new organisation 'never had quite the independence and flow of creative ideas that Inghinidhe na hEireann had displayed for thirteen years under the personal leadership of Maud Gonne',[41] while Maud's own conclusion, expressed more circumspectly towards the end of her life, was that Cumann na mBan 'worked less independently than we had, but was also very useful'.[42]

Les Mouettes, Maud's big, rambling summer home in Normandy, perched above the seashore at Colleville, had become a place of refuge, where many friends and relatives enjoyed Maud's easygoing, casual hospitality. Her cousin May, now Mrs Clay, lived with her after the disintegration of her marriage. She died in 1929; her life, sadly, never having fulfilled its potential. Willie Yeats first visited Les Mouettes in 1909 and he continued to go almost yearly until the war. It wasn't far from Iseult's boarding school in Caen, and once Sean began school at the Gonzaga College in Paris, the house was a haven for him also. Gretta Cousins, a suffrage militant who was gaoled in both London and Dublin for her activities, and her husband James, joint editor with Francis Sheehy-Skeffington of *The Irish Citizen,* were in France during the wet summer of 1912. Gretta had had an encounter with one of Maud's cousins, a Captain Edward Gonne, in 1910, when she had been part of an Irish contingent over in London to take part in the suffragette window-breaking campaign. Through some mysterious process the young officer had been appointed as their escort to Downing Street.[43] Gretta and James gave a delightful portrait of their experiences at Les Mouettes. They received a note from Maud suggesting that it was better to be 'drowned with friends' than 'alone in a strange village hotel. So come over here.' She added, 'Mr Yeats is here.' When they left the train they saw:

Yeats standing like an elongated rook . . . near a donkey cart in which Madame Gonne was apparently trying to pack things. She greeted us warmly. A young lad, thin, pale and dreamy, was introduced as Shawn. . . . He disposed of us quickly . . . we being only human beings, and busied himself over the important matter of the safe transit of a pet bantam cock home in the cart. . . . I was received with much friendliness and natural freedom by a tall, slender girl of great beauty of countenance and grace of form. This was Madame's niece, Iseult. She was accompanied by a dog and two cats. There were cooings in the background mixed with chirpings in different keys, and a sharp parrot-like exclamation . . . .[44]

At dinner, during which the bantam roosted on Maud's shoulders, Yeats was so engrossed in his discussion on poetry that he absent-mindedly piled in front of him all the dishes that were supposed to be passed to others, until Maud reminded him that 'there were others at the table and that their interest was not solely conversational.' After dinner they gathered around a large open fire, discussing astrology and mediumship until after midnight. The following day Maud went to church with Iseult and Sean and asked Gretta, although a Protestant, to accompany them as she was to present a new embroidered cloth for the altar. As they continued their holiday by listening to Yeats read prose he had translated from the Bengali poems of Tagore and travelled around the countryside with Maud in a large Normandy farm cart with hooped canvas covering, one receives an impression of a family grouping that was at peace with itself. Literature, rather than politics, formed the focal point of many of the discussions, but that no doubt was the influence of Yeats.

In May 1914 Yeats invited Maud to join himself and Everard Feilding, a member of the Psychical Research Society, to investigate a supposed miracle in Mirabeau, where a lithograph of the Sacred Heart was said to have dripped blood. They couldn't authenticate the miracle, but they were impressed by the piety of the old priest who, when they were departing, warned Maud to leave France as terrible events would shortly take place.[45] Maud hoped to return to Mirabeau that summer, but the care of her family prevented it. Sean had contracted chicken-pox while Iseult was diagnosed as having a weak heart, the doctor ordering her to 'give up smoking, to eat meat and to keep her window open', all of which the moody nineteen year old refused to do, as Maud wrote to Willie from Paris.[46] She also had Helena Moloney staying with her, recuperating from illness, as well as Diva Brat Mukerjea, a young Brahmin with whom Iseult was studying Bengali. Maud was concerned about his penniless state and only with immense difficulty succeeded in persuading him to accept 'a very small remuneration' for the lessons he was giving Iseult. Iseult and Mukerjea were translating poems of Tagore and Maud wrote to Willie of her pleasure that her daughter seemed at last to be 'really working and interested in the work.'[47] The worry that the imaginative and fanciful

Iseult would never develop a consistent interest in anything was a constant preoccupation. Maud, with her usual concern for everyone's well-being, hoped that Yeats could help Mukerjea obtain a professorship, and that he could ensure Helena was given some small part at the Abbey Theatre, once she was strong enough. In the meantime, she decided to take everyone to the Pyrenees, where Iseult could enjoy fresh air far away from tobacconist shops and Helena could recover her strength. Her friends, the Chirfils, were going also, 'so my duties of chaperone will be lightened', as Maud primly put it. While they were in their mountain retreat, England declared war.

On 26 August, Maud wrote to Willie in anguish, 'I cannot work, I cannot read, I cannot sleep. I am torn in two, my love of France on one side, my love for Ireland on the other. . . . This war is an inconceivable madness which has taken hold of Europe.'[48] She was desperate for news, while Helena longed to be back in Ireland with her Citizen Army comrades. But travel was difficult and in France, as the German army advanced, the numbers of dead and injured increased. Maud went to Argelès as a Red Cross nurse, 'patching up poor, mangled, wounded creatures in order that they may be sent back again to the slaughter' as she described her work to John Quinn.[49] Iseult and Helena were working as nurses' aides while young Sean was a page. Iseult hated it, 'an *abrutisement* life [that] leaves no room for the intellect' she complained,[50] but the soldiers loved her and her mother felt it was good for the dreamy young woman to have contact with the harsh realities of life. Never again would Maud accept violent action lightly. In November she wrote to Yeats that she was nursing the wounded from six in the morning until eight at night, 'trying in material work to drown the sorrow and disappointment of it all – and in my heart is growing up a wild hatred of the war machine . . . .'[51] War confirmed her in her belief that women were the guardians of the race:

> I always felt the wave of the women's power was rising, the men are destroying themselves and we are looking on – Will it be in our power to end this war before European civilisation is swept away. . . .[52]

Maud returned to Paris after three months of nursing in Argelès. Helena managed to get back to Dublin and took part in two productions at the Abbey in 1915. Most of the Irish inhabitants of Paris returned home, leaving Maud to feel totally isolated. Wartime censorship prevented her from obtaining any of the Irish political journals. She longed to be able to bring her family to Dublin, send Sean to Patrick Pearse's school and resume her place in the struggle, but now she could not even discover what was happening. And her own family had its share of sorrow. Kathleen's eldest son was killed in action in March 1915 and his mother's frail health collapsed. Maud devoted herself to nursing her sister until July when, together with Iseult, the two sisters offered their services at Paris-Plage, to work in one of the military hospitals there. Maud wrote to thank John Quinn for his 'generous cheque'. He was now sending her ten or twenty pounds every few months, money Maud put towards buying the wounded extra food to supplement their meagre hospital rations, occasionally also finding herself forced to obtain medical instruments. The months ground on, and Maud noted 'It is a strange absorbing life which brings one very near to the suffering and horror and waste of war.'[53]

The winter of 1915 was bleak. An attempted advance at Champagne packed the Paris hospitals which then began to empty with the arrival of spring, in readiness for the next bout of fighting. Kathleen's second son was badly wounded, while the third, at seventeen, was already an officer. Kathleen was having great difficulty in getting a passport and permission for herself and her daughter to go to a sanatorium in Switzerland, prompting Maud to write bitterly to Quinn that she didn't think United States' citizens would be treated in the same way. She thought she would come to live in America after the war, 'for Europe won't be a place to live in for generations'.[54] Maud was approaching her fiftieth birthday and feeling life could never again give cause for celebration.

CHAPTER 7

'MADAME MACBRIDE' RETURNS

On Monday 24 April 1916, the combined forces of the Irish Volunteers and the Irish Citizen Army marched out onto the Dublin streets as the Irish Republican Army, pledged to fight for the establishment of an Irish republic. The First World War was ostensibly being fought for the right of small nations to self-determination, and the republicans hoped that their historic action would win for Ireland its own recognition as a nation. The Easter Rising had begun. After all the years of struggle and dissension and endless organisation everything was now, as Yeats wrote, 'All changed, changed utterly'.

For six days the republicans fought against overwhelming odds to maintain the Irish republic which had been declared by a Proclamation read out by Patrick Pearse on the steps of the General Post Office, headquarters of the insurgents:

Irishmen and Irishwomen: In the name of God and of the dead generations from which she receives her old tradition of nationhood, Ireland, through us, summons her children to her flag and strikes for her freedom.

James Connolly was one of the leaders, and so was Tom Clarke, last of the treason-felony prisoners. Many of Maud's old friends were involved. From Inghinidhe na hEireann came Maire nic Shiubhlaigh, Madeleine ffrench-Mullen, Dr Kathleen Lynn, Helen Laird, Muriel and Grace Gifford, Helena Moloney and Constance Markievicz. Helena took part in the attack on Dublin Castle, during which her fiancé, Sean Connolly (who had once been a member of the Inghinidhe dramatic class), was killed. Constance Markievicz was Connolly's second-in-command, serving as a lieutenant in the Citizen Army at the Stephen's Green outpost. John MacBride, who knew nothing about the preparations for the Rising, was on his way home from a wedding when he passed by Thomas MacDonagh's post at Jacob's biscuit factory. He asked if he could join in and, as one of the few with actual experience of battle, played an exceptionally useful and courageous role as sniper.

On 29 April, with a large part of Dublin reduced to rubble by the British guns and the civilian death toll mounting, Pearse and Connolly decided to surrender in order to save further bloodshed. They knew that they would be executed, but few expected the savagery of the British reaction. Martial law was declared, nearly two thousand men and women were imprisoned and seventeen of the leaders were given death sentences. Constance Markievicz, the only woman to be court-martialled, had her sentence commuted to life imprisonment because of her sex and Eamon de Valera, as an American citizen, was also spared. But the early part of May witnessed what seemed an endless litany of vengeful executions. All seven of the signatories to the Proclamation were shot, including Connolly, who was so badly wounded that he had to be strapped to a chair. John MacBride was not a leader, but the British were glad to have got him finally in their sights. They had his treacherous role in the Boer War as justification. His death redeemed much of what had gone before, especially his bravery in facing the firing squad. He refused to be blindfolded, remarking that he had faced British guns before.

Maud and her family were spending Easter in Normandy when the first garbled reports of the fighting in Dublin began to filter through. She was in agonies of anxiety as she attempted to discover the facts, who amongst her friends had been killed and what the situation in Dublin was in the aftermath. Despite feeling 'wretched and powerless' she wrote to Quinn of her conviction that 'practically and politically their sacrifice will avail. They have raised Ireland to tragic dignity, and in the conference at the end of the war where the rights of small nations will be talked of it will be impossible to ignore Ireland.'[1] On 11 May, Yeats wrote to Lady Gregory of his and Maud's initial reactions:

> I had no idea that any public event could so deeply move me – and I am very despondent about the future. . . . Maud Gonne reminds me that she saw the ruined houses about O'Connell Street and the wounded and dying lying about the streets, in the first days of the war. I perfectly remember the vision and my making light of it and saying that if a true vision at all it could only have a symbolised meaning. This is the only letter I have had from her since she knew of the Rebellion. I have sent the papers every day. I do not yet know what she feels about her husband's death. Her letter was written before she heard of it. Her main thought seems to be 'tragic dignity has returned to Ireland'. . . . She is coming to London if she can get a passport, but I doubt her getting one. Indeed I shall be glad if she does not come yet – it is better for her to go on nursing the French wounded till the trials are over.[2]

On the same day, Maud wrote to Quinn from Paris, 'My dear friend, I have seen the English papers now and know the ghastly extent of the tragedy'. She told him that most of her best friends – people he had met at George Russell's – had been executed in cold blood, adding, 'Constance Markievicz was like a sister to me.'[3] She now knew what had happened to John MacBride. When Maud heard the news of her husband's execution she went to Iseult, the paper still in her hand, and looking pale said bluntly, 'MacBride has been shot'. She then went over to Sean, who was busily making a boat, and said, 'Your father has died for his country – he did not behave well to us – but now we can think of him with honour.'[4] Maud's old bitterness against her husband was now forgotten, although never forgiven. As she explained to John Quinn:

> My husband is among those executed. He and MacDonough gave themselves up from Jacobs biscuit factory to save the civil population of that crowded district from indiscriminate shelling by the English. He has died for Ireland and his son will bear an honoured name. I remember nothing else.[5]

In reply to Quinn sending her a poem published about MacBride's life and death, she said that she was keeping all such material for Sean's sake, 'He made a fine heroic end which has atoned for all. It was a death he had always desired.' Yeats incorporated his old rival into his poem 'Easter 1916':

> This other man I had dreamed
> A drunken, vainglorious lout.
> He had done most bitter wrong
> To some who are near my heart,
> Yet I number him in the song;
> He, too, has resigned his part
> In the casual comedy;
> He, too, has been changed in his turn,
> Transformed utterly;
> A terrible beauty is born.

But when he asked Maud to send the poem to Quinn, hoping that French censors would be kinder to it than British ones, Maud scathingly felt that no censor would bother to black out a poem which she considered 'not worthy of Willie's genius and still less of the subject'.[6] Its style was not heroic enough for her liking and she wanted no further reminders of the less romantic side of John MacBride. The Capuchin priests who attended the rebels were diligent in informing the relatives of the last moments of their loved ones. On 22 June Father Augustine wrote to Maud of Major MacBride's 'beautiful, heroic end' and she sent copies of all this correspondence to Quinn, presumably so that he could publicise news of the 1916 martyrs to Irish-American circles.[7] In many ways, Maud was becoming keeper of the flame. She tried to have MacBride's body exhumed from its quicklime grave in Arbour Hill but the authorities refused. 'I do not mind,' she wrote to Quinn, 'for he is with his comrades and England is powerless to dishonour their memories.'[8]

Maud was now a widow, free to remarry, and Yeats spent much of June and July attempting to obtain a passport so that he could be with her in Normandy. During this time Iseult, who as a French passport holder was free to travel, arrived in London to see him. She was carrying messages from her mother. Iseult said Maud was 'very sad', seemed 'lonely' and was 'sleeping badly', but Iseult always had a flair for the overstatement.[9] Although Maud was certainly full of sorrow at the loss of her friends and frustrated at her inability to join those who remained, her attitude was more positive than Iseult implied. At that moment her main concern was the fate of Helena Moloney, who was still in gaol. She wanted Yeats to find a lawyer for her friend, and having done that, to accompany Iseult back to Normandy. Willie found himself regarding Iseult in a very different light from his previous fatherly affection. Temporarily freed from the overwhelming presence of her mother, the twenty-year-old woman with the Pre-Raphaelite looks attracted the attention of the fashionable friends Willie now introduced her to. Yeats wrote proudly to Lady Gregory:

> She looks very distinguished and is now full of self-possession. She is beautifully dressed, though very plainly. I said, "Why are you so pale?" and she said, "Too much responsibility." She makes me sad, for I think that if my life had been normal I might have had a daughter of her age. That means, I suppose, that I am beginning to get old.[10]

By August, Yeats was in Normandy. He and Iseult were reading the works of French Catholic poets and Iseult was acting as his secretary while he worked on another book of memoirs. He mentioned marriage once again to Maud, but it was obvious that she hardly heard him as she mused over the possibility of getting a passport. As Willie ruefully wrote to his old friend, the actress Florence Farr, the death of Maud's husband had made no difference to their relations, 'She belongs now to the Third Order of St Francis and sighs for a convent.'[11] Maud was resolute that she wanted no man in her life again, apart from her son Sean.

Walking along the seashore with Maud that September, Willie recited the poem he had been working on. It was 'Easter 1916'. The sentiments most connected to Maud were 'Too long a sacrifice/Can make a stone of the heart', and during their conversation he implored her 'to forget the stone and its inner fire for the flashing, changing joy of life'. But Maud, who recounted this incident after Willie's death, said her mind was 'dull with the stone of the fixed idea of getting back to Ireland'.[12] She was determined to return with Iseult and Sean in October. 'I must have my boy brought up in Ireland. I must be near him. Besides, I feel my place is there.'[13] She also badly wanted to help the families of all those sent to internment camps in England and Wales. Yeats's proposal of marriage was repeated almost out of habit, as he had promised Lady Gregory before leaving for France that he would not marry Maud unless she 'renounced all politics, including amnesty for political prisoners'.[14] The Abbey Theatre was dependent on rich patrons for its existence, and these often had unionist politics. Lady Gregory was determined that they should not be offended by any awkward personal alliances. Besides, she felt Iseult would be a much more suitable wife than her mother, being uninterested in politics and very interested in literature. For his part, Willie was slowly falling in love, as can be deduced from this letter to Lady Gregory, written from Normandy:

> I believe I was meant to be the father of an unruly family. I did not think that I liked little boys but I liked Shawn. I am really managing Iseult very well. The other night she made a prolonged appeal for an extra cigarette. . . . I have stayed on longer than I intended, but I think you will forgive me under the circumstances – as father, but as father only, I have been a great success.[15]

It was a pathetic admission. The situation verged on the ludicrous with Iseult undecided about her feelings and Maud appearing to have resolved not to interfere. By September Maud still had no word about her passport and Yeats could not prolong his stay in France any longer. He went with them to Paris, promising to use his influence once he returned to England. Maud and her little family were again back in their apartment, hurriedly clearing it of all their possessions and optimistically removing everything, including themselves, to a tiny apartment on the seventh floor of the building. Maud was sure that they would soon be leaving, writing to Quinn that she hoped to live 'chiefly in Ireland now, so am only keeping a *pied-à-terre* here'. Her return to Paris and the reality of the continuation of the war made her very depressed, 'Nothing is left standing but the insolence of ammunition manufacturers, ship owners – and still the grim massacre goes on.'[16]

In November, Maud's passport finally arrived, but she was informed, on the day before her departure, that orders had been received from the British War Office to say she could go to England but would not be allowed into Ireland. She was further warned that if she went to

London to argue her case, she might not be able to return to France. 'Such is the liberty of the world we live in', Maud wrote angrily to Quinn. She wrote letters to everyone she could, protesting 'this monstrous and stupid piece of tyranny'.[17] The Irish MPs were not cooperative; their condition of support appeared to be for Maud to endorse the policies of the Irish Party, rather than Sinn Fein. She, Iseult and Sean had no choice but to stay there for the winter, shivering with cold in their cramped little attic, without coal and often in complete darkness as the electricity supply was cut off at irregular intervals. Food was rationed and, having thought they would soon be in Ireland, Maud had no supplies laid in. 'It is not gay', she commented drily. All came down with flu at Christmas, to be followed by a recurrence of Maud's old lung trouble. Despite their difficult living conditions, Maud's main preoccupation continued to be the situation in Ireland. She managed, with apologies for not having had time to copy it out neatly, to send Quinn the little book in which she had jotted down all the money she had spent for charity. She still had 520 francs in hand which, with his consent, she hoped to spend in Ireland, probably on food for the school children.[18]

The majority of the Irish population had greeted news of the Rising with bewilderment, jeering the defeated insurgents as they were marched off to prison. But the nationalist forces had quickly regrouped themselves, led by the redoubtable figures of women like Kathleen Clarke and Aine Ceannt, widows of the leaders. Another important figure at this time was Hanna Sheehy-Skeffington. Her husband Francis had been arrested while attempting to organise a citizens' militia to discourage the widespread looting of shops during the Rising. He had then been taken to Portobello Barracks and murdered in cold blood by a British army officer after witnessing atrocities committed by him. As a pacifist, Sheehy-Skeffington had not supported armed confrontation, but as a socialist he had sympathised with the aims of the rebels and did not want the Rising to be discredited by the looters. Determined to bring her husband's murderer to justice, Hanna went to America, where she spoke at over 250 meetings on Ireland's claim to independence and succeeded in obtaining an interview with President Wilson. The publicity generated by such women had an effect: many countries put pressure on Britain to show clemency, while the attitude within Ireland changed dramatically.[19]

When the first batch of prisoners was allowed home in December 1916 they were greeted as heroes, with bonfires lit on the hillsides in jubilation. The remaining prisoners were freed in June 1917 – Countess Markievicz was the last person to return home. Ella Young was there to watch her triumphal return through the Dublin streets, a radiant figure upon a float piled high with enormous bouquets, a Tricolour and small red flowers, symbolic of her socialist beliefs.[20]

Maud was still in France, and she, Iseult and Sean were spending yet another summer in Normandy, living on the potatoes and beans they had planted in the garden at Easter, and on torpedoed fish and other trophies washed up from the sea. Maud felt the only reason why the fighting continued was that the governments were frightened of peace because they would then no longer control the world. She felt certain that socialists would take over, making future wars impossible. She told Quinn of her hatred of militarism, an attitude that he, far away in America, probably did not share as he had not witnessed the horrors of bloodshed:

> But you, I believe, still see beauty in war. I did once, but hospitals and broken hearts and the devastation and destruction of all art and beauty have changed me and I bow to every peace advocate. They are the real ones who are showing moral courage at the present time in Europe.[21]

In August she received a letter from the Paris director of the British Passport Office, again refusing her permission to return to Ireland. Maud had hoped the release of the prisoners would have heralded a more tolerant attitude towards herself, and she enclosed the letter of refusal in a note to Quinn, asking for his help. Despite the danger, she, Iseult and Sean had made up their minds that they would not pass another winter in Paris under the present conditions. She hoped that Quinn would be able to use his influence to get them out if they were interned.

A week later, Willie was over again, combining a lecture series with a visit to Normandy. He proposed marriage to Iseult, who hesitated before giving her answer. On 12 August he gave Lady Gregory the latest news on the situation:

> Iseult and I are on our old intimate terms but I don't think she will accept. She 'has not the impulse'. However, I will think the matter undecided till we part. . . . It is very pleasant here. Maud Gonne is no longer bitter and she and Iseult are on good terms now and life goes on smoothly. Iseult herself seems to have grown into more self mastery after months of illness from cigarettes. She has only had one outbreak so far and that was only one cigarette and a half and was secret.[22]

On 21 August he wrote to say that Iseult had been ill in bed for two days and had come down 'full of affection' owing to a dream in which Willie appeared in sympathetic light. But he did not think he would change her mind. The letter went on to give a picture of the inner dynamics of the household:

The little boy is now quite tall and is going to be very clever and to my amusement has begun to criticise his mother's politics. He has a confident analytical mind and is more like a boy of 17 than 13. Life goes smoothly after one outbreak from Maud Gonne, the result of my suggesting that London was a better place for Iseult than Dublin. They go to London in the middle of September to try and get the government refusal to allow Maud Gonne to go to Ireland withdrawn.[23]

Maud was anxious to get Sean to Ireland for the start of the school term in September, but the situation was increasingly difficult. Although the British government, in order to conciliate foreign pressure, had released the prisoners people were now being rearrested as Sinn Fein started to reorganise. It had won two by-elections in succession, clearly demonstrating the extent of its popular support, and Sinn Fein workers found themselves subject to arbitrary arrest. Maud was, in Willie's words, 'in a joyous and self-forgetting condition of political hate' as she packed their possessions in preparation for their forthcoming trip to London. Before they left, Iseult at last refused Willie's offer of marriage. He was less upset than he might have been, finally realising that the young woman had always been more like a daughter to him than anything else. He confided to Lady Gregory that his chief concern was Iseult's welfare as she was sunk deep in melancholy and apathy, constantly accusing herself of sins of omission. Only in the country was she amused and free of that mood for any length of time.[24] One can feel deeply sorry for Iseult, it could never have been easy for her, the unacknowledged daughter of Maud Gonne.

On 17 September, they finally reached Southampton. Maud and Iseult were taken into a shed and searched for secret codes while their companion walked up and down outside, fuming under the drizzling rain and cursing the shamefaced, polite detectives. The boat train was held for them but no sooner had they reached London than Maud was served with a notice under the Defence of the Realm Act, forbidding her to proceed to Ireland. To Willie's enormous relief, Maud decided against any rash action and said she would take a flat in Chelsea for six months and study design at a London art school. A friend of Yeats was able to find Iseult a post as assistant librarian in the School of Oriental Languages. The pay was small but the hours were short and she would be amongst an interesting group of people. Ezra Pound, the poet, who had become a close friend of Yeats, would tutor Sean. Joseph Hone wrote in his biography of the poet that after all this had been arranged, 'Yeats burst into tears from sheer happiness.'[25]

Pound wrote to John Quinn that Yeats was back from Paris, 'bringing Maud Gonne, 10 canary birds, 1 parrot, 1 monkey, 1 cat, two members of M.G.'s family and the hope that she will lead a

Maud, Sean and Barry O'Delaney. The cross worn by Maud could be her cross of the Knights of St Patrick, which Sean wore when collecting money from members of the St Patrick Society in Paris. His proud look while clutching a bouquet of flowers would suggest this was such an occasion. (*Courtesy of the MacBride family*)

Constance Markievicz in Lissadell in 1904, a few years before she renounced her aristocratic background in favour of the nationalist cause. (*National Museum of Ireland*)

ean na h-ipeann

(THE WOMAN OF IRELAND)

Vol. I, No. 3.   éanaın — JANUARY, 1909.   PRICE—ONE PENNY.

MADE IN IRELAND.

THE
KILKENNY WOODWORKERS

MANUFACTURERS OF

Bedroom Suites,
Diningroom Chairs,
Chesterfield Couches,
Comfortable Easy Chairs,
In many shapes and sizes.
Writing Tables,
        Roll Top Desks,
        Bookcases,
        AND
Cabinet Making in all
        Departments.

NEW DEPARTMENT—
BASKET AND WICKER WORK,
PERAMBULATORS.

SHOWROOMS—
**6, 7 & 8 Nassau St.,
DUBLIN.**

MAUNSEL'S NEW BOOKS.

To Our Sisters.

The new year is the time for good resolutions and editorial sermons, and a good many pious sentiments and meaningless platitudes are preached from editorial arm chairs at this season. The **bean na h-éıpeann** does not like sermons. We believe there is in Ireland too much preaching and too little practice. The chief fault we find with men is that they talk very big and do very little, and we would like to foster amongst Irishwomen a desire to work, rather than talk about it in the columns of newspapers.

But because we are at the beginning of another year, it is well that we should consider what opportunities the coming year will afford us, and how we can make the best of them, for the advancement of Ireland.

In the beginning of this year, we who were women, we are glad to say—complained that we had not taken a brave enough position. Well, the **bean na h-éıpeann** wants to make in this first month of the new year a **Proclamation**, that she never intends to shirk any difficult problem, or subtle issue, and will always be at least brave enough to speak on the **side of Ireland and Ireland's Women** against the whole world, if need be. We are glad to know such fearless Irishwomen still exist, small though their numbers be in proportion to the great unthinking majority. Our *raison détre* is to awaken Irishwomen to their responsibilities and long neglected duties. An article by Lapaıppıona appearing in this issue deals exhaustively with this subject. There is little use in us women starting to abuse men and their methods of thought and action. We must remember the humiliating fact that they are largely what their women-folk have made them. Neither must we waste time bewailing our past disabilities. We must set about raising the present position of women in the social and political life of the country, and we must labour to make their present environment compatible with their moral and intellectual advancement, which incidentally means the development of the nation and of the race. Our desire to have a voice in directing the affairs of Ireland is not based on the **failure of men** to do so properly, but is the inherent right of women as loyal citizens and intelligent human souls. It is not our intention to countenance any sex antagonism between Irish women and Irish men. There are too few Irish hearts aflame with pure and **conscious love** of Mother Éıpe to have them divided by such an unnatural barrier; but we think that men would be the better for a little of women's unselfishness and spirituality, and we look for the advent of

and a purer atmosphere. We, Irishwomen, must learn to throw off our present diffidence, and assume our natural position in Irish life, and men will soon have to frankly admit that it is only by working hand in hand that we can hope to **make Ireland free.**

A great many, if not all, the various pressing social problems could be much more effectively dealt with by women than by men. The squalor and misery of the towns, with the poverty and dulness of the rural parts of Ireland, surely need some attention, and we believe women could relieve much of this distressing state of affairs without legislation or any kind of outside help. The grinding poverty of the rural population, and the town-dwellers ... its attendant horrors. To relieve them employment every woman has in her own hands one simple and swift remedy, the **support of Irish manufacture.** We cannot do better than go a step further and reiterate the advice given in our first number: to give preference to those Irish firms who pay their workers honestly for their labour and give them opportunities to live decent healthy lives. Much might be said of the disgraceful conditions under which women work, and we hope to deal with this matter in the near future. If well-to-do Irishwomen interested themselves a little more in their less fortunate sisters, we believe women workers would have many of their grievances redressed. There are many other questions that could be peacefully settled if women only took some real interest in their own country.

In this Number articles appear in Irish and English by Caitlín ní Ṡabann and Lapaıppıona, each treating this all-important subject of women's place in society from slightly different standpoints. Both writers are well-known to Irish-Irelanders. We hope our readers will take their message seriously to heart, and make it the foundation of a new year resolution—unique in this respect that it shall be **faithfully kept.**

The most pleasing memory of the old year was the Christmas Aonac, held in the Rotunda Buildings, Dublin. Owing to its great success we understand the Aonac of 1909 will be on a much larger scale. It will soon be looked forward to by Dubliners as the event of the winter. The Samain Festival which, up to a few years ago, was such a pleasant busy week, has unhappily been allowed to die out; we hope to see it revived again in all its glory, and we hope the Christmas Aonac will grow until it becomes as important to the trade of Ireland as its great prototype of Leipsic is to that of Germany, and that it will rival the splendour of its forerunners, the great

Front page of *Bean na hEireann*, journal of Inghinidhe na hEireann. The masthead, featuring a strong looking woman in Celtic dress, a rising sun behind her, was designed by Constance Markievicz. (*National Library of Ireland*)

Hanna Sheehy-Skeffington, life-long feminist and close friend of Maud. This photo was taken in 1917 while she was in America attempting to publicise the facts of her husband's murder by a British army officer during the 1916 Rising. On her return in 1918 she briefly joined Maud in Holloway Jail. (*Courtesy of Andrée Sheehy-Skeffington*)

Iseult Gonne as a teenager. (*Courtesy of the MacBride family*)

Maud in the widows's weeds she adopted after the 1916 Rising. (*National Library of Ireland*)

Maud, Francis Stuart and Mrs Stuart standing, while Iseult kneels in front with her children Kay and Ian. (*Courtesy of the MacBride family*)

Roebuck House, Maud's home for the last thirty years of her life. (*Courtesy of Anna MacBride White*)

Maud and Charlotte Despard in 1923 at the height of the WPDL campaign against the Cumann na nGaedheal government. The placard carried by Mrs Despard begins 'Prisoner's mothers, wives, sisters protest ...' (*Courtesy of Louie Coghlan O'Brien*)

Maud (centre) standing in front of a WPDL banner. (*Courtesy of the MacBride family*)

Maud in the mid 1930s addressing a meeting at the corner of O'Connell Street and Cathal Brugha Street. 'Dublin was a battlement in which she, Helen, walked triumphant.' (Francis MacManus) (*Courtesy of the MacBride family*)

Maud in the late 1930s, this time using a microphone.
(*Courtesy of Anna MacBride White*)

Willie Yeats at his home in Riversdale, where Maud visited him in 1938, a few months before his death. (*The Raymond Mander and Joe Mitchenson Theatre Collection*)

The novelist, Ethel Mannin, who was to become a close friend in the last years of Maud's life. (*The Mansell Collection*)

Maud and her grandson
Tiernan MacBride,
c. 1939/40. (*Courtesy of
the MacBride family*)

Sean MacBride at Roebuck
House in 1986. The painting
in the oval frame above the
mantlepiece is of Sean as a
baby, painted by Maud while
in exile in Paris.
Photo by DerekSpeirs/Report
(*Courtesy of Gemma
O'Connor*)

tranquil life'.[26] And life was tranquil for them, as they settled down amongst the writers and artists of London. On 20 October Yeats married Georgie Hyde-Lees, whom he had resolved to marry if Iseult turned him down. The Gonne spell was finally broken and at long last Willie was able to share his life with a woman who possessed the gift of happiness and an ability to help others to find happiness. Willie wrote to Lady Gregory that his wife was 'a perfect wife, kind, wise, and unselfish'.[27] It was what he had always wanted, and what Maud had always realised she could never be. Although there was much curiosity concerning Maud's reaction to Willie's marriage, it does not appear to have affected her unduly. In the main, she must have been relieved that Iseult had not become his wife, that she was still her daughter. Iseult and George Yeats, so close in age to each other, became friends, to everyone's surprise, and Iseult often stayed with the newly-weds. Maud knew she could always rely on Willie's support when necessary, and that was what mattered, not a romantic preoccupation with the past.

She continued to haunt the War Office in her determination to return to 'God's own country', as she wistfully described Ireland to Quinn. She met for the first time Charlotte Despard, founder of the Women's Freedom League, a convinced socialist, pacifist and feminist, who also happened to be sister to Lord French, Field-Marshal General at the battle of Ypres and, from 1918–1921, Viceroy of Ireland. The 63-year-old rebel had long ago rejected the values of her upper-class family, but her contacts would come in useful when she later visited Ireland. In December, Maud gave two lectures to the Workers' Suffrage Federation, Sylvia Pankhurst's organisation, on 'Sinn Fein Ideals and Personalities', where The Irish Citizen reported Maud held her audience spellbound with her attack on the British government for refusing to allow her son to visit Ireland and stand beside his father's nameless grave. She hailed Francis Sheehy-Skeffington and James Connolly as the modern type of patriot, exponents of a new definition of freedom which included the emancipation of women, the improvement of conditions for workers, and the feeding of school children.[28]

None of these activities brought Maud any closer to what she most wanted. Two months after her Workers' Federation lectures she decided she had been patient for long enough. With rags stuffed under her black skirt, a shawl over her head and her height disguised by a bent stoop, Maud boarded the Holyhead ferry to Ireland, accompanied by Sean. Recalling her exploits in her old age, she was amused to remember that Helena Moloney failed to recognise her as she waited at the station for her former president.[29] At first Maud stayed in the house of Dr Kathleen Lynn, before buying a house at 73 St Stephen's Green. Sean promptly joined the Fianna, the republican boy-scout movement that had been formed by Constance Markievicz in 1909. Once they reached the appropriate age, Fianna boys became full members of the IRA. Maud now called herself 'Maud Gonne MacBride', a name she had never before used. But from now on, even her letters to John Quinn contained this form of her signature. She had joined the ranks of the republican widows of 1916, although there were some who resented what they considered to be her insinuation into their tradition.

Dublin was a very different city from the one she had known before the war. Instead of busy days campaigning for school meals and lively evenings of conversation with friends from the political and literary worlds, there was now only determined opposition to the continuance of British rule in Ireland. The First World War was grinding on, and British losses were now so great that the government decided upon a course of action they had previously rejected as unworkable: the imposition of conscription on Ireland as a desperate measure to supplement their numbers. In Ireland, all shades of opinion, including the churches, united in outraged opposition. Women signed anti-conscription pledges, vowing that they would refuse to take the job of any man who was conscripted and a one-day strike was organised in every town in Ireland. Only Unionist-dominated Belfast remained loyal to the Crown. In order to defuse this opposition, the British concocted a 'German Plot', for which they never bothered to give any evidence. It was a flimsy pretext to round up everyone connected with Sinn Fein.

On the night of 17 May, seventy-three prominent Sinn Fein leaders were arrested and immediately deported to English gaols. Constance Markievicz was the only woman amongst them, but two days later she was joined in Holloway gaol by Maud and by Kathleen Clarke. Maud was arrested and thrown into a police van as she left AE's house one evening. Through the barred window she could see fourteen-year-old Sean running after her.[30] By the end of that year, he had joined the IRA. Sean pretended to be older than he was, deliberately hiding the fact from his mother, who was quite happy for him to be in the Fianna but who would have disapproved of a boy so young taking up arms.

Despite all Maud's years as an opponent of the British government, this was the first time she had suffered imprisonment and she found it a gruelling experience. Their conditions were punitive. Because they refused to sign a pledge promising not to discuss politics with visitors, they were unable to see anyone during the whole period of their confinement. The three women shared a landing – 'three wild Irish-women' – safely isolated from the other prisoners. They were not prisoners, having been charged with no offence, but internees who were locked up for twelve hours each night and allowed only one hour's exercise a day. Maud and Kathleen worried incessantly over the welfare of their children. Kathleen had three young children, and had suffered a miscarriage after the execution of her husband, but she did at least have a large family of sisters she could rely upon while she was imprisoned. Constance was also a mother, but she had long ago sent her daughter Maeve to be brought up by her mother, Lady Gore-Booth. Maeve hardly knew her own mother at all. Sean was a student at Mount St Benedict while Maud was imprisoned, but she fretted over her inability even to write a cheque for his keep. While Constance and Kathleen settled down with books and paintings, Maud found the claustrophobia of her environment so unsettling that she could do nothing. Kathleen Clarke recalled that all Maud seemed able to do was to talk to her caged canary, which she had managed to have sent in:

> She was like a caged wild animal herself, like a tigress prowling endlessly up and down. We were given the chance to apply to the Sankey Commission for release, and in her misery she said she would – said she'd point out that she hadn't been in Ireland during the war. Con said 'If you do that, you need never come back to Ireland,' and she tore the application up. After that she fell sick, or maybe feigned sick, she was such a good actress that you couldn't tell.[31]

In August their imprisonment was cheered up by the brief stay of Hanna Sheehy-Skeffington, arrested while making her way home from America. The seasoned suffragist immediately resorted to a familiar tactic, the hunger strike, and won her release after a few days. Maud envied her friend, but didn't feel capable of following her example. Her health was deteriorating and Constance's letters to her sister Eva reveal continuous anxiety over the health of her two cell mates: 'M.G. has been very ill with a rash, but she is on the mend and up again. We were most anxious for some days.'[32] 'Mrs C. is better again, thanks to a filthy bottle, a painted chest and being rolled in cotton wool for a week.'[33] While in gaol Maud learned of the death of Millevoye, although she must have kept that information to herself, and then in October the news was broken of the death of her sister Kathleen, who had never recovered from the shock of her son's death in battle. Maud became seriously depressed and her family and friends pulled every string they could to secure her release.

Yeats used his influential English friends on Maud's behalf, while in America John Quinn did the same. In late October she was finally allowed to be examined by a Harley Street specialist, who reported a return of pulmonary tuberculosis, recommending 'active medical and open air treatment in a suitable climate without delay'.[34] The report was sent to those who could influence government action, and after five and a half months of imprisonment Maud was released from Holloway to a London nursing home. She of course refused to remain there and a few days later returned to Woburn Buildings, where, to her indignation, Iseult had to sign papers accepting her mother into her care.[35] Iseult had stayed with Ezra Pound and his wife while Maud was in gaol, but she and Sean now rejoined their mother in Willie's old apartment. Kathleen Clarke was not released until the following February. Although she was at least as ill as Maud, she did not possess the latter's reputation or circle of friends. Constance Markievicz, yet again, was amongst the last to be released. On hearing of Maud's return to Ireland she wrote to Eva, 'Had she leave? I wonder if she'll be sent back. It's very mysterious why they ever took her, but they are, luckily, sometimes very stupid.'[36]

Soon after her release Maud wrote to Hanna Sheehy-Skeffington of her 'joy to be out of that awful place' and to be able to see Sean and Iseult, but she felt it was a 'heartbreak to leave Constance Markievicz and Kathleen Clarke. . . . They are so brave and so uncomplaining and so willing to suffer for Ireland.' She hoped that Constance would be elected to Parliament as 'she would be a splendid candidate on social and labour questions as well as the national question'.[37] The elections referred to by Maud were those called by the British government for 14 December, after the end of the First World War. They were the first elections in which women (over the age of thirty) could vote and be candidates – the culmination of the long suffrage campaign – and great interest was shown in both Britain and Ireland over the question as to whether or not women would be elected to Parliament. Sinn Fein decided on an all-out campaign to get as many of their candidates elected as possible, in order to demonstrate conclusively that the majority of the Irish people supported the demand for an Irish republic. There was much speculation on whether the three women imprisoned in Holloway might be put forward by Sinn Fein, and many women also hoped that Hanna Sheehy-Skeffington, for so long a campaigner for women's interests, would be selected also. The Labour movement agreed to stand aside in order to give Sinn Fein a clear run. In the event, only Constance Markievicz for St Patrick's division in Dublin and Winifred Carney for the Victoria division in Belfast were adopted. Winifred Carney's constituency was a hopeless one, but in Dublin women threw themselves into the task of ensuring that an Irish woman would be the first female member of Parliament. In Britain, the eighteen women candidates (including Charlotte Despard) were all defeated, but in Ireland the result was a landslide for Sinn Fein, which won 73 out of 105 seats, and Constance was duly elected. Instead of attending Westminster, however, Sinn Fein set up their own assembly, Dail Eireann, which had its first meeting on 21 January 1919. It was March before the second session was held, after the release of the 'German Plot' prisoners. On this occasion Eamon de Valera was elected President and Constance Markievicz became Minister of Labour.

Those who were elected for Sinn Fein were by now seasoned fighters; their credentials included participation in the Easter Rising and more than one term in gaol. They were at the heart of the nationalist movement in a way Maud would never be. And it was not a role she aspired to. As soon as she had recovered sufficiently from her gaol experience she again disguised herself and, accompanied by both Sean and Iseult this time, made her way back to Ireland and her house at Stephen's Green. As she wrote to Hanna, to whom she was becoming increasingly close, 'my mind is quite made up, I will go to no sanatorium in England ... and if put back in Holloway I shall hungerstrike at once ... what devils English officials are!'[38]

Maire Comerford, a member of Cumann na mBan, soon to be a worker for the White Cross and an indefatigable republican all her life, differentiated between the role played by Maud and that of members of republican organisations. While praising Maud's 'really splendid devotion' to Ireland, she regarded her as 'a person more of reactions, resenting injustice, going where places were burnt, where the military burnt towns, that kind of thing – she followed them as a protester'. And that was a much different role to the one played by those widows of 1916 who regrouped the remnants of the republican movement after the defeat of the Rising. Maud was 'extremely good and important in her own way ... but hadn't the same relationship to the Republican tradition'.[39] Maud could have joined Sinn Fein, or intimated her willingness to hold at least an honorary position in Cumann na mBan on her return to Ireland, but did not. Although there was a degree of public suspicion concerning her private life, with friends of MacBride always resenting her, attempts to explain Maud's reticence in the light of this do not do justice to her as a woman of great personal courage who had outfaced her accusers in the past. A more likely explanation comes from her son Sean, who felt that his mother agreed with Hanna Sheehy-Skeffington on many issues, chief of which was a reluctance to join any organisation that favoured the use of force.[40] Cumann na mBan was engaging in military operations alongside the IRA, albeit in an auxiliary capacity, and Maud's experience of the French battle-fields had left her with no taste for combat, even though she wholeheartedly supported the aim of Irish freedom and realised that the British had left them with no option but to fight. The effect of war-weariness, combined with a horror of prisons that had intensified since her own experience of confinement, was to give Maud her primary political causes for the rest of her life: campaigning on behalf of those most affected by the devastation of war, and agitating on behalf of those in gaol. In letters to friends she constantly reiterated her conviction that peace and justice were the two most important causes in life, and that they were indivisible.

While in gaol she had rented her house to Yeats and his wife, as George was expecting her first baby in the new year and they wanted it to be born in Ireland. Willie was taken aback by Maud's appearance on the doorstep, particularly as George was seven months' pregnant and just recovering from a bad bout of flu. Fearing a raid on the house, he refused to let Maud in and, angry and hurt, she stormed off. Iseult told Ezra Pound that they were 'equally to blame and both in need of keepers',[41] but the rift between the two old friends took a long time to heal. By Christmas, she had moved back into her house. Anne Yeats was born in February. Shortly after her birth Yeats wrote 'A Prayer for my Daughter', in which he hoped that the infant would never resemble the woman he had loved so hopelessly for thirty years:

> An intellectual hatred is the worst,
> So let her think opinions are accursed.
> Have I not seen the loveliest woman born
> Out of the mouth of Plenty's horn,
> Because of her opinionated mind
> Barter that horn and every good
> By quiet natures understood
> For an old bellows full of angry wind?

The War of Independence started in earnest at the same time as Dail Eireann's inaugural meeting. For the first time since the Rising, republicans engaged in armed action, and the battle lines were soon drawn. In response, political organisations were banned, arrests began again and a policy of terror was instituted following the introduction into Ireland of the band of mercenaries known as the Black and Tans, who raided and ransacked homes at will and resorted to indiscriminate murder as they attempted to terrorise the population into abject surrender.

International opinion was a vital element in the propaganda war between the republican forces and the British government, and the pressure of international opinion was one of the few weapons the beleaguered population possessed in their attempt to assert Ireland's right to self-determination. It was an area in which Maud was supreme and she now offered her services to the Sinn Fein publicity department. When the Dail was proscribed as an illegal assembly, its various departments were forced to meet secretly and the publicity section concentrated its forces in Frankfort House, home of the Coghlan family. Constance Markievicz was to live there for the rest of her life, and various of the Coghlan daughters, all active members of the nationalist movement, would, at the end of the civil war, be employed by Maud in her workshops to provide employment for republicans.[42] The ties between those risking all they possessed in the cause of Irish independence were, of necessity, very close. A young republican widow, Kathleen Kearney (later to remarry and become better known as the mother of Brendan Behan), worked for Maud for almost a year. She had asked Constance Markievicz for help in getting a job:

I went to her because I knew she would help a poor woman with children to support, and she did. She asked Madame MacBride, widow of Major John MacBride that was executed in 1916, to find me a job in her house at St Stephen's Green. It wasn't a bad job, though Madame MacBride paid very little (my meals and that and a little money besides), but then I wasn't really a servant —more a receptionist. I let the visitors in and answered the telephone. . . . So, although I got very little for it, I didn't feel degraded ever, and that was worth something.[43]

The prison issue was one where the government was vulnerable to criticism and republicans made every effort to draw world attention to prison conditions. At the end of 1919, leading women activists launched an appeal to their 'sisters in other countries', urging them to demand the formation of an international committee of inquiry into the conditions under which Irish political prisoners were being detained. It was signed by Constance Markievicz for Cumann na mBan, Helena Moloney for the Irish Women Workers' Union, Louie Bennett for the Irishwomen's International League, Maud Gonne MacBride for Inghinidhe na hEireann and Kathleen Lynn for the League of Women Delegates.[44] It was an impressive list, even if organisations such as the Inghinidhe were no longer in existence, and it had an impact in America, where women organised a lobby of Congress. In 1920 an American Commission on Conditions in Ireland held an inquiry into the situation. Membership of the Commission consisted of senators, congressmen, governors, mayors, teachers, trade unionists and writers – a deliberate cross-section of all shades of opinion – and the Interim Report of the Commission concluded that 'the sanctity of the family home is violated' by the 48,474 raids which were carried out on homes during 1920 alone.[45] From Britain, the Women's International League, the Labour Party and the British Society of Friends organised separate fact-finding tours, all of which condemned British policy in Ireland.

In December 1920, Maud sent Dorothy Macardle over to London to persuade Mrs Asquith to intercede to save a young man from execution. She had been asked by the Dail for her help with the case and during her few days in London, Dorothy was fascinated to observe British politicians in action, as one side denounced the other. The Irishman's reprieve was a mere pawn in the political game, but skilfully used by the republicans. Whether this was Maud's idea or not, Dorothy did not say, when she told her story to Maire Comerford while the two women found themselves sharing a gaol cell.[46] As Dorothy waited in London to learn of the result of the appeal, she called on Charlotte Despard at her Battersea home. Charlotte promised to go over to Ireland if her presence would help. They talked about starting a relief scheme for women and children, a sure sign that Dorothy had been briefed by Maud.[47]

The visit to Battersea was successful. In January 1921 Mrs Despard came over to Ireland, a guest in Maud's Stephen's Green home. Maud was also her guide on the fact-finding tour she immediately embarked upon. Martial law had recently been declared in large parts of the country and the two women braved considerable hazards as they drove around Cork and the south-west, constantly being stopped at road blocks by hostile troops. Mrs Despard was seventy-five, Maud was fifty-six, but neither fitted the conventional image of elderly or middle-aged women. Maud wrote to John Quinn of her experiences with Charlotte, whom she considered 'a most remarkable woman and intensely Irish in feeling'. As Lord French's sister she was able to talk her way through road blocks to visit places Maud could never have reached if she had been on her own. Maud was greatly amused by the 'puzzled expressions on the faces of the officers and of the Black and Tans, who continually held up our car, when Mrs Despard said she was the Viceroy's sister'.[48] Maud wrote an article entitled 'Devastation', an eye-witness report of the situation, hoping that Quinn would be able to sell it to an American paper for her. She also asked him for his help in obtaining regular work as a correspondent for an American paper, as the end of the First World War had left her financial affairs in ruins. The Gonne trust money must have recovered after this time, because from family testimony Maud's income, although reduced, remained adequate for the family's needs. Quinn did try to help, but with little luck. Maud was to be more successful in the following months, working for the relief organisation, the Irish White Cross.

The publicity generated by the American Commission's investigations, as well as all the publicity efforts by republicans, had paid off: in December 1920 the American Committee for Relief in Ireland was formed and approved of by President Harding. Over one million pounds for relief was collected in America alone. To co-ordinate and distribute all these donations, a relief organisation entitled the Irish White Cross was launched in January 1921, at a meeting chaired by Lawrence O'Neill, Lord Mayor of Dublin. Seven women were nominated onto the executive committee, including Maud Gonne MacBride, Hanna Sheehy-Skeffington and Kathleen Clarke, who was now an alderman (sic) on Dublin Corporation. Relief at the rate of 10s per adult and 5s per child a week was paid out to those 100,000 people who had been left destitute as a result of the destruction of homes and businesses. A Reconstruction Committee was also set up to examine requests for help to rebuild factories, businesses and homes, with low interest rate loans given. In Dublin alone, 10,000 children were fed by the funds of the White Cross, because the British government had withdrawn all grants to the local public boards, as penalty for their opting out of the British local government system and pledging allegiance to the Dail.[49] Maud's expertise in school feeding was an asset, and so was her knowledge of Donegal. During Easter she and

Charlotte Despard toured the areas that Maud had once known so well in her Land League days, and Maud wrote an impassioned letter to Arthur Griffith, then Acting President of Ireland in place of de Valera who was in America. She described scenes of near-famine, with the proud Donegal people starving in their homes, refusing to beg for assistance. In her estimation more than double the amount of money than that allocated by the White Cross would be necessary to alleviate the situation and create employment. It was a very emotional plea to an old friend, 'God forgive me for troubling you with all this, I know how hard your task is, and how unnecessarily hard it is being made for you by people who should know better. May you have strength to carry your great and unselfish work to completion.' She also asked for his help in obtaining assistance for the destitute Belfast refugees who had been forced to flee from the terror of the anti-Catholic pogroms.[50]

A long time ago, Maud had described herself as a 'freelance' in the Land League movement. During the War of Independence she in some ways performed a similar role, but with the important difference that she now had a strong and influential network – mostly composed of women – whom she could call on when necessary. Although she was on friendly terms with women like Constance Markievicz, many of her closest associates were people like herself, who were not formal members of any branch of the nationalist movement, but who associated with it on an individualistic basis. In this way Maud retained a freedom to act that suited her essentially instinctive approach to politics. Thus, when Sylvia Pankhurst came over to Ireland, although her arrival was 'most unexpected', it was in Maud's house she stayed,[51] and when Maud was asked to investigate the possible arrest and imprisonment of a young boy in Mountjoy, she was able to write to Sylvia, to George Lansbury and other members of the British labour movement, as well as the more routine task of sending letters to the editors of all the influential newspapers.[52] When the occasion demanded, Maud did not hesitate to ask Willie Yeats for help and, despite his new-found marital happiness, he proved as co-operative as ever. Desmond Fitzgerald, Sinn Fein's Director of Publicity (and head of the department Maud sometimes worked for), was arrested in February 1921, and his wife Mabel approached Maud in desperation at being unable to visit her husband in gaol. Maud asked Willie to use whatever influence he could, with the result that Mabel was allowed to visit Arbour Hill prison, and Fitzgerald's conditions of imprisonment improved. In her letter of thanks, Maud told Willie of Fitzgerald's great admiration for him, and his pleasure that he had taken the trouble to intervene. She also mentioned Sean and Iseult's welfare before concluding by sending love to his wife and daughter. It was the warm response of one old friend to another, personal considerations not forgotten despite the urgency of the political situation.[53]

Maud's concern for her children and pleasure in sharing her love of children with her women friends is very evident in all her correspondence. She was delighted to be able, at last, to introduce Sean to her Irish circle of friends and pleased that her friends liked the boy. Equally, she always enquired after the welfare of her friends' children. Boys like Owen Sheehy-Skeffington had been suddenly left fatherless, with mothers whose energies were being poured into the propaganda war. An expression of concern for their well-being was much more than an empty formula. In 1921 a young boy called Tommy Whelan was hanged for alleged complicity in an assassination plot and Maud comforted his anguished mother in her vigil outside the gaol. Twenty-five years later, in a letter to the writer Ethel Mannin who was visiting Galway, she recalled the occasion, wondering if Ethel had come across old Mrs Whelan. They had remained friends throughout the years, and Maud enclosed Mrs Whelan's address, mentioning that she had recently received a letter from her. That level of support was an important element in the web of friendship which would sustain those bereaved by war for many years to come.[54]

Sean's military development was as precocious as his political development had been. While his mother wrote proudly of his hard work in his law studies, he was, at the same time, surreptitiously leading an IRA active service unit. In September 1920 he was stopped while driving a car near midnight in Rathmines. In the car were Constance Markievicz and Maurice Bourgeois, an emissary from the French government. He and Bourgeois were released after two days, but Constance was tried by court martial for having organised the Fianna ten years previously. For that 'crime' she was sentenced to two years' hard labour.[55] Maud and her friends attended the trial, but were not allowed to speak to her. Maud visited Constance, who in her typically selfless way mentioned in a letter to her sister Eva that Maud looked so ill and worn she hoped the authorities would leave her alone.[56] Dublin was a terrible place to live in, as Maud described to Quinn:

> Hardly a night passes that one is not woke up by the sound of firing. Often there are people killed, but often it is only the crown forces firing to keep up their courage. One night last week there was such a terrible fusilade just outside our house, that we all got up thinking something terrible was happening. That morning, when curfew regulations permitted us to go out, we only found the bodies of a cat and dog riddled with bullets.[57]

Sinn Fein was attempting to set up alternative structures to the ones imposed by the British, in the hope that they would eventually supplant the British institutions. Like many other women, Maud acted as judge for the Sinn Fein courts, which were modelled on the ancient

Brehon Laws of Gaelic Ireland. Owing to the war situation, and the illegal nature of the courts, written judgements were not kept. All Sean MacBride could remember of his mother's role was that she would sometimes leave the house for a day or half a day without saying where she was going, and no one asked any questions.

Maud discovered Sean's membership of the IRA when the young man, while cleaning a rifle in the attic, accidentally let off a shot. The bullet went through the floorboards to the room where a priest, who used to visit Maud every Sunday afternoon while in a sanatorium recovering from his nervous breakdown, was relaxing. That particular Sunday afternoon couldn't have helped his recovery, and Sean was then obliged to confess to his mother. He said she 'came round'.[58] The fear of his death in action must have been her primary concern. It was the feeling of a mother, not a political activist.

Iseult was also staying with Maud. She had eloped to England with Francis Stuart, a young Ulsterman and would-be poet eight years younger than herself, and her mother, appalled at the prospect of her daughter forfeiting her respectability by this flouting of convention, insisted that the couple got married. Helena Moloney was dispatched to act as intermediary to arrange what was, in most people's eyes, a misalliance from the start. Maud's experience of being ostracised by polite society and her efforts to establish an accepted place within society for her illegitimate daughter were the obvious reasons behind her action.[59] Iseult's insistence that there had been nothing sexual in their relationship was ignored. Appearances were what counted. The Stuart marriage was eventually consummated, and Iseult was expecting her first baby in March. Spinal meningitis killed baby Dolores at three months and both mother and daughter grieved bitterly. Relations between Francis and Iseult were always difficult. Iseult lived an indolent, insecure existence of continual cigarette smoking and card playing, as if to deny the reality that surrounded her, while her eighteen-year-old husband was simply not ready for the responsibilities of marriage and hated his mother-in-law with a venom he later gave voice to in his strange autobiographical novel *Blacklist, Section H*. Stuart described himself as 'equally ill at ease whether Madame was caressing Iseult or talking in her impassioned way about Ireland. He didn't like her easy assumption of the absolute rightness and moral purity of the nationalist cause'.[60] Matters were so bad in the summer of 1920 that Maud asked Willie Yeats over to Ireland to act as arbiter between the two young people. The ex-suitor played the role of honest broker with little success.

Although the bloodshed was continuing all around them, neither side was gaining an advantage. It was an appalling deadlock which was eventually broken by Lloyd George capitulating to international pressure. On 24 June 1921 he proposed a conference to work out a peace formula. A truce between the British and Irish was finally agreed on 11 July. While calm prevailed, Maud felt she and her family needed the respite of a change of scene and so in August she took Iseult, Francis and Sean with her to Bavaria, to enjoy the music of Wagner. A favourable rate of exchange with the German mark was the only reason why Maud could afford the holiday. She felt ashamed of benefiting at the Germans' expense and tried to make restitution by giving money to the collections for the wounded and orphans that were held between acts at the opera house.[61] Maud enjoyed her much-needed rest but Sean could only stay a short while as his IRA duties were urgent, and the quarrelling young couple were less than ideal companions. She was beginning to wonder what was happening with the peace talks back home. It was time to return.

Chapter 8

WORKING FOR PEACE

During the period of the Truce, only the gaoled members of the Dail were released. Everyone else had to wait on the outcome of the forthcoming talks. On Hallowe'en night, four of the imprisoned women decided they had waited long enough and, in a daring escape, they climbed over the wall of Mountjoy gaol. Eithne Coyle, one of the escapees, sheltered in the home of Dr McLaverty until she learned that Maud had offered to help shelter the women. The young woman stayed quietly in the Stephen's Green house until she went home to Donegal at the end of November. She described Maud as a 'charming hostess', giving the impression that she had been a visitor to a country house, rather than a fugitive from the authorities. But grace and charm are words often used to describe Maud Gonne, regardless of the circumstances in which she was encountered. Eithne added that everyone in the house was kind and friendly, with the exception of a caged monkey which spat at her when she walked past. Constance Markievicz, not long out of prison herself, visited one day. She lent Eithne £5, a kindness the young woman never forgot.[1]

That October, five delegates from the Dail, invested with the powers of plenipotentiaries, had left Ireland to meet British representatives in London. Sean MacBride went as aide-de-camp to Michael Collins. On 6 December, under the pressure of Lloyd George's ultimatum of 'immediate and terrible war' if they did not sign, the five put their signatures to the 'Articles of Agreement for a Treaty between Great Britain and Ireland'. The Irish Republic was signed away. In its place came partition, with a twenty-six county 'Free State' and a six county 'Northern Ireland', where Protestants greatly outnumbered Catholics. All members of the Free State Parliament would be required to take an oath of allegiance to the Crown. Ireland remained within the embrace of the British Empire, and Britain ensured this by retaining control of Irish coastal defences.

Weeks of bitter, painful debate in the Dail and all over the country followed, as the merits of the Treaty were argued. All six of the women who had been elected under the terms of the Government of Ireland Act to the Second Dail, in May 1921, rejected the Treaty.

Constance Markievicz objected to what she considered a 'deliberate attempt to set up a privileged class'. She stood proudly by her beliefs, 'While Ireland is not free I remain a rebel, unconverted and inconvertible . . . I have seen the stars and I am not going to follow a flickering will o-the-wisp'.

Unlike Constance, Maud had not pledged herself to a socialist republic. The Treaty, while offering much less than the regenerated Ireland of myths and warriors she and Willie had dreamed of so long ago, was a substantial improvement on the Home Rule Bill that so many had welcomed as a first step in the years before the war. More importantly, acceptance of the Treaty would mean an end to the bloodshed that Maud found increasingly distressing. She did not accept the Treaty in the way that her old friend Arthur Griffith did. He was now President, in place of de Valera, who had resigned after losing the vote in the Dail. Maud's view was more akin to that of Michael Collins – the Treaty was a stepping-stone on the way to freedom. Sean MacBride, on the other hand, was passionately on the anti-Treaty side. He and Maud had heated discussions on the subject as the young man tried to convince his mother of his point of view. Sean was now Assistant-Director of Organisation for the IRA, travelling to Europe on various arms procurement missions (which no doubt he combined with his trip to hear Wagner), before eventually joining the anti-Treaty IRA forces in their Four Courts headquarters.[2]

Maud retained the confidence of the pro-Treaty side, and Griffith appointed her as one of the Free State representatives to the Irish Race Convention which was being held in Paris in January 1922. Delegates from seventeen countries gathered together to celebrate Irish talent and to see how Ireland's fight for independence could best be supported. Attitudes over the Treaty had hardened to such an extent that the Irish delegates, instead of presenting a united front of Sinn Fein solidarity, divided into two groups, each insisting upon its own organisation. The whole convention was marred by intrigue, despite the lustre of lectures by Willie Yeats, his brother Jack, Douglas Hyde and others, on Irish theatre, art and language. Nevertheless, Maud and Constance Markievicz, who were amongst the anti-Treaty group, maintained their personal friendship. Both women were appalled by the red-draped dais and throne, erected in honour of the Duke of Tetuan who had come from Madrid to preside over the Convention. Maud had mocked similar scenes in Paris many years earlier, when she had attended evenings organised by the Association du St Patrice. She had never expected to see a repetition of such nonsensical ostentation at an event intended to establish a permanent organisation capable of promoting Ireland's interests internationally. Although the Duke possessed the honorary title of 'The O'Donnell', in recognition of the ancestor who had been forced into exile in the seventeenth century, he knew nothing of Ireland except its horses, as Maud scathingly commented.[3] The initiative foundered because the Dail Cabinet refused to grant a loan to get the organisation off the ground until funds were obtained from other sources.

The creation of a sectarian six county state in the north of the province had left Catholics vulnerable to attack by unionist extremists. Catholic workers were brutally expelled from the shipyards while over two hundred people were killed and more than one thousand wounded in the first year of the state's life. Terrified Catholic refugees, jobless, their homes burnt to the ground, began to flee to the south. When Maud returned to Ireland, she felt their plight to be the most urgent of all the existing problems. She did not want to debate the merits of the Treaty and she was not involved in the various organisations then debating their next move; as usual, Maud's interest was with the immediate, and with how she could be most effective. But the refugees themselves were pawns in the battle between the pro- and anti-Treaty forces. Those opposed to the Treaty were pointing to the sectarian behaviour of the unionists as proof of the untenable nature of the northern state. Those in favour of the Treaty wanted the pogroms against the Catholics played down, believing British promises that a review of the border would eventually ensure the impossibility of a separate state continuing to exist in the north of the country.

The IRA was sheltering the refugees in Fowler Hall in Dublin, the property of the Orange Order. It was empty except for office furniture and when Maud saw 'women half demented and children sick with terror' grouped forlornly in the building, she went immediately to Griffith, believing it would be a routine matter for him to arrange for the supply of beds from the evacuated British barracks. But his first words were, 'The IRA have no right to bring down refugees from the North; it is not our policy and we are the government.' Maud's reply that their plight was similar to those made homeless in France at the start of the war, whom she had seen encamped in the Gare St Lazare, drew only the response that Fowler Hall was not a suitable place. 'What place', she asked, 'could be more suitable than the property of an Orange institution to house its victims?' Pale and harassed, Griffith remained unmoved by her pleas. His final argument was that the IRA was simply looking for trouble.[4] Maud's declaration that the issue was one of humanity, not politics, was obviously not his view: in the eyes of those struggling to establish the Free State the reverse was the case. But Maud was never a politician.

Elections to a Third Dail were held on 16 June. Those opposing the Treaty lost heavily, including most of the women candidates. The election, using an out-of-date register, was held amidst protests that the people had been unable to consider all the issues involved. The new constitution, for example, was only published on election day and Michael Collins reneged on an election pact that had been agreed upon by the two sides. Tensions were growing. On 22 June, Field

Marshal Sir Henry Wilson, military adviser to the Unionist government, was assassinated in London. Evidence points to this having been authorised by Michael Collins in retaliation for the pogrom against Belfast Catholics and the order never rescinded, but the finger conveniently pointed to the anti-Treaty IRA. At any event, it provided the British government with the necessary excuse to demand that the Free State government get rid of the Four Courts garrison. If they did not, the British Cabinet declared that the Treaty would be considered to have been 'formally violated'. They even lent the artillery for the bombardment.

Maud was again in Paris, apparently sent there by Griffith to publicise the creation of the new twenty-six county state. Her wide-ranging contacts with prominent French people could be put to good use, as Griffith knew well, but while over there she also took the opportunity to publicise the attacks being made on Catholics in the north. As this was an issue heavily emphasised by those opposed to the Treaty, the fact that Maud felt capable of giving voice to the preoccupations of both sides is a clear indication of the extent of her neutrality at this time. In August 1923, Hanna Sheehy-Skeffington was sent to Paris by the anti-Treaty republicans in an attempt to argue their case against the recognition of the Free State by the League of Nations.[5] Significantly, Maud was not a spokesperson on this occasion. It was possibly an indication that her original stand had been too ambiguous.

The French papers of 29 June reported the shelling of the Four Courts by the Free State government and Maud immediately rushed back to Dublin, realising that this was the start of the civil war everyone had been dreading. Her fear must also have been for Sean, although it is unclear whether she knew he was actually in the Four Courts at that time. When she arrived in Dublin, the two days of bombardment were almost at an end, but the Dublin Brigade of the IRA had commandeered various sites around O'Connell Street, snipers from both sides were taking their places on the roof tops and fighting was breaking out in different parts of the city, including some hand-to-hand encounters. The situation was desperate, and Maud was not the only woman to wonder frantically how peace might be restored. In several contemporary articles, Maud claimed that she met the Lord Mayor of Dublin, Lawrence O'Neill, on her return, and he asked her to 'Get together some of the women who are not afraid and who want peace. We will make a supreme attempt.'[6] In an article written in 1948, Louie Bennett, of the Irish Women Workers Union, said that she and some other women sent a message to their friends to meet at the Mansion House the following day.[7] The discrepancy is probably no more than proof that many women were trying to work for peace at this time. Certainly, both Maud and Louie Bennett were prominent figures on the various peace missions.

A formidable body of women grouped themselves together. From former suffrage ranks came Hanna Sheehy-Skeffington, Charlotte Despard and Meg Connery; from the labour movement there was Louie Bennett, Maire Johnson and Mary O'Connor, and from the nationalist side there was Maud herself, as well as Agnes O'Farrelly and Rosamund Jacob. The delegation, accompanied by O'Neill, decided to talk to the Four Courts garrison first. As they descended the steps of the Mansion House, news came of the surrender of the republican forces within the Four Courts. Out of the blackened shell, waving a white flag, marched one hundred and eighty prisoners, Sean MacBride included, bound for Mountjoy gaol. Their capitulation did not mean the end of hostilities, so the women decided to remain together as a peace committee, the Lord Mayor at its head, to negotiate with the opposing factions. Two delegations were formed, one to the government forces, the other to the republicans. In Maud's words, 'We claimed, as women, on whom the misery of civil war would fall, that we had a right to be heard.' They proposed an immediate ceasefire until the meeting of the Dail, scheduled for 2 July; during that time all combatants were to return home, without fear of arrest.

At twelve o'clock on 1 July a delegation composed of Maud Gonne MacBride, Charlotte Despard, Louie Bennett, Agnes O'Farrelly and Gertrude Webb were received at government buildings by Griffith, Collins and Cosgrave. Louie Bennett gave her impression of the men, 'Collins was excited: obviously excited. Griffith was utterly depressed; an old, broken man. Cosgrave was outwardly unmoved, frigidly cold.' Without a laying down of arms, they would not negotiate. Griffith's curt response was 'We are now a government and we have to keep order.' That was the last occasion the two former friends met. On 12 August Griffith died of a cerebral haemorrhage. Some called it a broken heart. His death was one factor in bringing to an end Maud's neutrality over the Treaty. She no longer had any bonds of friendship with those in the leadership of the pro-Treaty forces. Michael Collins was shot dead in an ambush ten days later, and the government was then headed by a triumvirate of William Cosgrave, Richard Mulcahy and Kevin O'Higgins, a bureaucratic, humourless trio of young men, whose ruthless suppression of all opposition was to galvanise Maud into a furious resistance.

The second half of the women's peace delegation had met the republican forces in their headquarters at the Hammam Hotel on the afternoon of 2 July. They had agreed to the peace terms, but insisted on holding onto their arms. That was unacceptable. There were to be no more talks. By the afternoon of 5 July, the Hammam Hotel, the last outpost of the republican forces in Dublin, had surrendered. A large part of the city centre lay in smoking ruins, sixty people had been killed and three hundred wounded. After the collapse of Dublin, the fighting moved to the countryside and the IRA fighters found themselves gradually pushed further southwards by their immeasurably better-equipped opponents, who had the benefit of continued British donations of artillery and armoured cars. The casualty rate was an appalling three hundred a month for both sides, while the prison population rose to over twelve thousand. The peace mission had failed, and the saddened, increasingly embittered women turned to the work of nursing the wounded.

Maud filled the ground floor of her house with beds, turning her home into a makeshift hospital for republican casualties. Iseult helped her mother obtain medical supplies from sympathetic doctors while her husband Francis carried slop pails full of bloody swabs and brought up trays from the basement kitchen. Josephine, Maud's old French cook, grumbled continually at the invasion of her territory by the young Cumann na mBan women who were also working in the house. Francis soon went off to the Continent, where he surprised even himself by succeeding in smuggling guns for the IRA. His delight in finding himself on the margins of conventional society was much greater than any sympathy with the republican cause. A short while afterwards he was picked up by Free State troops and interned.[8] With her son and her son-in-law in gaol, the welfare of the prisoners began to take up all of Maud's waking hours. They were badly in need of support.

In August, Maud accompanied a group of relatives to Mountjoy gaol to try to give clean clothes and food to the prisoners inside. They were refused entry. No one could get information as to the whereabouts of individual prisoners and, to make matters even worse, the authorities imposed a sentence of summary execution for the possession of arms, ammunition, or explosives. The sound of the firing squad began to be heard from inside the prison walls. As the IRA countered this by shooting deputies who had voted in agreement with this policy, the government retaliated with a dreadful strategy of official reprisals. It was a spiral of death that started in November and continued relentlessly. Seventy-seven men were officially executed, and there were many unofficial deaths as well. One of the worst examples was the unprecedented execution of four men – Liam Mellowes, Rory O'Connor, Richard Barrett and Joseph McKelvey – on 8 December. Sean MacBride shared a cell with Rory O'Connor and he too was woken up in the middle of the night and told to get dressed. He was later sent back to his cell, but his comrade from the Four Courts had no such reprieve.

The beleaguered republican forces, reduced to hiding out in remote country areas, were in no position to make any protest concerning the treatment of their prisoners. Her informal protest at the prison gate had convinced Maud that the relatives could only be effective if they organised. A meeting at the Mansion House inaugurated the Women's

Prisoners' Defence League (WPDL), to which Charlotte Despard was elected president and Maud secretary. The only qualification for membership was the payment of one halfpenny a week and a familial relationship to a prisoner. They were affectionately dubbed 'The Mothers' by those who had cause to be grateful for their courage over the next decade. Their offices were the open streets outside the gaol gates, where anxious relatives came looking for their sons and daughters, pooling information with the women of the WPDL so that the whereabouts of the missing ones could finally be discovered.

Sheila Humphreys, a prominent member of Cumann na mBan, paid tribute to the support Maud gave to the relatives who flocked to the WPDL for help – 'they were the poorest, most disadvantaged members in the movement. They were the ones with nothing, who had nothing, and that's who she worked with.'[9] Solicitude for the weakest sections of the population, those with neither financial support nor the backing of any organisation, was a characteristic of every cause Maud adopted. There was no hint of the 'Lady Bountiful' about this, as she never remained aloof from those she worked with. On the contrary, she would immerse herself in a situation with such intensity that her own self became submerged within the drama of the moment. And – perhaps unconsciously at least – that is what she wanted and always aimed to achieve.

The intricacies of Maud's life were hidden from most people, apart from what Yeats wrote and made public, but her 'air of gay gallantry covering tragic experiences' was evident to anyone sensitive enough to go beyond first impressions. Helena Swanwick, a suffrage friend of Charlotte Despard's, had first met Maud at the Dublin house of historian Alice Stopford Green while visiting Ireland in 1921. She was then on a fact-finding tour for the Women's International League. Maud's 'beauty and dare-devilry' had been a legend to Helena for years and she found the flesh and blood woman lived up to her reputation. Maud had a way of creating a court wherever she went, so that everyone became her 'willing courtier', while the 'gay gallantry' appeared to emanate from having 'thrown all she had, memories as well as dreams, into the cause she believed in'.[10] In 1926, Helena Swanwick returned to Dublin to attend the Fifth Congress of the Women's International League for Peace and Freedom. This time she was to stay in Roebuck House, where she discovered the mesmerising effect of Maud remained as potent as ever. 'I have sometimes felt as if I might have committed any folly against my judgement if she had desired it.' But she recognised that Maud possessed another dimension; within her domestic circle her 'homely charm' was as compelling as the 'radiant personality' which shone in society. Helena was an astute observer, who recognised the complexities of Maud's character: 'More than ever she seemed to me the Diana who would set off diamonds, or light a cottage fire, or be welcome at a deathbed.'[11]

Maud's years of experience of fighting for the treason-felony prisoners, combined with the old suffragette tactics of poster parades and demonstrations that Charlotte Despard and Hanna Sheehy-Skeffington made skilful use of, made 'The Mothers' a highly effective organisation. Every Sunday, week after week, no matter what the weather was like or whether the government had banned public meetings, Maud Gonne and Charlotte Despard, majestic in flowing black robes, headed their procession of women protesting against the imprisonment of republicans. The march always ended on 'ruins corner' in O'Connell Street, which British guns in 1916 had reduced to a pile of rubble. Sheila Humphreys was again impressed by Maud's dignified, conscientious devotion to her self-imposed duty:

> Madame would prepare her speech with the same care as if she was giving it to Congress in America, where often there would only be a rabble to hang around and listen. Mrs Despard and others would take part too, but often, often it was Madame on her own. She never missed a week.

From all the evidence, Maud was obviously the mainstay of these demonstrations. At one point, when she was absent, Mrs Despard wrote to ask Constance Markievicz to take over as speaker. The elderly suffragette, despite her decades of experience with political causes, was very conscious of her very different background and upper-class English accent. She was always reluctant to take too prominent a role – she was keeper of the flame, and that flame was Maud Gonne:

> Dearest Con,
>   Can you – will you – speak for me next Sunday at O'Connell Street. Maud, as you know, is in Paris and I am on my own. Come, if it is at all possible, and let me have a word as soon as you can.
>   You see I have a sense of responsibility about the meeting. . . .[12]

Their demonstrations were broken up, they were shot at and had hoses aimed at them, but still they protested. In November, Maud and Mrs Despard were speaking at a meeting to publicise the fact that Mary MacSwiney (the sister of the Lord Mayor of Cork who had died in 1920 after a hunger strike of seventy-four days) had gone on hunger strike herself, when a lorry-load of pro-Treaty troops pulled up and opened fire on the crowd. Fourteen people were wounded and hundreds hurt in the panic-stricken confusion.[13]

All those who protested against government policies knew that they faced continual harassment and the threat of imprisonment, no matter who they were. Dorothy Macardle, a teacher at the prestigious Alexandra College, bastion of the Protestant Ascendancy, was living in the top rooms of Maud's house, when she was raided and carted off to Kilmainham gaol. When word spread that she had not turned up to give her lectures because she had been arrested, Lilian Dalton, one of the few pupils sympathetic to her teacher's political views, went to call at the house to find out what had happened. She arrived on the doorstep at the same time as Maud:

> Very overawed and shy at being confronted with this notorious Maud Gonne, the legendary beloved of Yeats, I followed her up to the top flat. Here was a shambles, evidently the work of the Free State soldiers. Everything was strewn around the floor, drawers and shelves were overturned, obscene graffiti scrawled on the walls. I remember Madame MacBride exclaiming dramatically, 'Who can we get to see all this?' and even in that moment thinking to myself that the professional political agitator took precedence over any other concern. . . .[14]

Dorothy put her imprisonment to good use, becoming a prolific correspondent for the republican press with her vivid descriptions of life behind bars. The Free State troops ransacked Maud's house again while she was out and, in an act of vindictive revenge, piled up a heap of papers in the middle of the road before they left, making a bonfire of it. All Maud's most treasured letters, relics of a lifetime of devotion to political causes, were destroyed.

At this time Maud was in the process of vacating her home in order to share a house with Charlotte Despard in the Dublin suburb of Clonskeagh. Roebuck House, a substantial Georgian mansion, was surrounded by gardens and outhouses, giving ample scope for the various schemes which its two inhabitants would devise over the coming years. For the moment, it was to serve as refuge for those on the run and as convalescent home for those in need of a break before they returned to active service. Only Maud's pet dogs were unwelcoming, but having braved them it was said that any person could walk in and ask for dinner or asylum for life. Charlotte Despard, who had lived in a very different world from the conspiratorial, twilight existence imposed on those who were challenging the government of the Free State, found the furtive footsteps and whispered conversations that seemed to emanate from all parts of the house once night fell, most alarming. Although the dedicated pacifist had the purpose of these nocturnal visits explained to her, it was still an effort not to be frightened. The British and Irish political traditions had some fundamental differences, as she was beginning to find out.

The WPDL was amongst the organisations banned by the government at the beginning of 1923 and this time Maud found herself joining the prisoners on whose behalf she had been so energetically campaigning. Yeats had been appointed a senator in the Free State the month previously, a fact which infuriated Maud, who condemned him for accepting the legitimacy of a state 'which voted Flogging Acts against young republican soldiers still seeking to free Ireland from the contamination of the British Empire'.[15] But as soon as he heard of Maud's arrest he broke off the letter he was in the process of writing, explaining to Olivia Shakespear, the recipient:

> I cannot write any more as I have just learned that Maud Gonne has been arrested and I must write to Iseult and offer to help with the authorities in the matter of warm blankets. The day before her arrest she wrote to say that if I did not denounce the Government she renounced my society for ever. I am afraid my help in the matter of blankets, instead of her release (where I could do nothing), will not make her less resentful. She had to choose (perhaps all women must) between broomstick and distaff and she has chosen the broomstick – I mean the witches' hats.[16]

In the mood Maud was in, warm blankets would have been refused with contempt, but they were not needed. The woman described by London's The Times as 'one of the most prominent Republicans in the country' was only kept overnight in Mountjoy. She was released the next morning and quickly used her experience to publicise further the scandalous prison conditions. She was 'grateful to the ignorant young ape of a Free State officer', who in arresting her had enabled her to obtain up-to-date information on the current situation, including the lack of medical facilities, overcrowding and drunkenness amongst the prison officers. As she also pointed out, in a letter to Max Wright of the Daily Express, other women arrested with her were still in gaol:

> I was released because I happen to be well known abroad and in America, and Mrs Despard hastened to make my illegal arrest known to the press. My arrest is typical of hundreds of the arrests now taking place. If anyone is in a house that is being raided and the . . . Free State officer does not happen to like his or her face he arrests at pleasure without warrant or order. The prisoner is then lodged in jail in secret, no communication with the outside world permitted, no solicitor allowed in, no redress possible.[17]

The only weapon the prisoners possessed was that of the hunger strike. Prison conditions deteriorated further as the authorities found themselves unable to cope with the twelve thousand prisoners – a number which included four hundred women. The tactic of the hunger strike was resorted to with increasing frequency. But the government, knowing that the anti-Treaty forces were nearing military defeat, was reluctant to make any concessions. The public at large was disheartened and war-weary, and it was only the determined actions of the small groups of women in the Women's Prisoners' Defence League and the Cumann na mBan organisation, the Prisoners' Dependants Society, that provided any support for the actions of those inside the prisons. Mary MacSwiney had been released on 28 November, after twenty-four days fasting, but only after full-scale protests against an Irish government daring to let a MacSwiney die like the British had let the Lord Mayor of Cork starve to death. Other hunger strikers had less support for their actions.

At the beginning of April, another hunger strike was embarked upon by a number of women, the fourth to be undertaken by female prisoners. Ninety-one women in Kilmainham won their demand to receive and send out letters – the cause of the dispute – but the government began a crackdown on those who were organising outside support. On 10 April, Maud Gonne was rounded up, and so were a number of other prominent women: Kitty Costello, Nell Ryan, Annie O'Neill, Kate O'Callaghan and, once again, Mary MacSwiney. Nell Ryan was the sister-in-law of the Defence Minister, Richard Mulcahy (an example of how the civil war had divided families), and Kate O'Callaghan and Mary MacSwiney were the only two women members of the Dail. The two TDs had been travelling by train to Tipperary, to attend the funeral of Liam Lynch, the IRA chief-of-staff, who had just been killed in battle. The government feared that their presence would exacerbate an already emotional situation so they were arrested as they left the train. They were being held without charge, while the others were charged with the minor offence of disseminating anti-government publications. Nell Ryan initiated the hunger strike, which Maud joined as soon as she was arrested. In Holloway gaol she had felt unable to follow Hanna Sheehy-Skeffington's method of securing a quick release, but now she had no hesitation. The intervening years had hardened her resolve and she was determined not to show any weakness in confronting a government she had come to despise as much as she had ever detested British rule over Ireland.[18]

Mrs Despard, on hearing of her friend's arrest, rushed to the gates of Kilmainham in an anguish of helplessness. With so many of those who could have been relied upon to organise effective protests now inside, the veteran campaigner resorted instead to an individual display of solidarity. She confided to her diary that she was 'moved to a sudden resolution' and she immediately sat down outside the gates of Kilmainham, remaining there throughout the twenty days of Maud's incarceration. Dr Kathleen Lynn offered a camp bed, but all she would accept was a chair. It was a real test of friendship and political commitment, enduring 'strange nights and days, bitterly cold. . . . Oh the bitter cold and the *length* of those nights', as she ruefully described the experience.[19] Large-scale demonstrations were impossible, but many influential people did appeal on the women's behalf. Lord Glenavey, chairman of the Senate, urged the government to consider clemency; Archbishop Byrne warned that 'their deaths would cause a wave of sympathy throughout the country'; and of course Yeats once again rushed to intervene on Maud's behalf. He urged President Cosgrave to consider that she was 'fifty-seven and [could] not be expected to stand the same strain as a younger woman'. Cosgrave retorted that it was not possible 'to consider these women as ordinary females'.[20] He insisted that women had no business in politics and should stick to tending the sick, but despite his personal hostility towards Maud and her friends, it was obvious that the government could not allow that particular group of women to die.

The prison doctor told Maud she was the most cheerful hunger striker he had ever met. Her reply was 'Why wouldn't I laugh, when I win either way?'[21] If they were allowed to die, the government (and, by implication, the Treaty) would be utterly discredited; if they won, they would have defeated the government on that point at least. After twenty days Maud was carried out on a stretcher. An ambulance was requisitioned and Mrs Despard joyfully left her lonely vigil to leap in beside her friend, off to help her recuperate in Roebuck House. The civil war was almost over by the time the pair had recovered their strength.

The government was only persuaded to deal leniently with the prisoners when a deal was agreed between the opposing forces that in the future 'the fact of a prisoner being on hunger-strike should not affect the merits of the question of detention or release'. In other words, the government gave due warning that it would not give way to the moral pressure of a hunger strike on any future occasion. The prisoners had won their release in this round of the battle, but the government was determined to win the war. For no obvious reason, Kate O'Callaghan and Mary MacSwiney were not released until the twenty-fifth day of their hunger strike, and then only after women prisoners in Kilmainham had refused to allow themselves to be transferred to the North Dublin Union, because it would have meant leaving their hunger striking comrades behind. A brutal battle between the women and their captors had ensued and after the details were made public, the women were released. Again, it would seem that the reputation of 'Ireland's Joan of Arc' was such that she escaped the worst of the reprisals.

The intensification of the struggle inside the gaols and internment camps was one indication that the civil war was nearly at an end, with the republicans suffering defeat after defeat. Finally, on 24 May, Frank Aiken, the new chief-of-staff, issued the order to dump arms and cease fire. And now more prisoners were added to the numbers already incarcerated, and the bitterness of the defeated increased. The military struggle was over, but the government seemed determined to wipe out all traces of opposition. They also decided to hold another election, on 27 August, to secure an unambiguous mandate for their policies.

It was a travesty of the democratic procedure. The government called the election, and then harassed every republican that dared to speak at the hustings. When de Valera came out of hiding to speak at a meeting in Clare, the Free State troops forcibly broke up the meeting and arrested the former president. As so many of the republican candidates were in gaol and unable to speak for themselves, the voice of the Women's Prisoners' Defence League became a substitute for the political party. Maud and her small group took great delight in outwitting the government, holding impromptu meetings in coffee houses, plastering the hoardings with their posters, speaking at every street corner they could. Although Maud was not a Sinn Fein candidate, she contributed diligently to their paper. The work of herself and Mrs Despard did not go unnoticed. On 17 August, *Sinn Fein* reported that there had been an attempt to set fire to Roebuck House, followed by the planting of a bomb in an outhouse the following night. The report went on to say:

> Madame Gonne MacBride brought it to Rathdrum Police Station and handed it in, saying, 'I return your property. You will be able to send it on to the particular force that placed it in Mrs Despard's outhouse.' Mrs Despard, sister of Lord French, is speaking at election meetings in the south.

Despite their efforts to prevent their opponents from electioneering, the result was not a resounding victory for the government forces: the republicans won 44 seats while the government won 63. The remaining 46 seats were won by Labour, Farmers and Independents. Mary MacSwiney was returned for Cork, Constance Markievicz regained her seat in Dublin, and two other women – Dr Kathleen Lynn and Caitlin Brugha (whose husband Cathal had been killed as he left the Hammam Hotel outpost) – were also elected for the anti-Treaty forces. The only pro-Treaty woman elected was Michael Collins's sister. This was the first occasion in which women between the ages of twenty-one and thirty could vote, five years before British women gained that right.

The war of attrition continued. On 20 November Constance Markievicz was arrested while she and Hanna Sheehy-Skeffington were collecting signatures on a petition calling for the release of the prisoners. At the time of her arrest, a mass hunger strike was being conducted by the prisoners, in a desperate attempt to gain their release. Hanna was refused permission to accompany her friend, but was able to hold two more meetings without interference. The government was now selective in who it wanted to lock up. They and the British shared a keen desire to put the 'Red Countess' away as frequently as possible. Discovering Constance to be held without charges in Pearse Street police station, Hanna and Maud went to see if she needed warm clothing and food, but she declined their offer. She joined the strikers.[22] Day after day during October and November a grim-faced trio of Maud, Charlotte Despard and Hanna Sheehy-Skeffington could be seen leading the same little group of demonstrators through the streets of Dublin, their placards reading 'Freedom or the Grave'.

The strike was called off on 23 November by a demoralised republican leadership who, after the death of two of their comrades, realised that the government was fully prepared to see them all starve to death. The fear of an influenza epidemic amongst the weakened prison population was a more urgent reason for the government to begin releasing the prisoners. During December thousands were let out, including all the women. Candles of thanksgiving were lit in many homes that Christmas, including Roebuck House. Sean MacBride was not there, but neither was he in gaol, having escaped while being transferred from Mountjoy to Kilmainham during the hunger strike. He had gone on the run, working for a greatly weakened IRA which was beginning to reorganise itself. Francis returned to Iseult and his marriage, entering Roebuck House for the first time. Yeats came to visit him there, to announce in person that the young man's book of poems had been selected for a prize by the Royal Irish Academy. The poet was now not only a senator but also the holder of the Nobel Prize for Literature. Francis was honoured by the visit, but Yeats deliberately did not ask to see Maud. He thought it would be 'unwise' for them to meet.[23]

The WPDL formed a Released Prisoners Committee, to welcome back those who were emerging from the gaols. They set up a rota of volunteers to meet the trains, while their headquarters in the old Sinn Fein offices in Harcourt Street became a meeting point for the prisoners and their families. Many were desperately grateful for the food and clothing distributed by 'the Mothers' in those hard times. Most had no jobs and no prospect of finding one in a state slowly recovering from a war that had cost an estimated £17,000,000. Republicans found themselves boycotted when they looked for work and as they refused to take the oath of allegiance, employment in the state sector was out of the question. Many were unable to return to their profession – Hanna Sheehy-Skeffington lost her job as teacher of German in a technical college; Dorothy Macardle had been officially sacked in March 1923 for 'not attending to her duties', and there were countless others in similar situations. Maire Comerford was sent on a nine-month long mission to America, to raise money for the establishment of a fund for the released prisoners, but the few thousand dollars she collected were only a drop in the ocean in comparison to what was needed.

John Quinn, Maud's old friend and benefactor, was a sick man absorbed in disposing of his vast art collection. He died in July 1924 and there was no one to replace him or his generous donations. The inhabitants of Roebuck House had only their greatly depleted private funds, but they threw all their resources into the task of providing work for destitute republicans. The outbuildings became part of the 'Roebuck House' jam-making enterprise, supervised by Mrs Despard, while her companion revived artistic skills from a bygone age when young ladies were taught to be creative. A room within the house was turned into a workshop for making intricate ornaments of varying size from sea shells. Roebuck House still contains examples of this work, which resembles art deco designs rather than the gruesome seaside souvenirs which one might have imagined.

The jam factory was less successful than they had hoped. Although in season it could employ up to fifteen workers, Mrs Despard found the hard work a most unrewarding way of creating employment. The fruit had to be grown and harvested, the workers trained in boiling and bottling the jam, local shops urged to take orders, and advertising copy for *An Phoblacht* written – exhorting readers to 'Eat Pure Jam' – but at the end of it all, she was forced to admit that cottage industries could not solve the problems of chronic unemployment. To make matters worse, she discovered that someone had stolen money from her jam factory, leaving her with barely enough to cover wages and expenses before bowing out of the business.[24]

Sean MacBride had married Kid Bulfin in January 1926 and the young pair went first to Paris and then to London, returning to Ireland in 1927, where they joined the fluctuating population of Roebuck House. Catalina (Spanish for Cathleen), known as Kid because she was the youngest in her family, was one of a highly unusual group of young women who shared a flat in Dawson Street. Most had degrees and interesting jobs, all had taken an active role on the republican side during the civil war, and they possessed an appreciation of European culture which was rare in the conservative atmosphere of this essentially rural society. Kid was the daughter of William Bulfin who had left Ireland for Argentina when only nineteen. He became the owner of a successful Buenos Aires newspaper – amongst its coverage of Irish affairs had been the marriage of Maud to John MacBride – but he eventually returned to Ireland where his book, *Rambles of Ireland*, led to a Dublin street being named in his honour. Todd Andrews, at one time an IRA associate of Sean MacBride, gives a vivid description of the young Kid, who appeared to have all the qualities necessary to be a daughter-in-law to the cosmopolitan and unconventional Maud:

Kid Bulfin, who was the youngest and most sophisticated of them, had read unusually extensively. She was a typical woman of the Twenties, elegant, smoking cigarettes through a very long holder, short skirted and not sparing decolletage. It was she who introduced me to Aldous Huxley, who was just then causing much literary excitement with the publication of *Crome Yellow*. . . . As well as the regular visitors to the flat many IRA men, still more or less on the run, dropped in for an occasional chat. . . . The conversation which ranged through books, the theatre, politics and religion was always stimulating and to me of unfailing interest.[25]

Sean, as a senior IRA member, was one of those still on the run from the Free State Special Branch. His visits home would be brief and shrouded in secrecy for many years. While Kid and their daughter Anna settled happily into what would become their family home, Anna remembered her father as being 'always ready to go'.[26] Kid, of whom Maud was to say fondly that Sean was the lucky man when he married her, began to take over the running of house and jam factory. Although the jam factory still made no profit, some order was introduced into its running and sixteen-year-old Louie Coghlan, whose sister was making ornaments with Maud, was persuaded to leave her secretarial course in order to work in the office and devise some system of book-keeping. She went to evening class to find out how to do that, but soon discovered that there was little to be done in organising the affairs of a concern employing no more than three or four workers. But life at Roebuck was never dull, particularly with the presence of the exotic Gonne–MacBride family. Louie soon became Sean MacBride's secretary. He was now the IRA Director of Intelligence and she found there was more than enough work for herself.[27]

In July 1927, Kevin O'Higgins, the Minister for Justice and the man responsible for ordering the execution of the republican prisoners during the civil war, was assassinated. No one was ever convicted of the murder, but Sean MacBride, on 24 August, was amongst those arrested and charged with the killing. The evidence against him was that of a gardener, who identified him as one of the assassins. He had in fact been travelling back from the Continent at the time and was able to prove it, but instead of being freed, he was then charged under the Public Safety Act and interned in Mountjoy gaol. While he was inside his mother, outraged at this blatant victimisation by the government, worked incessantly to publicise the draconian powers being misused by the government. In a letter to Thomas Johnson, Labour leader and senator, she angrily concluded 'If this is the law in Ireland, one must feel ashamed of being Irish.'[28]

The writer Richard M. Fox and his wife, Patricia Lynch, author of

The Turfcutter's Donkey and other wonderful children's stories, were close friends of Maud. Fox was in Dublin at this period and he witnessed the powerful effect Maud's presence had in mobilising opposition to a state which was daily becoming more repressive:

> Next Sunday, at mid-day, the weekly Prisoners' meeting was due. O'Connell Street swarmed with uniformed and plain clothes men. An atmosphere of terror had been worked up. Covered vans, a few nights before, had patrolled up and down O'Connell Street, each filled with men armed with sticks for the purpose of preventing demonstrations. But, at the time the meeting was announced, a laneway opened through the vast throng of people who packed the street, and Madame MacBride headed the slow procession, in single file, of her Defence League women. She carried a huge bouquet of flowers and looked radiant. Her followers bore placards. In some strange fashion her presence filled that great audience with a sense of irresistible power. The meeting was held, and she spoke the first words in public against the methods of savage repression current then. When the prisoners were released, it was recognised that she was right.[29]

Although her son was eventually released, Maud's hostility to the Cosgrave government deepened. Andro Linklater, writing of Charlotte Despard, believed that the shock of MacBride's arrest for such a brutal murder 'jolted [her] from her tacit acceptance of the IRA's violent tactics', leading to a growing alienation from her friend Maud.[30] It is dubious whether this was the case, as Mrs Despard herself, under the Public Safety Act which the government rushed through in the aftermath of O'Higgins' murder, was declared a dangerous character, liable to expulsion from Ireland. That threat was never carried out, but it says a great deal about the nature of the Free State, that it would consider deporting an 81-year-old woman because she opposed its policies. It is, however, true that the older woman's role within the Roebuck household became that of financial provider, rather than anything more collaborative. Mrs Despard was returning to her primary political commitment – the development of a socialist movement – and to that extent a parting of the ways was inevitable. But the coming to Roebuck of Sean and his family transformed life within the house. Maud was obviously delighted to have her family – her beloved Sean in particular – around her. No matter how welcoming the family circle, those outside of it are always, to some extent, on the periphery.

Another elderly inhabitant of Roebuck was Barry O'Delaney, Maud's old supporter from her Paris days, who had always been relied upon to keep things going during her prolonged absences. She was fanatically devoted to Maud and to Sean, whose baby scrapbook she had religiously kept up to date. It was she who had hailed him as the future 'King of Ireland' and life without the MacBrides was unthinkable. When they left Paris, so did she. Now in her seventies, she was a permanent fixture in Roebuck, as accepted and as taken for granted as Maud's menagerie of pets. She was there until she died, an object of affectionate derision, whose only skill appeared to be an ability to keep small children enthralled with her stories. She earned a small income by writing excruciatingly bad religious poetry; a typical unmarried woman of a particular era, whose hard work and devotion were often essential to their adopted causes, but who could never be considered a social asset. As Louie Coghlan remarked, 'she wasn't a decoration to any occasion'. Only someone with the kind heart of Maud Gonne could have welcomed her into her home. That Maud did regard her with a genuine affection can be seen in a letter written to Ella Young in 1943, in response to an unexpected letter from her old friend. Maud described who was living in the house with her, adding 'Barry O'Delaney still in the land of the living and though well over 80 hobbling around, she was delighted at your remembrance of her. . . .'[31]

When Sean was arrested again in 1929, in an effort to get him out on bail Maud described him as a 'managing director of the family firm', urgently needed at home to help sort out their financial affairs. This was nothing but the usual propaganda on a prisoner's behalf – Kid, not Sean, looked after the business – but it is significant in marking a final shift away from the partnership of Maud Gonne MacBride and Charlotte Despard to that of the MacBride family alone.

The jam factory was sold off around 1930, while Maud's ornament-making continued a little longer, although no more successful a business venture than the jam. It was always, unquestionably, her own individual concern. Kid knew better than to attempt to take that over. A few young women worked in the house, making up the opalescent ornaments – to that extent it did provide some employment – and Maud undertook their sale as seriously and as diligently as all the other undertakings she had worked for during the past half century. Her little granddaughter Anna remembered accompanying the stately black-clad figure to Christmas and Easter fairs at places like Ballsbridge, where Maud would walk majestically up and down, publicising her stall of wares. A long mirror from the house was always taken along for the ornaments to sit on and be shown off to their best advantage. The larger arrangements were popular in cinema foyers. It had cost her £50 to start the sea shell business. When she sold off its assets she recouped the £50, but that was all.

Just as die-hard republicans would motor out to Clonskeagh especially to buy their jam and therefore keep a few of their comrades in work, so too must many have bought a Roebuck House table decoration. But no amount of hard sell from Maud could create adequate employment opportunities for those who had opposed the creation of the state. The realisation that only government action could provide meaningful employment, combined with working with close women friends who were all socialists, had a radicalising effect upon her opinions. In *Eire,* she wrote an angry protest to her former friend AE (who supported the Treaty), berating him for attacking communism while, in the name of humanism, praising the Free State. Had he forgotten the Lock-Out of 1913, when he had denounced the society which permitted such horrors as the Dublin slums to exist? In her eyes, the Free State was a continuation of such a society, which would only end when a new order was created:

> In Ireland an obscure prejudice, born of slave teaching, surrounds the words Socialism and Communism, which even the clear thought and noble life and death of James Connolly failed to entirely dispel. Humanism in this case would be a true title, for Communism is the apotheosis of Christ's teaching of the brotherhood of man and the upraising of humanity. As a triumphant world wave, it will eventually reach Ireland and will find no contradiction in the Republican ideal; but the Free State based on Imperial connection and endowed with a fiercely capitalistic constitution is its very antithesis.[32]

They were strong words, but Maud's political beliefs were not always so unambiguously on the side of the communists. The national ideal would, for her, always come first. In the years to come, as her friends visited Soviet Russia and attempted to introduce class politics into Irish political life, Maud's contribution to this new departure would be largely confined to her constant concern for the welfare of political prisoners within Irish gaols on both sides of the border. She never hesitated to work with any organisation that opposed the Free State, but her priorities were not always those of her comrades.

Chapter 9

'The Mothers'

In the sullen years that followed the end of the civil war, those who opposed the Treaty found themselves surviving in a state that seemed determined to stifle every form of political dissent. There was little opposition to the government from within the Dail as the anti-Treaty republicans refused to swear an obligatory oath of allegiance to the British Crown and were therefore debarred from taking their seats. Slowly, people began to recover from the nightmare of that bitter war. The demoralised republican groups, painfully coming to terms with the political and emotional consequences of being on the losing side, contained as many different viewpoints as before. Within Sinn Fein there were those who believed that only the members of the Second Dail (elected in 1921 and who, because they rejected the Treaty, refused to accept the dissolution of that assembly), could be regarded as the true inheritors of the republican conscience, while for others a regenerated IRA was the only hope of defeating the Treaty and winning the republic – and its members were not in agreement over whether or not to embrace a radical social programme.

The lack of an effective opposition enabled draconian laws to be passed with little dissent, and the prisons once again began to fill up. Economic survival was the main preoccupation of many, as they found themselves having to put considerations of work and family before anything else. They had experienced the euphoria of victory during the war of independence, only to suffer the bitterness of defeat at the hands of former comrades. Some wanted nothing more to do with politics, while others were consumed by one overriding objective: the ousting from power of the triumphant Cumann na nGaedheal government.

As the republicans began to come to terms with their situation, Sinn Fein, in March 1926, held an Ard Fheis (annual conference) to consider a way out of the political impasse. De Valera argued strongly that once the hated oath of allegiance was abolished there would be nothing to stop those who opposed the Treaty from taking their seats in the Dail. They could then begin to dismantle all the contentious arrangements that had been insisted upon by the British. The organisation split down the middle as they debated the issue. In the end, de Valera resigned as president of the organisation and he and his followers left to form a new political party, Fianna Fail. Constance Markievicz was one of those who joined him. Other prominent women, including Dorothy Macardle, Kathleen Clarke and Hanna Sheehy-Skeffington, were also elected onto the executive of the party. Although they were all close friends of Maud's, she did not follow their lead. She and her son had quarrelled over their different views on the Treaty, a divergence of opinion which he later admitted was 'very unpleasant while it lasted, because normally we got on very well'.[1] But that was their last major difference of opinion. From now on, Maud's political allegiances were to closely follow those of her son.

In the June 1927 election Fianna Fail did well at the polls, gaining forty-four seats, while Sinn Fein kept only five. Constance Markievicz regained her seat while Kathleen Clarke became a senator. Those who were anti-Treaty had voted against a continuance of abstentionism and therefore those most closely associated with Sinn Fein fared badly. Mary MacSwiney, the most intransigent of them all, lost her seat. Maud made it quite clear that she was not joining in the wave of enthusiasm for Fianna Fail when she sent her this letter of commiseration, 'I am very disappointed that you were not elected. Your clear brain and unfailing courage are so necessary – elected or not you will always be one of the contributors of our nation.'[2]

The introduction of a new Public Safety Bill was not the only consequence of the O'Higgins assassination, which had occurred less than one year after the formation of Fianna Fail. The government also rushed through a bill to ensure that every candidate for election would, on nomination, swear to take the oath if elected. There was also provision to disqualify anyone who subsequently failed to take that oath. It was a direct threat to Fianna Fail: if they did not take their seats now, they would be unable ever to enter the Dail. De Valera argued that the oath was simply an 'empty formula' and he took up the challenge. In August he and his followers signed the book containing the oath and they settled down on the backbenches of the Dail. All, that is, except for one of their most prominent members. Constance Markievicz had entered Sir Patrick Dun's hospital for an appendectomy. True to her socialist convictions, she insisted on taking a bed in a public ward and there, amongst the Dublin poor, she died on 15 July, at the age of fifty-eight. It was five days after O'Higgins' murder and so she was spared the dreadful moral dilemma of whether or not to join de Valera in taking her seat.

The deep divisions between the opposing groups were painfully evident at the time of Constance Markievicz's death. The government – despite the fact that she was an elected representative of the people and a former comrade – refused permission for her remains to lie in state in any civic building. Despite this, enormous crowds came to pay their respects at the Rotunda, and she had one of the largest funerals anyone had ever witnessed. Maud Gonne MacBride and Charlotte Despard headed the delegation from the Women's Prisoners' Defence League, as all the organisations the Countess had ever given her energies to marched together in procession. The groups intermingled with bands and floats of flowers, along streets lined with the hungry, sorrowing faces of the Dublin poor, who were paying their own respects to one who had always championed their cause. Free State detectives patrolled the grounds of Glasnevin cemetery, preventing a volley from being fired over the grave, while de Valera gave the funeral oration: 'Ease and station she put aside.... Sacrifice, misunderstanding and scorn lay on the road she adopted, but she trod it unflinchingly.'[3]

No one will ever know which choice Constance Markievicz would have made, but for Hanna Sheehy-Skeffington, one of her closest friends, the issue was plain: the oath of allegiance was anathema to all true republicans, and while it existed Fianna Fail should not have entered the Dail. Hanna had always had a personal antipathy to de Valera, whose anti-feminism had been evident since the time he had refused to allow any woman to serve under his command in Boland's Mill during the Easter Rising, so this issue probably gave her the let-out she needed. She was able to resign on a question of principle and return to concentrating her energies upon the causes most dear to her: feminism and socialism. Hanna was convinced that the repressive measures of the Free State government would eventually lead to its downfall, so the task was to speed that day by mobilising opposition from as many quarters as possible.

Charlotte Despard had turned her attention away from both jam-making and Sinn Fein, to what she hoped would be more fertile ground: the development of a vigorous socialist party firmly based amongst the Irish working class. Roddy Connolly, the son of the martyred leader of 1916, was her hope for this regeneration. Her money was now used to pay Connolly a wage so that he could be full-time organiser for the newly formed Workers' Party of Ireland, and also in subsidising their paper, the *Hammer and Plough*. For a time, Maud lent her support to this venture, partly out of loyalty to the memory of James Connolly, her old friend and associate, as well as from loyalty to Mrs Despard. Both women were on the executive of the WPI and in May 1926 they were speakers at a commemoration meeting, organised by the WPI around the anniversary of Connolly's death.[4] However, by the following year the fledgeling organisation had dissolved, reluctantly obeying instructions from the Communist International, which refused to recognise the group as the official representative of Irish communism. It was a casualty of internal divisions within the communist movement, particularly the emergence of Stalinism as the dominant force. The fact that Maud was involved, even though the venture was ill-fated, does show that the divergence of views between herself and Mrs Despard was not as conclusive as many have claimed.

Mrs Despard continued her association with the Women's Prisoners' Defence League, whose work remained as essential as before, but her hopes that a constructive political movement could emerge from the embittered and conservative atmosphere of the Ireland she was living in had faded to nothing. She fell into an acute depression, 'Everything is sad and perplexing, and I have had difficulty in holding the balance of my mind.'[5] A visit to Russia in the summer of 1930 was to renew her old optimism for the future, but in the meantime, while she despaired, her friend Maud remained in the forefront of opposition to the Free State, organising her weekly demonstrations, writing angry articles on the prisoners' behalf, and thriving on the experience of being at the heart of her family.

One notorious event of this time – the furore over Sean O'Casey's play *The Plough and the Stars* – had its origins in the frustrations and disillusionment of many of those activists who found themselves in the galling position of seeing the hard-headed men take power and begin forming a state in their own image, lacking any trace of the idealism which had been at the heart of the nationalist cause. Law and order and the necessity to impose harsh economic measures, particularly amongst the poorest sections of the population, replaced the old ideal of the Republican Proclamation that all the children of the nation would be cherished equally. The women of Cumann na mBan, in particular, found it difficult to adjust to the lack of any programme of action. While the men of the IRA had begun to debate future strategy, its female counterpart waited impatiently, its role little more than a reminder of past struggles. It was a member of Cumann na mBan who alerted her organisation to what she considered the vilification of those who took part in the Easter Rising. The women then set about organising a co-ordinated protest for the Thursday night performance.

The Plough and the Stars attempted to convey the experience of 1916 through the lives of the Dublin working class. O'Casey's message was determinedly anti-heroic and unromantic. Jack Clitheroe is a Citizen Army member, but one who lacks any trace of idealism. His wife Nora begs him not to get involved and goes to the lengths of burning the letter confirming her husband's promotion to officer rank. The Tricolour is brought into a pub frequented by prostitutes as the men drink and wallow in sentimental attachment to Mother Ireland. In the end, Clitheroe's participation in the Rising, which has been prompted solely by his vanity, leads to his wife's miscarriage and subsequent madness. He is killed and so too is an innocent neighbour. The message of the play is that nationalism has no relevance for the working class. The uproar with which it was greeted in the Abbey Theatre was on two counts – those who objected on moral grounds to the presence of a prostitute and the implication that the men of 1916 took a drink, and those who felt that it betrayed the idealism of those who had given their lives for the cause. Hanna Sheehy-Skeffington was the person who articulated the republican objections most forcefully. Once again, when nationalist women needed someone to speak on their behalf, Hanna came to the fore. Cumann na mBan delighted in organising noisy protests, but by and large its members shrank from having to speak in public. Hanna did not take part in the deliberately staged riot of protest, but she did make a dignified statement as the objectors were roughly shoved out into the street.

> We are now leaving the hall under police protection. I am one of the widows of Easter Week. It is no wonder that you do not remember the men of Easter Week, because none of you fought on either side.... All you need do now is sing *God Save the King*.[6]

A public debate between Hanna and O'Casey, organised by the Universities' Republican Society, eventually took place. Maud had sat in silence in the theatre while those around her shouted their anger and Yeats, harking back to the *Playboy* riots, had taken the stage, revelling in telling a Dublin audience that they had disgraced themselves once again. Her lack of response was a result of so many old memories flooding her mind. While women shouted 'our men didn't drink' as they objected to the pub scene, Maud's studious silence was a reflection of her own knowledge that her man had not only been a drinker, but a French court had attested to this fact. The appearance of Rosie Redmond, the prostitute, was greeted with outraged calls to 'get that woman off the stage', and on the question of whether or not all Irishwomen led blameless lives, Maud again was forced into silence. Her own past was still a subject for speculation amongst the Dublin gossips. Maud's claim to be a widow of Easter Week had always been clouded with controversy and on this occasion she did not join those who claimed that honour. It was significant. Ironically, Ria Mooney, the actress who played the part of Rosie Redmond, remembered one young man in particular shouting up to her that she was 'a disgrace to her sex'. She later identified her heckler as Sean MacBride.[7] Given all this, it was therefore even more notable to find Maud as the second speaker backing up Hanna in her debate with O'Casey. Surely only the bonds of deep friendship led to her agreeing to lend Hanna her support?

O'Casey came out badly from the encounter. Hanna was a practised orator, natural and relaxed in style and capable of witty and memorable phrases while the playwright suffered from poor eyesight and acute nerves. According to Ria Mooney, Maud attacked his plays and mentioned specifically 'Mary Bentham and her child', by which she meant the character Mary Boyle, from *Juno and the Paycock,* who is made pregnant and then abandoned by Bentham, the schoolmaster.[8] Presumably Maud disagreed with O'Casey's portrayal of Mary, but it was an extraordinary example for her to have taken issue with.

In his account of the affair O'Casey described Mrs Sheehy-Skeffington as 'a very clever and a very upright woman' whom he acknowledged wanted to raise the controversy above the level of fights and abuse, but despite the fact that Hanna, not Maud, was the main protagonist against him, it was 'Madame Gonne-MacBride' for whom the playwright reserved his invective:

> She was clad in a classical way, with a veil of dark blue over her head, the ends flowing down over her shoulders. She turned slowly, only once, to glance at him; and Sean saw, not her who was beautiful, and had the walk of a queen, but the Poor Old Woman, whose voice was querulous, from whom came many words that were bitter, and but few kind. . . . Here she sat now, silent, stony; waiting her turn to say more bitter words against the one who refused to make her dying dream his own. There she sits stonily silent, once a sibyl of patriotism from whom no oracle ever came; now silent and aged; her deep-set eyes now sad, agleam with disappointment; never quite at ease with the crowd, whose cheers she loved; the colonel's daughter still.[9]

The accuracy of such savagery is highly questionable. O'Casey undeniably felt enormous hostility towards upper-class women who adopted the Irish cause. His resentment of Constance Markievicz eventually led to his resignation from the Citizen Army and he pilloried her unmercifully in his writings as a braying Lady Bountiful, motivated by egoism. Francis MacManus, who arrived in Dublin as a young man in the year following *The Plough and the Stars* controversy, has left us with a very different picture of Maud Gonne MacBride and her ability to communicate with an audience.

One afternoon, as he picked his way around the piles of rubble that continued to litter the streets of Dublin, the aftermath of years of warfare, he heard a burst of cheering from a meeting taking place near the Parnell Monument:

> A woman was speaking. Before I could catch a glimpse of her beyond the heads and shoulders of her audience, I heard her voice. It was a voice no man forgets. Never had I heard a voice like it. . . . I had not to be told that she was Maud Gonne MacBride. She appeared to be a tall woman, dressed from head to foot in wispy, lacey black. Black, they say, is absence of colour, she made it as vivid as scarlet or turquoise. . . . What she said I never remembered as words but only the effect of it: an

effect of fluent, stern and even slightly theatrical speech; and more than that, an effect of intense feminine vitality and of great hope.[10]

Even when Maud walked along the street afterwards, MacManus continued to be mesmerised by her presence. Although Maud must have been conscious of her effect upon people, the actress within her would never have dreamed of revealing that awareness. That would have shattered all illusions:

> She held herself erect; her pace was stately; her wispy black clothes fluttered. People turned to look after her as I would see them turning to look in the many years to come. She walked as though all her story were around her. . . . Dublin was a battlement on which she, Helen, walked triumphant.

The welfare of prisoners had been Maud's obsession for almost the whole of her political life. If interest in their welfare dwindled, then there was all the more reason for her to redouble her efforts on their behalf. In the past, the British government alone had been responsible for the gaoling of young Irish men and women, but since the establishment of the Free State and the Northern Ireland state, British and Irish governments were equally repressive in their treatment of those who continued to fight for full independence. In Maud's view, support for the prisoners was unconditional; their actions, after all, had been motivated by the selfless desire to secure Irish freedom.

Yeats, still a supporter of the Free State although it had fallen far short of his ideal, was scathing in his dismissal of the sacrifice made by the new generation of republican fighters, but he was forced to acknowledge the steadfastness of his old friend as he wrote 'These dead cannot share the glory of those earlier dead, their names are not spoken aloud today except at those dwindling meetings assembled in O'Connell Street or at some prison gate by almost the sole surviving friend of my early manhood, protesting in sybilline old age, as once in youth and beauty, against what seems to be a tyranny.'[11]

As secretary of the WPDL Maud toured London, Glasgow, Liverpool and Manchester in support of IRA prisoners in British gaols. The freedom of Irish prisoners could be achieved, she wrote in a leaflet, if 'the thirty millions of the Irish Race living in Free Countries' rose up and demanded 'the release of Irish prisoners of war as slaves of England'.[12] But the real Maud was never as fierce (apart from the occasions when she was in direct confrontation with those she opposed) as this quotation would imply. After speaking in Liverpool she attended a concert which had been arranged for her at the local Irish Club. Matt Curran, who had arranged the event, described her delight in watching the children performing Irish dances. 'She had a charming personality and you could feel quite at ease in her company. We had tea together, and I always look back with pride to have had the honour of meeting such a great Irish Woman and Patriot.'[13] Two of the prisoners Maud had been campaigning for, who had been sentenced in 1922 to ten years, were finally released in 1930. She held a triumphant reception for them in Roebuck House.

While in Lancashire Maud addressed a meeting jointly with the Indian nationalist Saklatvala, demanding the release of both Indian and Irish hostages. Maud had been close to exiled Indian leaders, particularly Bhikaji Cama, during her years in Paris, and she retained those personal and political links. Madame Cama finally succeeded in returning to India in 1935, one short year before her death, but the India of British imperial rule was still in existence.[14] Indian nationalists were regular visitors to Ireland (often staying in Roebuck House), discussing the development of their own fight for independence with those who had so recently defeated their common enemy. In October 1932, Maud became Chair of the Indian–Irish Independence League.[15] When Sean MacBride visited India in later years he made a point of visiting the street in Bombay which was named in honour of Madame Cama, a staunch revolutionary and treasured friend of his family.

In 1929, Maud and her son joined Comhairle na Poblachta, a short-lived attempt to give a political voice to non-Fianna Fail republicans. Although the Free State police sourly noted that the sole purpose of the new organisation was 'the overthrow of the State by force of arms', in reality it contained people of such conflicting views – socialists, militarists, purist republicans amongst them – that it soon began quietly to disintegrate.[16] There was an urgent need for a viable political alternative, but the circumstances were still highly unfavourable. There had to be greater agreement on what they were campaigning for and, in the meantime, small groups continued to come and go.

In July 1929 an Irish Labour Defence League – its members drawn from the trade unions and the IRA – held its first national convention. This was the first time that the Dublin membership of the IRA had ventured into radical politics. Sean MacBride had been in prison for the first five months of the year, held on remand on charges related to Comhairle na Poblachta, which was a possible reason for him not to be closely associated with the new group. He was also still hesitant about how far the IRA should become involved in social issues. Maud had no such doubts, and she became an executive member of the League at the July convention.[17] More cynically, one could also surmise that her son was able to capitalise on his mother's willingness to join anything that might offer a way forward. It meant that he received full reports of all discussions without having to commit himself to the organisation. As it was partly an IRA venture, he could have been instrumental in encouraging her to stand for election.

Maud had always been a tireless campaigner, an inveterate joiner of new ventures, and she now had the influence of very different people – her friend Charlotte and her son Sean – who had vastly different political leanings, but who would obviously both want the illustrious name of Maud Gonne MacBride to enhance their chosen groups. A memorandum from the Department of Justice concerning the sudden proliferation of new organisations shows that the Free State detectives had also noted Maud's burst of energy:

> The number of these revolutionary organizations all of which have something in common, is bewildering and each week so to speak gives birth to the new ones. . . . It is also of interest to note that much the same people appear to be behind several organizations, Mrs Maud McBride [sic] being as ubiquitous as it is possible to be.[18]

All these various short-lived initiatives had at least the merit of influencing steadily greater numbers of people into support for some radically alternative conception of a future society. The vague call for a 'republic' would soon not be enough. In an Ireland beset with economic depression, the demand for a 'workers' and farmers' republic' began to make good political sense. Republicans on the left, like Peadar O'Donnell, David Fitzgerald and George Gilmore, had always urged the forging of alliances with workers and small farmers, so that their economic grievances could be fought as part of the process of winning the republic, thereby strengthening both the military and political wings of the movement. There were many right-wing members of the IRA – often in commanding positions within the organisation – who were suspicious of any hint of communism, but they were for now a minority. Visitors to Russia were returning to Ireland full of enthusiasm for what they had seen, and radical ideas began to gain acceptance amongst the IRA and Cumann na mBan. The leadership of Sinn Fein, composed mainly of an older generation of nationalists, was exceptional in continuing to distrust the influx of new ideas.

The IRA's move to the left eventually gave birth to another new organisation – Saor Eire – whose object was to organise 'the working class and working farmers to overthrow British imperialism and its ally Irish capitalism'. It was publicly launched on 26 September 1931 at a meeting in Dublin which was attended by 120 delegates. Amongst the women on its executive were Helena Moloney and Sheila Dowling (who had both visited Soviet Russia along with Charlotte Despard and Hanna Sheehy-Skeffington), together with Sheila Humphreys and May Laverty, both Cumann na mBan members. Sean MacBride was a prominent member on the IRA's behalf. A chorus of public disapproval greeted the appearance of Saor Eire. A 'Red Scare' swept through the country. The Catholic hierarchy denounced both Saor

Eire and the IRA by name, while the government took this opportunity to amend the constitution with Article 2A, giving itself the power to set up military tribunals which could impose the death penalty. Twelve organisations – including the IRA, Saor Eire, Cumann na mBan, the Women's Prisoners' Defence League, Friends of Soviet Russia and the Revolutionary Workers' Groups – were banned. Saor Eire collapsed, still-born as a result of this onslaught, and everyone affected by the ban braced themselves to face what was to come.[19]

IRA members went on the run, newspapers were suppressed and raids on houses increased. The only paper the republicans could produce was *Republican File* – composed solely of reports taken from other papers – and Hanna Sheehy-Skeffington took over as editor once Frank Ryan joined his comrades in gaol. There were no mass arrests as the government hoped that locking up the leadership would be sufficient to scare off the rank and file. Nevertheless the total arrested, which included a few members of Cumann na mBan, began to increase. And so too, inevitably, did the protests mounted by the Women's Prisoners' Defence League. As the organisation had been banned, it reappeared under the name of the People's Rights Association. Maud's years of experience in outwitting the forces of law and order were to stand her in good stead. The women were evicted from their offices in Middle Abbey Street and found it impossible to acquire other premises, so the committee arranged to hold weekly teas in Woolworth's café. When they become too well known they alternated their sessions by going to nearby Bewley's café. Impromptu press conferences were held in the safety of the crowds that surrounded them. Many people were wary of Maud's love of the dramatic, regarding her tendency towards the theatrical as stemming from a desire for self-enhancement and, as such, vastly different from their own selfless commitment to the cause. But in times of crisis, that very theatricality became a weapon in the struggle and Maud came into her own. She was at her most incomparable, her private self indistinguishable from the public persona.

The first Sunday after the introduction of Article 2A was an important occasion. Huge crowds waited in O'Connell Street to see if the women would turn up to defy their suppression. Squads of uniformed police and CID also stood around. At the usual time, a lorry-load drove up bearing the inscription 'People's Rights Association'. As it was not on the list of banned organisations, the police could not prevent them from speaking. Charlotte Despard and a number of other speakers then mounted the platform. Maud, who was chairing the meeting, announced that, at a time when the liberties of the people were being taken from them, the People's Rights Association had come into being to defend those liberties. When it came to Helena Moloney's turn to speak she impudently grinned and quoted Shakespeare, 'A rose by any other name would smell as sweet!' She was greeted with a roar of applause.[20]

Seamus O'Kelly's eye-witness account of one of those meetings is a vivid testimony of the women's courage and determination. It was street theatre of a deadly kind:

> It was then that I saw the most extraordinary public meeting of my life. The speakers ... broke into sections, and kept moving up and down O'Connell Street, speaking as they walked along. Instead of Cathal Brugha Street being the venue of the meeting, all O'Connell Street became the venue.
>
> The public moved behind the speakers, the crowds followed the police, and Madame MacBride scored a singular success by keeping the demonstration going for two hours. She repeated the same tactics the following Sunday, and announced: 'For every meeting the Government bans, I will hold three.'
>
> The result was that no more meetings were banned, and Madame MacBride carried on her prisoners' agitation until the republican prisoners were released.[21]

Until their meetings could be resumed as normal, the women resorted to many ingenious devices to maintain their tradition. As Maud had promised, they did hold multiple meetings in defiance of the ban, these taking place in country areas which had not been affected by the government's decree. On some occasions meetings were held in Dublin on the Friday or Saturday and in places outside the city boundaries on the Sunday. One week saw Charlotte Despard and Helena Moloney heading a poster parade of women along O'Connell Street to announce that, because of trouble in Portlaoise gaol, the usual meeting was being conducted outside the gaol by Maud Gonne MacBride and 'John Brennan'. The dozen posters they held were painted with the various paragraphs of the speech which they were forbidden to utter aloud. Other women who regularly joined in this defiance of the government were Dorothy Macardle, Hanna Sheehy-Skeffington and Madge Daly, a sister of Kathleen Clarke. Taking their message to those who lived outside the capital paid dividends in politicising a whole range of people who might otherwise never have come into contact with the persuasive powers of these propagandists. As Maud joked, the government eventually realised that 'those damned women' were doing more harm than when they spoke from the same place to their usual audience, and they then stopped proclaiming meetings. Although the League returned to its usual corner in Cathal Brugha Street they continued to arrange for meetings to be held after Mass in country areas until the elections.

Amongst the many sinister powers that Article 2A conferred upon the authorities was the power it gave the police to search and detain anyone they chose, women included. The Women's International League for Peace and Freedom passed a resolution of protest against this, viewing with particular concern the 'moral danger' in which it placed women who could be searched and detained at will by any man in the police force.[22] Maud was convinced that if they could focus public attention on such sections of the Act, the public would be so appalled that the Cosgrave government would be brought down 'in ignominy'. At a public meeting following the arrest of three members of Cumann na mBan – Sheila Humphreys, Kathleen Merrigan and Maeve Phelan – Maud angrily claimed that 'those who were striving to carry out the Act had shown that the respect for womanhood which should exist in a Catholic state, was fast disappearing'.[23]

Support for the prisoners in terms of who would publicly speak out on their behalf was not really all that great, probably because of a fear of arrest, and often it was only the same few stalwarts who dared to protest. On Christmas Eve 1931 it was again the indomitable figures of Maud Gonne MacBride and Charlotte Despard who led a small parade through the streets of Dublin in protest against the governor of Mountjoy's refusal to allow the prisoners any Christmas parcels.[24] The efforts of the women unquestionably had an effect upon the nerves of government ministers. By the start of 1932 one minister went so far as to say that his government was 'going to put down people like Mrs Despard and Mrs MacBride and those who were trying to bring in Soviet conditions . . . and if they persist, and if it is necessary, we are going to execute them'.[25] Even the British government at the height of the Black and Tan horrors would have repudiated such sentiments.

One other consequence of this unflinching disregard for their personal welfare was the constant series of raids which the inhabitants of Roebuck had to endure. 1931 was the worst year of all, even before the introduction of Article 2A. In May the CID arrived so early that Mrs Despard and Kid MacBride were still in bed. The house was well gone over, but July saw an even more thorough attempt. It was blatant revenge for the women's sustained campaign against government policies, but it was also connected with the activities of Sean MacBride, who was still unable to be more than an occasional visitor to the house. That July saw him busily trying to organise the IRA down in Kerry, when he and seven others were arrested. A local judge ordered their release, ruling that the police had not produced sufficient evidence. Perhaps in retaliation, Roebuck House found itself surrounded by scores of CID men, armed with revolvers, iron rods and wooden handles, walking sticks and torches. Maud was not at home and it was the ageing Mrs Despard who witnessed the systematic destruction of large parts of the house. Personal possessions were turned out, letters and papers read, fireplaces had their grates removed, pictures were ripped from frames, vases of flowers hurled to one side. One wall was gutted in case it contained an arms dump. Its hollow sound turned out to be caused by the straw used for insulation purposes. At six o'clock they finally left, leaving the house as if 'a party of particularly destructive chimpanzees had run amok in it', described Mrs Despard in a newspaper article.[26] She and Maud wrote angry letters to the press, informing people that this had been their eleventh raid in a few years. As long as the Cumann na nGaedheal government remained in power, such unwelcome attention would continue to be paid to all its opponents.

Elections had been held in 1927, and the government was not constitutionally obliged to hold another until September 1932. But just as the IRA began to consider the possibility of taking up arms as the only way of defeating what was steadily becoming a reign of terror, a complacent Cosgrave, convinced that his opponents no longer posed a threat, decided to call an early election for February. Coercion as a method of maintaining order could not be resorted to indefinitely, so the sooner an election was got out of the way the better. The decision took everyone by surprise. Peadar O'Donnell was in the office of *An Phoblacht* when he heard the news. He immediately decided to emblazon the front page with a call to 'Put Cosgrave Out!' People felt that a victory for Fianna Fail would end repression and secure the release of the prisoners. Republicans hoped that they would then be able to put pressure on de Valera to repeal the Treaty provisions and finally declare the Republic. The Cumann na nGaedheal government was also unpopular because of its economic policies which had recently included a reduction in pensions and a wage cut for those in public service. The Censorship of Publications Act of 1929 dismayed all those with socially progressive views and many writers were beginning to feel that the new Ireland had no place for them. Altogether, there were many reasons why a majority of the electorate wanted a change of government.

Grassroots republicans were prominent in the election campaign, although being careful not to endorse specifically any of Fianna Fail's policies, and the women of the WPDL concentrated their energies in hounding government ministers when they spoke at election meetings. Those responsible for the prison population came in for particular attention. Mrs Despard shadowed Fitzgerald, the Minister of Defence (on whose behalf Maud had persuaded Yeats to use his influence so that his wife could visit him in gaol in 1921), even setting up her own mobile platform a few yards away from his lorry. When her voice tired, Mrs Woods took over and the incessant barrage of questions concerning the plight of the prisoners, coupled with pointed remarks about the minister's past record as a prisoner, continued for several days in different locations.[27] As Maud later explained, their objective was to prevent the 'murderers and traitors' of the Cosgrave government from addressing the citizens of Dublin. She claimed that the crowds always respectfully made way for them, 'the mothers of the executed ... the accusers'. In an emotional recollection she declared:

We did this for the honour of Ireland, we did it at risk and suffering, for it is not easy for women, some of whom were old and feeble, to come out like this. Though often roughly handled and bruised, and our clothes torn, we saved Ireland's capital from the disgrace of allowing murderers and traitors to triumphantly flaunt their crimes and treason before a cowed and quiescent people.[28]

Examples like this of Maud's prose style help to convey the impact of her tremendous speaking presence, when she would 'give herself to the people', feeling that the great energy of the crowd gave her back even more than she originally imparted. This was, Maud firmly believed, a result of a National Trinity of the people, the land and the spirit. Her obsession with this mystic trinity was greater than the more conventional religious Trinity of the Godhead. It provided her with the inspiration to continue during the most testing of times.

The result of the election was a narrow victory for Fianna Fail and one of de Valera's first actions was, as promised, the release of the prisoners. On 13 March a tumultuous crowd of 30,000 packed into College Green to rejoice in their homecoming. The figures of Hanna Sheehy-Skeffington, Maud Gonne MacBride and Charlotte Despard were prominent on the platform of welcome. Many tributes were paid to the role played by women in defeating the Cosgrave government: Frank Ryan singled out Hanna Sheehy-Skeffington, who had kept publication going while he was in gaol, and Hanna herself, along with other male speakers, gave special praise to the courage of the members of Cumann na mBan who had defied the military tribunals 'and helped by their splendid and defiant attitude in no small way to break down that infamous machine'.[29] The work of the women of the Women's Prisoners' Defence League was not given any individual prominence, but its two leading lights were recognised by virtue of their inclusion in the platform group. Newsreel footage of Maud speaking to the crowd shows a gaunt, impassioned figure, restlessly pacing as she declared the people's victory over Cosgrave and the coercionists. Maud was convinced, even if de Valera was not as radical a republican as she might have wished for, that progress from now on would be sure and steady. The Women's Prisoners' Defence League announced that it would now be disbanding, its work accomplished.

Maud's honeymoon with de Valera was shorter than that of the IRA. By July she was announcing, in the pages of An Phoblacht, that 'The C.I.D. are reverting to their old methods of persecution. Next Sunday the Womens's Prisoners' Defence League will resume the weekly Prisoners' meetings in Cathal Brugha Street and continue them while the necessity remains.' But despite her words, these were different times. De Valera had abolished the oath of allegiance; he had suspended operation of the notorious Article 2A; he had stopped the payment of land annuities and in the process precipitated an economic war with Britain; he was soon to dismiss O'Duffy, the hated police commissioner; and he had instituted a series of moderate social reforms on such matters as pensions for veteran republicans. For many, tired of years of war and unrest, this was enough to be going on with. De Valera had also made it plain to the IRA that he did not consider it necessary for them to continue in existence. But members of the IRA and Fianna Fail had fought a civil war together and ties were still close. Frank Aiken, the new Minister of Defence, offered Sean MacBride a commission as Major-General in the army which he refused indignantly, but it demonstrated how warm the honeymoon period was while it lasted.

Despite Maud's claim that the police were once again harassing political activists, there is little evidence that republicans or socialists suffered adversely from the new government until almost the end of 1933, when the volatile political arena changed once again. Initially, the state concentrated its attention upon the growing Blueshirt movement – Ireland's home-grown fascists. The IRA was much in evidence in preventing 'free speech to traitors' and local IRA volunteers co-operated with Fianna Fail members in fighting fascism off the streets. IRA activism, however, was only tolerated as long as it was focused where it could not challenge the stability of the Fianna Fail government. The republican movement generally had flourished in the wake of the Fianna Fail victory and its ranks were swollen with new recruits. Their dilemma concerned their future role. De Valera appeared to have no intention of declaring a republic, but could the IRA force his hand on the issue? Would they have to challenge the state and take up arms once again? Those on the left realised that de Valera was cleverly outflanking them, and the enormous support he possessed could only be challenged by concentrating on social and economic issues, so that new political alliances could be made. The women of Cumann na mBan were not content to stand idly by while their male counterparts debated future strategy and they relaunched their 'Boycott British Goods' campaign. Bass Ale was added to the list and numerous scuffles between republicans and Blueshirts centred around the question of the disposal of Bass Ale. It was not a very constructive contribution to the debate on the way forward but it highlighted the corner that republicans found they had backed into as a result of the Fianna Fail victory.

The division of Ireland into two separate entities still remained and de Valera had given no indication of what he proposed to do on the issue. The question of partition saw Fianna Fail at its weakest and opened up new opportunities for propaganda. In 1932 there was a brief and unprecedented unity between Protestant and Catholic workers in the Outdoor Relief Movement, organised to protest at the cutting of relief rates at a time when thousands were being thrown out of work. Cumann na mBan organised a flag day to raise money and the IRA in the north backed the Unemployed Workers' Movement, but everyone's hopes collapsed once the Unionist government managed to play one group off against the other and sectarianism again dominated political life in the north. The Unionists also took this opportunity to ban all meetings and round up as many republicans as they could.

In January 1933, Hanna Sheehy-Skeffington accepted an invitation to speak at a meeting in Newry, held to demand the release of the republican prisoners. The government had forbidden her entry into the six counties because of her undesirable politics, and she deliberately defied that exclusion order. She was sentenced to one month's imprisonment in Armagh gaol as she refused to be 'of good behaviour'. Her defence was an impassioned statement against partition, 'I would be ashamed of my own race, I would be ashamed of my own murdered husband if I admitted that I was an alien in Armagh, Down, Derry or any of the thirty-two counties.'[30] Eithne Coyle, the president of Cumann na mBan, travelled to Dundalk to meet her after her release while thousands waited in Dublin to welcome her home. She was a popular woman, one of the hardest-working and most committed of socialist republicans, and her action in defying the Stormont government succeeded in temporarily lifting the spirits of those in the twenty-six counties who were continuing to debate their future strategy.

A short while later, on 21 March, over seventy women attended a supper party hosted by the Irish women's Franchise League in honour of their founding member. It was not only a celebration of her safe return from her prison cell, but also a reunion of those who had been fighting for one cause or another since the start of the century. Some had been imprisoned for their suffragette activities, some because of their nationalist beliefs, and a few – like Hanna herself – had combined both causes throughout their lives. Meg Connery declared that 'Mrs Skeffington has started a fire which will end the hated partition of Ireland', and in her speech Maud agreed that Hanna had done more than anyone to end partition. She also presented her old friend with a medal on behalf of the Women's Prisoners' Defence League in recognition of her role in helping to end Cosgrave's coercion acts.[31]

Hanna was a comparatively young fifty-six years of age at this time. Maud herself was sixty-seven. Although their goal of a free Ireland where women could participate equally in the affairs of the nation remained a far-off dream, their advancing years did not curtail their activities. That generation of activists remained as steadfast as ever, but their friends were becoming conscious of the passing of time and the necessity for some public recognition of their contribution, before time ran out. In the spring of 1932, some of Maud's closest associates decided to stage a public tribute 'in recognition of her fifty years' heroic efforts in the cause of Irish independence and of Irish political prisoners'. She tried hard to prevent them, to the extent of publishing an open letter in the *Irish Press* in which she begged her friends 'to stop all talk of thanks or honours'. She agreed that 'we women, by publicity, have perhaps succeeded in shortening some imprisonments', but the 'medieval torture of prisoners in Arbour Hill' had continued and so any tribute to her endeavours on their behalf was inappropriate.[32]

Despite these protests, a presentation was held that December and Brigid O'Mullane, who had been secretary of the People's Rights Association, began the evening by referring to Maud as 'one of the greatest Irishwomen that ever lived'. She commented on her reluctance to have any honour conferred, agreeing only to the 'trifling mementoes' of a gold wrist-watch and gold key brooch, symbolising her efforts to open prison doors. 'John Brennan', the next speaker, and friend from the early days of the Inghinidhe, referred back to those times when Maud had helped open the minds of the Irish people to the nationalist ideal. George Gilmore, who had spent from October 1931 to February 1932 naked in a windowless cell because of his refusal to wear prison clothes, expressed his heartfelt thanks when declaring that 'it was hardly possible to exaggerate the good work done by the Women's Prisoners' Defence League in looking after the comfort of the prisoners and making things hot for the jailers'. Helena Moloney, the ever-loyal friend, was one of the four other speakers.

Maud was very touched by the 'loving comradeship' that surrounded her. She said she was glad to see young people entering the republican movement, but warned her audience that coercion had not ended: Fianna Fail had permitted the arrest of Tomas MacCurtain, whose father had been murdered by the Black and Tans. She presented silver medals to thirty-three members of the WPDL and small purses to others who had assisted in its work. It seemed, despite Maud's warnings against complacency, as though the members of the Women's Defence League were awarding themselves their own golden handshake, so sure were they that the terrible experience of the past few years could never be repeated.[33]

Charlotte Despard was of course present during this ceremony, but the paths of the two women were beginning to diverge. While Maud remained within the orbit of republican politics, her friend was immersed in another attempt to raise working-class issues amongst the Dublin masses. In 1933 she bought a house in Eccles Street which she planned to use as a base for an Irish Workers' College, and as premises for Friends of Soviet Russia, for which she acted as secretary. Neither of the women ever divulged whether or not their parting was acrimonious. It was inevitable, given their different views, once the Cumann na nGaedheal government had been defeated. When that occurred, Mrs Despard's energies no longer needed to be limited to the most urgent task of fighting coercion. Although some accounts have implied that Roebuck House was simply left to Maud by her friend, this was not the case. During the 1930s the Gonne trust fund was broken by Sean MacBride so that capital could be removed from America and more patriotically invested in Irish government stock. Charlotte Despard's share of Roebuck House was bought from her. It would have been unlike Maud to allow anyone to leave empty-handed, and the Despard finances were not vast enough to allow for an unlimited acquisition of property.[34]

Mrs Despard's stay in Eccles Street was short. Anti-communist feeling was gaining in strength, fuelled both by the ideology of the Blueshirts and also by the Catholic Church, some of whose clerics were particularly adept in working up their congregations into a frenzy of anti-communist fervour. Connolly House, headquarters of the Communist Party of Ireland, was under mob siege for two days before it was finally set alight. The crowds, emboldened by the lack of police resistance, then marched on Eccles Street. The building was looted and wrecked, although the 89-year-old inhabitant escaped unharmed. The IRA had been ordered not to become involved in public support for notorious bastions of left-wing propaganda, but many rank and file members ignored their orders. Charlie Gilmore, while defending Connolly House, was arrested for possession of a revolver, even though none of the attackers were arrested by the police. Such partiality on the part of the forces of law and order was the final straw for Mrs Despard. If the republicans had unambiguously come out in support of the besieged buildings, showing the kind of enthusiasm they had displayed against the Blueshirt presence, her disillusionment might not have been so acute. Yet again, Hanna Sheehy-Skeffington was one of the few to immediately demonstrate her support during the riots. In the process she was assaulted by gangs screaming 'Up the Pope!' and 'Down with Russia'. A blow to her left eye was severe enough to cause a haemorrhage – 'For faith & fatherland', as she noted caustically in her diary.[35] It was also Hanna, only recently back from her prison sojourn, who advised a very distressed Mrs Despard to move to Belfast, where she felt conditions were much more suitable for left-wing agitation. The Eccles Street house was left to the Friends of Soviet Russia and that extraordinary nonagenarian moved north, to spend the last six years of an incredibly prolific life in trying to spread her gospel of Christian socialism amongst the bitterly divided working class of Belfast.

Her absence from Roebuck could not have been greatly missed as the household was enlarged still further by the birth, in 1934, of Tiernan MacBride. The flat at the top of the house was rented to Bill Sweetman of the *Irish Press* and his wife, and sometime after they moved out Louie Coghlan, who was now Louie O'Brien, moved in with her new husband. The Second World War had begun, public transport was limited and, as Louie explained, Sean wanted a secretary whose time was not curtailed through having to catch the last bus home.

Maud's two other grandchildren – Kay and Ian Stuart – were often in evidence as Iseult called frequently to see her mother, gaining comfort by confiding the details of her unhappy marriage with a husband whose interest lay more with the race track than with his family. True to his conception of the artist as outsider in society, he remained on the margins of all that was conventionally acceptable. He and Iseult had originally lived in a small thatched cottage at Glencree, but by 1928, with the addition of a son and daughter, it had become far too small for their needs and Maud gave them the money to buy a place near Glendalough – Laragh Castle. The money came from the sale of Les Mouettes, the French house in Normandy, which Francis Stuart insisted was Millevoye's gift to his daughter. The implication behind that claim was that his wife had possibly been defrauded out of some part of her inheritance – but that was only another manifestation of his estrangement from his mother-in-law.[36] Iseult received no inheritance from her father and if it were not for Great-Aunt Augusta's legacy, she would probably never have received anything at all.[37] Maud's desire to give her daughter some financial security could not have been realised through the Gonne trust fund. Presumably, if Maud had married according to her social class and status, her husband's income would have been sufficient to settle money upon their offspring. When Thomas Gonne made his will he did not envisage his beautiful daughter failing to contract a suitable alliance.

Willie Yeats rarely visited Roebuck House, which his biographer, Joseph Hone, attributed to a reluctance to meeting Mrs Despard, whose views he abhorred. But he kept in contact with the family through visits to Iseult, and he and Maud were partially reconciled once Yeats had retired from the Senate in 1928, thereby at least slightly distancing himself from the hated institution of the Free State. In 1932 the Yeats family moved back into Dublin, to the suburb of Rathfarnum, and the two old friends continued to communicate through letters and by the occasional dinner at a Dublin restaurant. As politics remained a dangerous subject between them, Willie would try to be amusing with his stories about the 'bright young people' he knew in London. These tended to be attractive young women: Dorothy Wellesley, Margot Ruddock and Ethel Mannin were prominent figures in this circle of poets and writers. But he was not very successful. Rather primly, Maud later remarked to Joseph Hone that she had not cared for his 'butterfly' talk; she thought it out of character.[38] Both she and Yeats, in their different ways, remained as prolific as ever. While the poet wrote some of his most powerful verses during his last years, Maud not only began to write her own account of an action-packed life, she also maintained all her old concerns, redoubling her efforts as if to compensate for the dwindling numbers of the faithful.

Chapter 10

A SERVANT OF THE QUEEN

Partition and the prisoners remained two burning injustices that Maud could not ignore. During the late twenties and thirties, when her rheumatism became unbearable she would return to the spa towns of France, the country which had been her home for so long, but with which she had now few personal ties. Nancy O'Rahilly, the American-born widow of The O'Rahilly who had been killed during the Easter Rising, was Maud's companion during these trips. Although Madame O'Rahilly had worked alongside many well-known nationalist women on behalf of the White Cross relief fund, she was not one of the most prominent of the widows of 1916. However, in a humanitarian rather than overtly political capacity she was very active, and worked for twenty-five years with the Children's Relief Association, created after the winding up of the White Cross to look after the interests of the one thousand children orphaned as a result of seven years of war. The rest of her family was more political. She was the aunt of Sheila Humphreys, the vice-president of Cumann na mBan, and her son Mac was a close friend of Sean MacBride.

A network of friendship, based on common experiences and similar attitudes, was an important source of support for those unyielding republicans who refused to accept any erosion of the nationalist dream. The short twelve o'clock Mass in Whitefriars Street was known as the 'republican mass', as so many of the older generation attended it, often remaining outside the church doors, unreconciled to the authority of the bishops, but revelling in the opportunity to catch up on the news. And after the Mass, Maud would hurry off to her weekly meeting of 'The Mothers' at Cathal Brugha corner.

Fianna Fail was riding high in the popularity stakes: the Blueshirts had been driven off the streets, another election had increased de Valera's majority and he had introduced service pensions for those who had fought on the republican side up until 1923. Those who accepted a pension out of dire financial necessity often felt they had compromised themselves politically and they left the Republican movement, whose ranks were decimated still further.

The question of pensions was always contentious, but while die-hard republicans poured scorn on those who accepted the bribe of Free State gold, the women of the Defence League saw another aspect of life: the misery of so many of those relatives who had lost loved ones, yet were not entitled to a small pension themselves. In a very angry article in *An Phoblacht,* criticising the de Valera government for putting IRA men before a military tribunal, Maud described some of the suffering she had come into contact with:

> Has Fianna Fail forgotten? Their government is two years in office, and while bills for the pensions of traitors are passed, the Defence League had to rescue the old father of one of the first executed boys from the workhouse, and the mothers and grand-mothers are in dire want while a well-paid Pensions Board investigates endlessly whether the dependants of those who died for Ireland should get a niggardly pension or be relegated to poor law relief.[1]

Economic depression was beginning to bite. In the towns, industrial development was slow and insufficient to meet the demand for jobs; in the countryside, where the majority still lived, schemes to encourage more tillage had little impact when the basic problem was that the land simply could not support the people. Left-wing republicans were convinced that economic discontent could be harnessed to the fight for the republic and they were impatient to begin the process of making alliances. The next radical initiative was the formation, in 1934, of the Republican Congress. The IRA split down the middle over whether or not to participate and, in the end, those who went over to the Congress group were expelled. The memory of the clerical denuncia-tion of Saor Eire was too recent for them to wish to repeat the experience. Sean MacBride stayed with the IRA and Maud had no links with the Republican Congress. Several people like Helena Moloney, although prominent in Saor Eire, also stayed away.

At an IRA-sponsored rally on the question of fascism and imperial-ism, held in College Green that June, the main speakers were Mick Fitzpatrick, Sean MacBride, Helena Moloney, Hanna Sheehy-Skeffington and Maud Gonne MacBride. The *Republican Congress* report was scathing on the emphasis placed by the IRA leaders on perfecting the military machine in order to challenge state forces on both sides of the border, but both Helena and Hanna stressed the need for a unity of forces.[2] The split between the IRA and the Congress group was bitter and long-lasting but it seems to have been confined to the male members of those groups. Maud's contribution to the rally was not recorded but it was sure to have centred around the question of prisoners. Cora Hughes, one of the most dedicated members of Congress, later shared a platform with her at a WPDL meeting in September 1935.[3] That level of co-operation was all the more notable when one remembers that the IRA attacked contingents carrying Congress banners at the Bodenstown commemoration of June 1934. Although Cumann na mBan, as the female section of the republican movement, stood firmly at the side of the IRA during this period, it would appear that many women activists were distressed by this internal dissension and unwilling to lend their support to either side.

The Republican Congress itself was beset with controversy and divided into two factions almost immediately. By 1936 the venture had petered out, some of its best-known members leaving to fight for the republican side in the Spanish Civil War. It was recognition that they felt there was no place for themselves in Irish political life. However, for almost two years the Congress group did inject some much-needed debate into the ranks of the republican left. Amongst the issues raised by them was the controversial question of women's status within Irish society. They were also, perhaps because George Gilmore was one of the group, appreciative of the continued efforts of the Women's Defence League. The first issue of their paper, on 5 May 1934, made the point that 'outside of the meetings held by the Women's Prisoners' Defence League – the mothers who never forgot – the agitation for the release of Republican political prisoners had apparently collapsed'.

Relations between the various republican groups and the government of the day were, once again, at a low point. When labour disputes began, the IRA decided to show its sympathy for the workers, to prove that it was not only the Republican Congress who had socialist sympathies. Their tactics were purely military, however, and their contribution to the Dublin bus and tram strike of March 1935 consisted of shooting at the tyres of strike-breaking army lorries. Two gardai were wounded and the government had the excuse it needed to reactivate the military tribunals previously used against the Blueshirts. De Valera stated that he had been patient for three years but this was the final straw. By 20 April, 104 republicans were in prison. *An Phoblacht* was regularly censored and occasionally suppressed, its last issue finally appearing in July.

As political tensions continued to escalate on both sides of the border, the worst sectarian violence of a generation took place in Belfast during the summer of 1935. Eleven people were murdered and 574 injured and Charlotte Despard's dream of working-class unity was irrevocably shattered. Her new political role became little more than giving what help she could to the victims of the unionist pogroms. Maud had kept in touch with her former partner and at the end of that year she travelled up to Belfast to see the situation for herself. She gave two lectures in the small town of Lurgan, and was then arrested at the home of the friends she was staying with. Remembering Hanna Sheehy-Skeffington's experience at the hands of the unionists, Maud had bought a single train ticket. As she expected, she was given an escort to the border. She was now seventy and presumably the Unionist government had the wit to realise that the imprisonment of Maud Gonne MacBride would not be the wisest of measures.[4]

That March, those who had remained within the IRA launched a new political party – Cumann Poblachta na h-Eireann (Republican Party of Ireland) – as their response to the Republican Congress. It had nothing new to offer, being based on abstentionist principles and lacking the radical appeal of Congress. Sean MacBride was the main instigator, hoping to be able to pose an alternative to the Republican Congress, against the objections of Moss Twomey, the chief-of-staff, as well as many other colleagues who were also tired of these abortive entrances into the political arena. MacBride, however, had little to do with the organisation once it was founded. It was a terrible time in which to launch a new party. Twomey was arrested in May and sentenced to three years and three months and MacBride was forced, yet again, to go on the run. On the other hand, Maud was much in evidence, and as political parties were never a particular interest of hers, especially at a time when concern for the mounting numbers of prisoners was occupying her energies, we can safely speculate that her role was to ensure a MacBride presence within the organisation and to encourage others to work for its success. The party contested the local government elections of June 1936 (as did the Republican Congress) and Maud stood as a candidate for Area 5. She polled 689 votes, a similar figure to the other republicans.[5] None of them was elected. At Cumann Poblachta's Ard Fheis in November, Maud tried unsuccessfully to rally support with encouraging words on how the election results were 'not too bad in the circumstances'. She was elected onto the national directorate of the party, but by that time it was more or less defunct.[6]

In June the IRA had been declared an illegal association – de Valera using the same provision of the constitution that Cosgrave had used five years earlier – so Maud's explanation for their poor showing in the elections was, if anything, an understatement. The annual Bodenstown pilgrimage to the grave of Wolfe Tone, scheduled for the week following the ban, was itself banned. A small group from Sinn Fein and Cumann na mBan tried to force their way past the cordon of police but in the end the indefatigable Hanna Sheehy-Skeffington was forced to stand at the side of the road in order to read an oration by Mary MacSwiney, which she was too ill to deliver herself, to a small dispirited group of the faithful.

The bad times were back. *An Phoblacht* was suppressed, the *Republican Congress* paper had collapsed, and it was becoming impossible to create an effective opposition to Fianna Fail. The majority of people regarded the IRA as an anachronism, unnecessary in the independent twenty-six county state. The republic had not been declared, but de Valera was the man they believed strong enough to eventually obtain it.

With this decimation of forces on the republican side, the role of the Women's Prisoners' Defence League remained as essential as ever. It was not only the numbers of young men sent to prison that concerned Maud, but also the inhumane treatment of those incarcerated in the prison system. She interviewed prisoners released from gaols in Britain and from gaols on both sides of the Irish border and was appalled to discover that the prison regime in the twenty-six counties was by far the worst. Some have suspected that the prisoners were simply a political weapon with which Maud could attack the enemy – be that Britain or the Free State – but this was not the case. Once Maud had seen, by her visit to Portland gaol and then by her own incarceration in Holloway, what imprisonment did to people, she was utterly and passionately a believer in the necessity of creating a humane alternative to the hideous system which was capable of driving people insane. If it were not for the unresolved national question, around which all other political issues were subordinate, she could have made her name as an informed advocate of penal reform. Her knowledge of the prison system was voluminous – from personal experience and from the painstaking accumulation of evidence that was one of the most important aspects of the work of the Defence League.

Once the weapon of the hunger strike was resorted to, the O'Connell Street rallies resumed some of their old importance. In July, Maud wrote a letter to *Irish Freedom* (a Sinn Fein-based journal which had escaped the rigours of the censor owing to the organisation's low profile), detailing the latest examples of prisoner mistreatment. She also announced that as a result of the arrest of Patrick McKenna, who was sentenced to eighteen months by the military tribunal after he had spoken at her weekly meeting, she would 'invite none but women to speak at these meetings'.[7]

While republican opposition to de Valera continued on its spasmodic course, another section of Irish women were also protesting against Fianna Fail policies – this time concerning the rights of working women. The Conditions of Employment Bill of 1935 allowed the Minister for Industry to prohibit or limit the numbers of women working in particular industries. Many suspected that it was the first stage of a move to get rid of women from the workforce. De Valera himself unquestionably favoured that option. The Irish Women Workers' Union initiated the fight against the Bill and Louie Bennett, Helena Moloney, Dorothy Macardle and Hanna Sheehy-Skeffington were much in evidence at the subsequent protest meetings. Within the Senate, Kathleen Clarke fought angrily, citing the 1916 Proclamation in her support. These were all old friends of Maud's, yet she does not appear at any time to have lent her name to the campaign. A National Council of Women in Ireland was also set up, to scrutinise all legislation of relevance to women in order to ensure that their interests were promoted, but again, Maud did not take part. Her work for the WPDL, which by this time was very much a one-woman show, was what most preoccupied her, but as well as that, her political views were now closely linked with those of the MacBride faction within the IRA. Her participation in Cumann Poblachta na h-Eireann had been on an abstentionist basis and she therefore had no scruples in becoming involved. But anything that smacked of acceptance of the Free State or constitutionalism was to be avoided at all costs. Such purist attitudes were never shared by someone of the flexibility and political acuteness of Hanna – who sought alliances wherever they could be made in her efforts to promote the twin causes of feminism and socialism.[8]

Maud's personal antipathy to de Valera and his tough stance on law and order did not prevent her from attending a reunion in the Mansion House on 1 September 1936, of those who had been on the original council of the White Cross. De Valera was there, together with the Lord Mayor of Dublin, the Chief Rabbi, ex-senators and many of the women who had been involved, including Madame O'Rahilly, Dr Kathleen Lynn, Kathleen Clarke and Maire Comerford. Hanna Sheehy-Skeffington and Dorothy Macardle were amongst those who sent their apologies. Perhaps they did not want to mix with such august company?[9]

Further evidence for Maud's political leanings during this period is shown in her work to reprieve Michael Conway, sentenced to death in May 1936 for the murder of a young IRA man who had been shot for giving evidence against his IRA comrades. According to Seamus O'Kelly, who was a member of the Conway Committee, it was on Maud's initiative that a small group of people 'representative of various shades of thought' were mobilised to fight for the life of Conway. Rosamund Jacob, a well-known writer who had been an independently-minded member of early Cumann na mBan and a close friend of Maud's and of Hanna Sheehy-Skeffington's, volunteered to write a pamphlet outlining the case for the defence. The only evidence was a fingerprint on a car taken from a garage where Conway worked, plus the fact that he was a well-known member of the IRA. Over fifty thousand copies of the pamphlet were produced and it was widely reviewed, not only in Britain and Ireland, but also in Europe. As O'Kelly remembered:

> Madame MacBride, through her knowledge of French and of Paris, was altogether responsible for this. It was she who got the committee together. It was she collected the money to make the publication of the pamphlet possible, and it was she, through her Women's Prisoners' Defence League, who undertook the most important task of securing adequate circulation.[10]

On 4 May 1938, Conway was released. He later became a monk in an enclosed order of the Catholic Church.

In May 1937, in response to the suppression of republican journals, a small four-page news-sheet appeared. It was called *Prison Bars* and it was produced monthly until the end of 1938 – edited, as it was modestly stated, 'by a woman of no importance'. That woman was, of course, Maud Gonne MacBride. Roger McHugh, later to become a professor of English, helped her in this venture. Although the bulk of its contents concerned the welfare of prisoners on both sides of the border, it also contained articles on other matters dear to Maud's heart – such as monetary reform, the control of banking by the nation, the rise in emigration and the economic situation generally. A poem by Barry O'Delaney was printed in one issue, which also partially reprinted the leaflet produced by Maud and James Connolly in 1897 and which, it was now claimed, 'because enough people heeded it, helped to stop a famine in the West of Ireland'.

The July 1937 issue of *Prison Bars* was almost entirely devoted to de Valera's new constitution, which was bitterly opposed by republicans. But while they rejected it on the old familiar grounds of partition and the republic, many women were outraged at the clauses relating to the future role envisaged for them in the new state of 'Eire'. Articles 41 and 45, in particular, were unmistakeable attempts to ensure that Irish women would return to hearth and home, leaving the public sphere of work to the male section of the population:

Article 41

2-1 In particular, the State recognises that by her life within the home, woman gives to the State a support without which the common good cannot be achieved.

2-2 The State shall, therefore, endeavour to ensure that mothers shall not be obliged by economic necessity to engage in labour to the neglect of their duties in the home.

Article 45

4-2 The State shall endeavour to ensure that the inadequate strength of women and the tender age of children shall not be abused, and that women and children shall not be forced by economic necessity to enter avocations unsuited to their sex, age or strength.

It was a solicitude for women's welfare that had the most sinister of undertones. For some, it heralded an outrageous denial of basic civil rights, and Hanna Sheehy-Skeffington was given much space in that particular issue of *Prison Bars* in which to voice her objections:

Never before have women been so united as now when they are faced with Fascist proposals endangering their livelihood, cutting away their rights as human beings. . . . Mr de Valera shows the mawkish distrust of women which has always coloured his outlook. . . . He has refused to restore 1916 Equal Rights and Equal Opportunities for women.

She was, of course, one of the most vocal of the protesters, whose ranks ranged from trade unionists to university graduates. Unfortunately, the protest was spearheaded by the older generation of women, who had all been active in their various spheres since before independence. A resigned apathy seemed to affect their younger counterparts. The republican women of Cumann na mBan took an abstentionist line on the issue, feeling that a movement which demanded changes to the constitution was tacitly accepting the institution of the state. Maud did not attend the public meetings either, but she made it quite clear that she did not support the introduction of the new constitution. Her point of view was that of the traditional republican, but she was also concerned for the welfare of women and of prisoners. It was a neat summation of her lifetime's concerns:

We have the Proclamation of the Republic as a noble, clear, concise Document, as our Charter of Liberty. . . . The substitution of another Document is a weakening of our national position.
If, when Ireland is free, a more detailed Constitution were needed, the Article concerning women and the Articles providing for Special Courts in Mr de Valera's Draft Constitution would damn it in my eyes.

The result of the referendum on acceptance of the constitution was a half-hearted victory for de Valera. Thirty-one per cent of the electorate abstained, but the figures were immaterial. The Free State was gone and in its place was 'Eire'. Irish women had suffered a crushing defeat and the partition of the country remained as controversial an issue as it had ever been.

What to do next was the question that faced republicans. Bodenstown, that litmus paper of republican fortunes, remained out of bounds to the IRA in 1937. Cumann na mBan led the small group of 1,500, a far cry from the crowd of 30,000 only two short years before. This time, Maud was a prominent figure amongst the women, joining unyielding republicans of the calibre of Mary MacSwiney and Leslie Price Barry, whose husband Tom had recently been elected chief-of-staff of the IRA.[11] Barry replaced Sean MacBride, who had a brief term as head during a time when the organisation was deeply divided over its future strategy. Eventually, in April 1938, Sean Russell became the new chief-of-staff and a bombing campaign for England was approved. Sean MacBride left the organisation, after twenty years of full-time involvement, and went off to complete his long-delayed law studies.

A drive against partition was one of the few options open to those who wanted to maintain some semblance of political opposition. In August 1938, Maud and Helena Moloney were both active members of the Anti-Partition League, speaking at a meeting in Bundoran, County Donegal, just a few miles from the border. Seamus O'Kelly was also involved, but he was able to travel to Bundoran by train, unlike Maud, who had to go to Sligo by car and then travel to Donegal. The more direct route went through Enniskillen, where it was felt Maud was sure to be arrested because the Exclusion Order which had been served upon her by the Unionist government was still in operation. Although Maud wanted to defy the Order, the committee of the Anti-Partition League decided against it.[12] She was now seventy-three, but the increasing years had little effect upon her ability to rise to the demands of the occasion. Her speech would have echoed a four-page pamphlet distributed by the Women's Defence League that June, which described the persecution of Catholics in the north, the plight of prisoners in Belfast gaol and the lack of civil liberties as a result of the notorious Special Powers Act. Maud wanted a relief fund to be established to assist the families of political prisoners and those who had been deprived of their jobs because of religious discrimination. As she said in a letter to the *Irish Press* of 6 August, 'A little help is of more value than much sympathy' and she hoped that all shades of political opinion would contribute to the fund because 'we should not remain indifferent to the distress of our own flesh and blood'. Her hope was that a constant portrayal of the evils of partition would bring pressure to bear on both the British and Irish governments to bring that unsatisfactory compromise to a speedy end.

After what was considered to have been a very successful meeting, the speakers travelled back to Dublin by car, arriving at well after five in the morning. Their one stop was for a meal in Roscommon and O'Kelly had his travels enlivened by Maud's reminiscences, which continued for the entire length of the journey.

Maud's past campaigns on behalf of the Land League and the Fenian prisoners, as well as the many friends she had known over the past half century were more than usually present in her memory just then. She had been working hard at writing her memoirs and her autobiography, *A Servant of the Queen*, was published in October of that year.

There were several reasons why she eventually decided to write an account of her life. To earn some money was certainly one of them. Until Sean left the IRA and qualified as a barrister in 1937, he had no income of his own. Even when he began to practise, as many of his clients were members of the IRA with no money either, payments were few and far between. Kid had begun to run the Irish Sweep-stakes in 1932, which was, apart from the Gonne trust, the only contribution to the household budget. Maud's income had greatly diminished after the capital from her trust was reinvested in Irish government bonds. But that was not the only reason. So many people had asked her about her adventures and urged her to write them down. And so many of her friends were writers. Yeats, in particular, wrote much autobiography, constantly adding new dimensions and thoughts to his chronicle of life and friendship. Maud must have ached to present her own account of events. And there were plenty around to give support and encouragement. Dorothy Macardle's definitive history, *The Irish Republic*, was published by Gollancz in 1937 and she persuaded Victor Gollancz to consider her friend's manuscript for publication.

Each morning, Maud would begin the task of recalling the past, writing down her adventures for Iseult to type later into manuscript form. The loss of her papers was a serious handicap and partly accounted for the many inaccuracies and almost complete absence of dates. Maud's own vagueness was exacerbated by Iseult's total lack of interest in politics. Her daughter's interests were literary and philosophical and her approach to events was blissfully ahistorical, oblivious as to whether or not incidents were related to the time in which they occurred. It explains why two chapters in the book are out of sequence: the typist simply didn't notice.[13] The question of what to put in and – more importantly – what to omit, became a subject for family discussion. Gollancz, anxious about possible libel action, insisted on the deletion of some names of political adversaries, but it was details of Maud's personal life that most concerned members of her family. Sean was adamant in his insistence that his mother maintain a discreet silence about aspects of her past life.[14] He did not want the general public to know that his grandfather's illegitimate daughter Eileen was married to his father's brother. Neither did he want people to know that he had an illegitimate sister as a result of his mother's affair with a Frenchman. He most certainly did not want the murky details of his parents' divorce to be dragged up once again. In the event, the book ended with Maud's marriage to MacBride, Eileen was disguised as 'Daphne' and Iseult remained her 'adopted' daughter. How frank Maud would have been if left to her own judgement is debatable, but she must have wanted to elaborate on her story to some extent or there would not have been such heated argument. Would she have admitted her relationship with Millevoye? So much time had passed since those years, but she still spoke of him, and to some of her younger friends she would say that he was the only man she had ever loved. Despite herself, the pain of their parting is certainly tangible in those pages.

The title must have puzzled a British audience, but it referred to

Ireland: Queen Maeve or Cathleen ni Houlihan. As she explained at the beginning of her book, she once had a vision of Cathleen ni Houlihan while sitting, utterly exhausted, looking out of a train window after a famine relief visit to Mayo. As she stared at the bleak landscape, watching a tall, beautiful woman springing from stone to stone over the treacherous bog, she heard a voice say 'You are one of the little stones on which the feet of the Queen have rested on her way to Freedom.' That was the role she believed she had played over the past half century and she wanted to call her book 'One of Those Little Stones'. As a title, it lacked impact, and Gollancz rejected the suggestion. They eventually agreed upon *A Servant of the Queen*.

Yeats wrote a typical letter of support when she asked for permission to use his poetry, and as usual he insisted upon clarifying his own views:

> Yes of course you can say what you like about me. I do not however think that I would have said "hopeless struggle." I never felt the Irish struggle "hopeless". Let it be "exhausting struggle" or "tragic struggle" or some such phrase. I wanted the struggle to go on but in a different way.
>
> You can of course quote those poems of mine, but if you do not want my curse do not misprint them. People constantly misprint quotations . . . [15]

Irish reaction to the appearance of Maud's memoirs was enthusiastic. From what was said, as well as what was left unsaid, reviewers were obviously aware of the compromises she had made in describing her past. E. T. Keane of the *Irish Independent* felt Maud had depicted matters of a possibly intimate character 'with frankness but with discretion' and concluded that no student of Irish affairs could afford to neglect the book.[16] M. J. MacManus, literary editor of the *Irish Press*, ended a glowing review by describing the book as 'the frank, unconventional narrative of a woman who has lived her life for a great cause and who has found adventure at every turn of the road. Gifted with rare courage and surpassing beauty, she has used these as weapons in the service of the only queen to whom she has ever given allegiance – Cathleen ni Houlihan.'[17]

British response was less enthusiastic. Rumblings of war were beginning. The Irish, with de Valera's protestations of neutrality, were again appearing to stab Britain in the back and the IRA's disastrous bombing campaign of Britain began to spread panic and hatred in the streets. Only fifteen hundred copies were sold and the unbound pages went up in flames when the warehouse was hit during the Blitz. But it was reissued in Dublin in 1950 and by Gollancz in 1974.[18] Maud's story continues to fascinate.

The bombing campaign led to a renewal of repression against

republicans in Ireland. The IRA were completely out of touch with current opinion, believing that their actions would lead to their residual support being mobilised and that de Valera would not come down hard on them. After all, they were not planning any activity in Ireland. But de Valera, having regained control of Irish ports from Britain, was determined as the shadow of war drew nearer that Irish neutrality would be maintained, and he was furious at the IRA bombings for compromising his position. The Offences Against the State Act, allowing for internment without trial, was promptly introduced.

The inhabitants of Roebuck House were soon aware of the increased interest shown towards known republicans by the state forces. In May 1939, little Anna MacBride was leaving the house to take part in a May procession organised by her school. Detectives waiting outside demanded to see what was in her school case. Maud was, as usual, still in her room as she rarely came down before midday and she was 'very superior, very disdainful' as the Special Branch looked around her bedroom. Grandmother Bulfin was also there at the time and Anna was highly amused to see her other grandmother marching around after the men, berating them for what they were doing and telling them they should be out ploughing the fields instead of wasting their time. She came from a farming background and compulsory tillage to make Irish agriculture self-sufficient was government policy. Both women were well used to the experience of being raided and reacted in their different ways; one as a plain-speaking country-woman, the other with all the considerable hauteur that an upper-class background enabled her to manifest.

Intermittently, for the rest of her life, Maud worked on a sequel to *A Servant of the Queen*. It was entitled *The Tower of Age*, and was supposed to bring her story up to date, although she was unsure if it would be for publication. But she never got that far with it. She complained to Ethel Mannin of the 'horrid mental lethargy' which prevented her from finishing any of the three books she had begun – one was on prisons – and that she found it impossible to summon up the emotional and mental energy required.[20] If Maud was going to write a follow-up, she would have to start with an account of her separation from John MacBride, and she simply could not face reliving the pain of that time.

There was never that problem in remembering her friendship with Willie Yeats. They had had another political disagreement over the question of partition when Maud had wanted him to speak out against it and he had replied, half-seriously, 'that he found the inhabitants of the lost province of Ulster so disagreeable that he hoped they would never reunite with the rest of Ireland',[21] but in the last few years of Yeats's life they managed to resurrect what was, for both, a cherished friendship. In the late summer of 1938 Maud visited him at his home at Riversdale. She was to recall the occasion in an affectionate and moving article about her old friend, written for *Scattering Branches*, a collection of tributes to the poet:

> as we said goodbye, he, sitting in his armchair from which he could rise only with great effort, said, "Maud, we should have gone on with our Castle of the Heroes, we might still do it." I was so surprised that he remembered, I could not reply. The whirlpool of life had sent the current of our activities wide apart. We had quarrelled seriously when he became a Senator of the Free State which voted Flogging Acts against young republican soldiers still seeking to free Ireland from the contamination of the British Empire, and for several years we had ceased to meet. I stood speechless beside him with the song of Red Hanrahan echoing through my mind, "Angers that are like noisy clouds have set our hearts abeat" – "Like heavy flooded waters our bodies and our blood", and I realised that Willie and I still "bent low and low and kissed the quiet feet" and worshipped Her, who is "purer than a tall candle before the Holy Rood".[22]

To the last Yeats continued to admire, often despite himself, Maud's unchanging commitment to the republican cause. A few days after that last meeting he read in the newspapers that a portion of a letter, signed Maud Gonne MacBride, had been found by the British police on an IRA captive. He was supposed to have thrown up his arms in elation as he exclaimed 'What a woman! What vitality! What energy!'[23] And he wrote to Sir William Rothenstein to beg him to find some way of making a drawing of Maud that he could use as an illustration for a definitive edition of his work, 'No artist has ever drawn her, and just now she looks magnificent. I cannot imagine anything but an air raid that would bring her to London – she might come to see the spectacle – do you ever go to Dublin?'[24]

On 28 January 1939, Yeats died in a hotel on the Riviera and was buried high above the village of Roquebrune. Maud had once written to him: 'I will fight until I die, against the cruelty of small ambitions.'[25] In the year before his death, in the preface to his revised edition of *A Vision*, he had paid tribute to Maud's integrity of purpose: 'Grown gaunt in the injustice of what seems her blind nobility of pity'. It was a tribute that could equally have been applied to Charlotte Despard, although he would have shrunk from making any such comparison. But that gallant fighter of causes had spent six years in the most inhospitable of places, still holding on to the hope that one day a new age would dawn. On 9 November 1939, she too, at the age of ninety-five, was dead. At her graveside at the Republican plot in Glasnevin it was a weeping Maud who gave the final oration, remembering the devotion her old friend had shown to her while she was in gaol:

she was like a white flame in the defence of prisoners and the oppressed. As President of the Prisoners' Defence League, she left her home to work all over the country for human liberty, and I, like many men alive today, owe my life to her.[26]

Mrs Despard had been a committed opponent of fascism and a noted speaker at anti-fascist rallies in Britain and Ireland. Her political views remained unchanged, although at times one particular cause was given prominence over others. Before the war it was suffrage, afterwards it was Ireland. When she grew tired of Maud's anti-Britishness she retreated to the north, but she never lost interest in the cause of working-class Ireland.

Maud's own political beliefs were motivated by an emotional concern for the poor and the underprivileged, fuelled by an inveterate hatred of Britain. While she remained fervently attached to her chosen path, her views lacked the internal coherency which a more theoretical understanding of society might have provided. The result was that she could make some very strange comparisons. In one of her best-known articles, 'Fascism or Communism', published in *Ireland Today* in March 1938, when the threat of war was drawing ever closer, Maud's disillusion with the Ireland she was then living in was contrasted with what she felt were the progressive young countries of Germany and Russia:

A generation ago in Ireland, heroic youth, daring in thought and act, proclaimed the Republic. The Proclamation of the Republic embodied a social policy based on equal rights and opportunities for all citizens, men and women. It left no place for land grabbers or usurers. When this generation abandoned the Republic it seems to have abandoned all constructive thought. . . . Ireland may not want to be either Communist or Fascist, but let us have the courage to look at the good points where the two contrary systems agree.

The good points shared by these two systems basically boiled down to state intervention in crucial areas: a planned economy which raised the standard of living; government control of finance which eliminated the scourge of absentee landlordism and unproductive land; state intervention to ensure the health of children, prospective mothers and workers; the harnessing of science to the national good. This unrecognisable description of Stalinist Russia and Hitler's Germany is important, not so much as a demonstration of political naïvety, as an example of Maud's willingness to have state intervention. In her eyes it was the only effective means of ensuring the well-being of all citizens, and she was scathing about 'British social muddle' which relied on 'the uncertainty of private charity', leaving the state indifferent to the needs of those without money. The question of state intervention became, as we shall see, a controversial political issue in the early 1950s. In this article Maud reveals herself to be on the side of progress and so I prefer to think of her as a social democrat, whether or not she would have described herself in those terms. She did express anti-Semitic views, condemning English alliances with 'Jewish money powers', and while she cannot be completely exonerated, her long association with the Boulangist faction in France would have influenced her in thoughtlessly voicing her political objections to Britain in such terms. While Maud could never be described as right wing in her views, Millevoye and his comrades were on the far right of French political groups and against Dreyfus, the Jewish army officer who in 1894 had been wrongly convicted of giving military secrets to Germany. The Dreyfus affair, as it came to be known, brought anti-Semitism out into the open and split French political life into two. The struggle to gain justice for the imprisoned man continued until 1906, when it was finally acknowledged that the evidence against him had been fabricated. Dreyfus was then decorated with the Legion of Honour. Perhaps Maud is culpable by association. Her conclusion to the article was typical: a reaffirmation of the importance of never standing idly by while human need was so urgent: 'Any policy is better than drift and apathy. Fear is a rotten counsellor, let us not be afraid of thought or of action.'

The MacBride family might have been considered as supporters of Germany during the war. Ireland retained its neutrality throughout, the German ambassador remained in residence in Dublin, and was entertained in Roebuck House on several occasions. No one knew anything about the more horrific aspects of 'state intervention' in Germany. News of the concentration camps only began to filter through towards the end of the war. Sean MacBride maintained that he was anti-German and on several occasions argued with his mother on the question.[27] This would seem to evade the reality of the first years of the war, when Irish people generally were pro-German for the simple reason that Germany was fighting the traditional enemy – England. Old republicans had romantic memories of the First World War, when 'England's difficulty was Ireland's opportunity' and German arms had helped plans for the 1916 Rising to get off the ground. There was also the Stalin–Hitler pact to confuse those whose loyalties lay with Soviet Russia. It was not as clear-cut as it appears in retrospect. People clustered around their radios listening to Lord Haw-Haw, enjoying the prospect of a British defeat. There was speculation as to what would happen to Ireland in that eventuality: Germany was their old friend, the Republic would be declared and a new age would dawn. Such wishful thinking. The heavy censorship of newspapers, imposed by de Valera to curb any public awareness of the desperate struggles of the imprisoned IRA members, may have contributed to the general ignorance of the awful reality.

Maud never said what she thought of the camps or of what the Nazi programme was really all about. Towards the end of the war, when people had some awareness of what had been happening and the victorious allies were on the march, her concerns were all with the plight of the starving children of Europe. She was almost bedridden by 1942, as the muscles of her heart weakened. Letter-writing was one of her sole remaining activities and she wrote to a Dublin newspaper to urge that food be shipped to feed German children.[28] There were many who dissented from such a suggestion but Maud defiantly maintained that the children's hunger was not an inevitable consequence of the war, but the result of action by 'self-appointed apostles of Peace and Liberalism'. She admired the work of her old friend 'John Brennan', who had found homes in Ireland for four hundred of these children, and had raised a thousand pounds to transport and support them. It was reminiscent of the 1913 Dublin Lock-Out, when Transport Union supporters had incurred the wrath of the bishops by trying to send the children of those locked-out to the homes of English sympathisers for the duration of the dispute.

Those who felt that the MacBrides were sympathetic towards Germany were also able to point to the fact that, after the outbreak of war, Iseult's husband had gone off to live in Berlin. He had been offered a post at Berlin University, following a lecture tour undertaken before the war. No moral qualms were involved in his decision to accept. Both family and country were to be left behind while Francis Stuart further developed his role as creative artist through living outside socially acceptable norms. He met and fell in love with a young German woman, remaining impervious to all Iseult's pleas to come home. Iseult died of coronary thrombosis in 1954 and he came back for her funeral; a most unwelcome figure as far as the MacBride family was concerned. It was 1958 before he returned to live in Ireland.

Francis Stuart's sojourn in Germany was responsible for Iseult's arrest on charges of aiding a German spy. The IRA had persuaded Stuart to ask the Germans for assistance and in response Hermann Goertz, a liaison officer, complete with radio transmitter, made a parachute landing into Ireland and turned up at Laragh, where he had been told Iseult would direct him to the IRA. She was arrested in May 1944 when clothes left by Goertz in the safe house in which he had been hidden were traced to purchases made by Iseult. The ever-faithful Helena Moloney, who had a close affection for Iseult which was not always reciprocated, was then dispatched by Maud to Laragh, to redirect Goertz, should he manage to find his way, to another safe house. The unfortunate spy was eventually arrested a year later and interned until the end of the war. Iseult was tried in secret and found not guilty of involvement in intelligence activities; that much would have been patently obvious to anyone.[29]

While Iseult had her private difficulties, her brother's career was rapidly gaining momentum. By 1943 Sean had become a Senior Counsel of the Irish Bar, responsible for some of the most important of the legal actions to be taken against the de Valera government. The military tribunals imposed the death sentence on several prisoners and in one instance soldiers fired on a group of prisoners, killing one of them. The inquest was immediately closed when MacBride asked the question, 'Why was Casey shot in the back?'[30]

In 1946 another inquest was to have important repercussions. Republican prisoners had refused to wear prison clothes and as a result were held in solitary confinement. They were also deprived of visits and exercise. One prisoner, Sean McCaughey, having been held for five years, went on hunger and thirst strike to force an end to these conditions. Republican women continued to campaign on the prisoner's behalf, but there was no longer a Women's Defence League. Maud was only able to vent her great anguish in letters to the press. On 10 May she wrote to the *Irish Times*:

Sir
Those unable to serve can *demand* nothing; therefore, I, who am almost 80 and bedridden, make my last *request*. . . . I make it to the people and to the Government: Let no more young lives be sacrificed to uphold an old British rule of Victorian origin; be speedier than death in releasing young McCaughey; please, with him, release the others from Portlaoghise Jail who have been fighting that old British rule with the same spirit of courage and endurance which liberated twenty-six of our counties and among whom is the son of our comrade Lord Mayor McCurtain, who, dying for Ireland, entrusted his own children to her care. Only when this is done can our Government and people unitedly, without hypocrisy, demand that the ill treatment of prisoners in our six occupied counties shall cease.[31]

McCaughey died the day after this letter was published. At the inquest, Sean MacBride was able, for the first time, to bring out in public the conditions under which the prisoners were being held. He forced the prison doctor to admit that he would not treat a dog in the way the prisoners were being treated. For many people, this was a shocking revelation. The fact that the ill treatment continued after the war, which had been the original justification for it, was to cause a great deal of disillusionment amongst supporters of Fianna Fail. De Valera, the great leader, was now no better than the old Cumann na nGaedheal.

Chapter 11

A PRISONER OF OLD AGE

In her tribute to Willie Yeats, Maud had described herself as a 'prisoner of old age, waiting for release'. She was, increasingly, to feel she had lived too long. For one of her free spirit, who had always valued her own personal freedom and who had spent fifty years railing against the inhumanity of prisons, it was doubly hard to endure the restrictions imposed by the infirmities of age. The death of Hanna Sheehy-Skeffington, on 20 April 1946, deeply affected her. In a letter to Brigid O'Mullane, who had worked with both women in the Defence League before Fianna Fail's victory, she reflected upon Hanna as both colleague and friend:

I loved her very much and for half a century she was perhaps the one with whom I was most closely associated in work and though we sometimes thought differently it never made the slightest difference in our friendship. I think she was the ablest of all the fearless women who worked for Ireland's freedom and she is a great loss to Ireland.[1]

In a note to the novelist Ethel Mannin, written soon after Hanna's death, Maud appeared utterly bereft, a realisation beginning to dawn upon her that she would soon have outlived all her old friends: 'Our dear dear friend Hanna is gone – she was almost the dearest friend I had and the woman I admired most on earth. Her loss to Ireland is terrible and Dublin won't be the same place without her. Can't think of anything else since heard last night of her death.'[2]

Ethel Mannin, a prolific writer, was a friend and correspondent of Yeats during the last few years of his life. In 1938 she bought a small cottage near Mannin Bay in Connemara, believing that an early ancestor must have given it that name. Emma Goldman had urged her to get in touch with Hanna Sheehy-Skeffington when she visited Dublin and Ethel did so. She was deeply impressed by the experience. Writing in 1939, she declared that 'there is no woman living for whom I have a deeper admiration, or whose friendship I count a greater honour. I should like to possess as indomitable a spirit, and as great a moral and physical courage.'[3] The prospect of meeting Maud Gonne does not seem to have occurred to her, although she obviously knew much about the woman who was so closely associated both with Yeats and with Hanna. War interrupted her visits to Ireland but in 1946, when she returned, she finally paid a visit to Roebuck House.

The young woman made an immediate impact on Maud who so rarely now had the delight of a new acquaintance. She later told her new friend 'when I first saw you standing in the twilight in my big bare drawing room at Roebuck . . . I knew we would be friends'.[4] It was to be an important friendship for both women, and perhaps most especially for Maud, who was to write almost thirty letters to Ethel in these final years. It was only Maud's body which had aged, mentally she remained as alert and as full of the same passionate interest in people that she had always possessed. She was convinced that this new friendship proved the existence of a closely knit spiritual relationship, consisting of Ethel, Maud, Willie, Iseult 'and others whom we may never have met in this life'. She found the thought consoling when she felt lonely for Hanna, and she believed that this mystic bond explained why Ethel, 'whose life is so full and active, feels at home and happy with an old useless woman of 80'.[5] Almost pathetically she thanked Ethel 'who is so full of life and energy, sparing time and thought for an old woman and I can't tell you what joy I get from your visits'.[6]

She confided in the young Micheal MacLiammoir: 'they talk about the beauty of old age, don't believe a word of it, it's HELL!',[7] but she was careful not to upset the family by expressing her private feelings too forcefully. While her family loved and admired her and she delighted in the friendship of Kid and the development of her grandchildren, her letters provided a very necessary outlet for the voicing of small frustrations. Traces of those feelings of helplessness are evident in many letters. Before Christmas 1947 she explained that she would not be sending any cards, because she was unable to get out to the shops to buy any, and she didn't like those which her grandchildren had queued up at the shops to purchase.[8]

In 1949 Maud fell and broke her hip, but recovered. She also suffered from bouts of flu and pneumonia but, almost despite herself and her weak heart, her body persisted in hanging on to life. She envied Willie for having escaped 'into the freer life of the spirit'.[9] The prospect of death held no terrors for someone with such an eclectic mixture of spiritual beliefs and besides, she had always remembered her father's instruction to be afraid of nothing, not even death. In a newspaper interview in 1968 her son recalled that his mother 'tried to get me to conquer fear as a child much as she had deliberately set herself out to do when she herself was a child. Never to be afraid of death. I was always taught that as a youngster and it has always been a very dominating influence on my life.'[10] She was as successful with Sean as her father had been with her.

Louie O'Brien remembered with an affection tinged with pity those last years of the legendary Maud Gonne. Plain girls, as the young Louie described herself, would never have to suffer what Maud suffered: 'She had been the world's most beautiful woman and then she grew old and lost it totally and had to live so long afterwards.'[11] As friends died and fewer came to share the big batch of scones which Kid would bake for Sunday afternoons, Maud was left to entertain her young friends and grandchildren with tales of the past. She was proud of her Russian adventure and relished the cloak and dagger intrigue of that mission. Drifting back in time she remembered those days with Willie, listening to the land singing to the pair of them as they lay on the Dublin hills. Now, when no one could be scandalised, she confessed that Millevoye was the only man she had ever loved, although for her grandchildren's consumption she would maintain that only her beloved father ever filled that position. She was proud to remember how small her waist had been, although Tommy disapproved of corsets and bustles, and so her society portrait showed her wearing a loose-fitting dress. She had also, despite all her travels and her renunciation of her life as a débutante, kept two of her most favourite ball gowns. One was her presentation dress, worn by a nineteen-year-old young woman who could have had no idea how famous the portrait of her wearing it would become in later years. Would other revolutionary women have clung on to such mementoes? Constance Markievicz would surely have roared with laughter at the very idea. That Maud had done so was endearing evidence of an enduring vanity. It was a trait successfully hidden but never entirely suppressed.

Maud's interest in dress and beautiful objects never left her, even though the Ireland of her last years was a far different place from the Paris of her youth. The actor Micheal MacLiammoir was one of the younger generation who befriended Maud in the 1930s, and who continued to delight her by his visits when many in Dublin assumed she must be dead. He had once seen her earlier, in 1917, when he had expected a 'tall rose'. Instead, he found himself confronted by a 'black orchid'. He remembered her as being 'blissfully indifferent to anything she ate or drank, or anything at all except clothes – she was interested in her dress. . . . Her clothes were well-worn but they were French, and exquisite material, exquisitely cut, and she had gold ornaments on her hair, and looked the part of the tragedy queen to the life.' She confided in him that she got her clothes in Paris because she thought the average Irish revolutionary woman was 'so *dowdy* and so bad for the cause', although she felt guilty for not patronising Irish industries.[12]

Her undeniable stylishness and sense of occasion had been a useful attribute throughout her public life. It enhanced that inimitable flair for the dramatic gesture, which was a large part of her allure, and which also remained with her until the end. When a prisoner under sentence of death was forbidden to attend the Christmas concert for Mountjoy prisoners, Maud sent the largest of her boxes of chocolates (given by friends while she was in hospital with her broken hip), to his condemned cell. It was a spontaneous gesture, but it helped her to make a telling point concerning proposed prison reforms when she next wrote a letter to the *Irish Times*.[13]

Only in extreme old age did she have the leisure to recall the gaiety of her youth and the emotional distance to be able finally to accept her background without too much anger or bitterness. In one of her letters to Ethel Mannin she recalled her English mother, whose blood in her 'makes me able to understand English people and appreciate the good qualities in them . . . even while my Irish blood obliges me to fight their government'.[14] It was one of the rare occasions when Maud allowed herself to acknowledge anything good in the English. MacLiammoir recalled that Maud preferred to sit in a low chair. He was convinced that this was to enable her to emphasise her point: 'every time she'd mention England, she'd bash her fist on the floor, as if England lived definitely in the coal cellar and Ireland lived somewhere on the roof. Because she'd say, "Strike a blow for Ireland," and point a long hand up at the ceiling. And her eyes would go cold with hatred when she mentioned England'. Only on the subject of England did he ever see Maud show anger. Her 'fanatical attitudes and statements' he regarded as 'being part of a sort of grand, romantic dottiness'. She was 'quite, quite wonderful' and he loved her dearly.[15] Although his appreciation of Maud was sensitive and warm, this emphasis upon her eccentricities, which no doubt old age had accentuated, fails to do justice to the other side of Maud: the serious political activist who endured countless committees, vigils, meetings and protests in her endeavours to free not only Ireland the country, but also its people, and most especially the poorest sections of the population.

Those last years were filled with memories, as she found herself being sought out by scholars fascinated to know more about the muse who had inspired the passionate devotion of W. B. Yeats, whose stature as a poet was increasing with every year that went by. Joseph Hone produced the first biography and Maud greatly enjoyed the experience of being interviewed by him, 'Talking to you helps me to dig out of my memory old forgotten things, which made life interesting.'[16] But she was not only a relic of a famous poet's life. Maud remained an important figure in her own right; her contribution to the nation not fully recognised perhaps, but appreciated by those who knew of her selfless devotion to the numerous causes she had espoused over the years. She was delighted to be asked, in 1949, to give a series of radio broadcasts on Inghinidhe na hEireann, to commemorate the fiftieth anniversary of its formation. She took the occasion very seriously, researching her subject thoroughly beforehand. The process revived her pride in the Inghinidhe, 'whose work was so amazingly fruitful' that it demonstrated the value of women's work, as she later wrote to Ethel Mannin, describing her thoughts during this time. But Maud was not simply indulging in nostalgia. Her judgements were still acute and immediate political considerations remained uppermost in her mind. She declared that she wanted 'a similar organisation today of young girls ready to do the job to hand, whether by themselves or in cooperation with men'. She lamented that Cumann na mBan, which worked 'less independently' than the Inghinidhe, although also 'very useful' was now doing 'nothing worthwhile' although Ireland had as great a need as ever of women's work.[17] It was plain what Maud Gonne would be busy doing, if only she could still be in her prime.

The producer of the series was the same Francis MacManus who had been so captivated by his glimpse, twenty years previously, of Maud speaking to the Dublin crowds. He was nervous, uncertain what to expect of an old woman of more than eighty years of age, of whom friends had warned him that 'Pallas Athene' was showing more than her years. He later rhapsodised that what no one had told him was 'this spirit was luminous in her as it had been when Yeats compared her complexion to the apple blossom through which the light falls'. And no one had told him about 'the serene wisdom, even the good humour, with which she accepted what the years had brought'. As always, Maud rose magnificently to the occasion. For the time being, all the pain of old age was forgotten as she proudly recorded for posterity the achievements of her middle years. MacManus once again succumbed to the magnetism of that physical presence. His description gives a vivid impression of someone still totally aware of herself and the effect she continued to have upon people:

> Her age had its beauty. Her hair, fine as silk and still glossy, was whorled over her ears in an antique way.... Deep furrows lined her cheeks in close parallel and when she smiled her face was all laughter. Above the fine aquiline nose, the calm, bright eyes were lively as a young girl's.
>
> A table was moved closer to her to carry a microphone. She was eager to have everything perfect. She raised her papers and leaned forward with an effort, then relaxed and settled back again, her long body in its narrow black gown as slim as a girl's.... She uttered not one single word without sharp awareness. The position of words, the run of sentences, and the sequence of paragraphs were altered, for the sake of clarity, for the sake of naturalness. She talked calmly and easily with prolonged rounded rhythms ... echoes of old-fashioned oratory and of classic patriotism sounded delicately.
>
> There was witchcraft in her voice. She was aware of it ... she, with her voice, her eyes, and her intense spirit, defied history and

made valid again, for a few minutes in the hollow room all that language which was spoken at crossroads and street-corners, lecture-halls and theatres in the days before walls in Dublin city were shaken down.

When she finished, she was a little flushed from the effort but her energy was still astonishingly bright. She smoked a cigarette and talked in quieter tones.[18]

It was a wonderful performance from an old trooper, but it took its toll. During the last of the six recordings she broke down and was forced to retire to bed with no visitors until she had recovered her strength.[19]

The programmes were broadcast on Irish radio at the end of 1949 and the start of 1950. Maud's voice was firm and melodic; its tone that of someone many years younger than eighty-four. Some of her sentiments were uncompromisingly tough, but expressed in a manner which revealed the oratorical abilities of someone who knew how to use her voice to full effect: 'Force is the only remedy for a people who have let a stranger get hold of their land'. She added that talk was good in its place, 'but if it has not force behind it, it cuts no ice'.[20]

It was an interesting time in which to express such views. Would her son have been in agreement? The Irish political scene had been radically overturned two years previously, when Sean MacBride had formed a new political party, Clann na Poblachta (the Republican Family), to capitalise upon the general disillusionment with Fianna Fail. Sean himself had won a seat to the Dail at a by-election in 1947, when Maud briefly left her 'prison house' in order to proudly cast her vote. A general election was called for February 1948 and Maud described the excitement this provoked in a letter to Ethel Mannin:

> Not only my grandchildren, but every young thing I know were working, talking, and thinking of nothing but the elections, ever since the amazing and inexplicable rage of the Government over Sean's being made a TD at the by-election. . . . I never saw as much voluntary work given by young people since the early days of the Sinn Fein movement.[21]

The result was the defeat of Fianna Fail and the formation of an inter-party government in which Clann na Poblachta, with ten deputies, succeeded in obtaining two Cabinet ministers: Sean MacBride became Minister for External Affairs while his socialist colleague, Dr Noel Browne, became Minister for Health. A thirty-two county republic remained a distant dream, but the new government formally severed the last links with the Commonwealth and on Easter Monday 1949, at a ceremony at the historic site of the GPO, a (truncated) republic was declared. Maud was photographed leaving the Pro-Cathedral after a celebration Mass. Sean MacBride was also the minister responsible for overseeing the return of the body of Willie Yeats from its lonely grave at Roquebrune to its final resting place beneath the Sligo mountains. Maud was pleased that Willie had at last come home, but she was too weak to be able to attend the ceremony herself.

It was ironic, given Maud's lifelong concern for the well-being of children and their mothers, that the inter-party government should collapse in recriminations over Noel Browne's scheme to introduce a free health programme for mothers and children. The Catholic hierarchy declared his 'Mother and Child' proposal to be socialised medicine and, as such, contrary to the teaching of the Church. MacBride attempted to initiate a compromise settlement by proposing a means test, in the hope that the bishops would relent and agree to the scheme, but Browne was adamantly opposed to any capitulation to clerical pressure. By April 1951 he had been expelled from the Clann for insisting upon continuing his attempted defiance. Sean MacBride was a prime mover in this act.

Browne, who has retained his bitterness over this abandonment by his former colleague, later recalled that Maud had once shown him a photograph of her son as a child, over which she had written 'Man of Destiny'. It led him to speculate on the extent to which the 'powerful and dominating personality of this notorious rebel mother' was responsible for MacBride's career. Had his mother, either through fear or through love, influenced her son's actions?[22] The answer must surely be 'no', if this question implies some inability on the part of MacBride to think for himself and to make his own informed decisions. As Willie Yeats discovered while helping the family to leave France, the young boy was a precocious political thinker with a resolutely independent mind. He had joined the IRA without his mother's knowledge and immediately commanded respect, rising rapidly through the ranks. What Maud did provide was an environment which was intensely nationalistic, coupled with a not-unrealistic conviction – given the stature of both parents – that Sean would grow up to be someone of importance to Ireland. The boy seized the opportunities that presented themselves and the man fulfilled those expectations.

But although mother and son were often linked politically, in some respects Maud was less conventional than her son. Remnants of her unorthodox younger self never totally left her. In common with well-known members of the aristocracy who were also converts to the Catholic faith (Constance Markievicz and Charlotte Despard being the two most obvious examples), she cheerfully took what she needed from Church dogma and discarded what she felt was irrelevant. Sean MacBride unquestionably took his religious faith from Rome, despite his former military activities. Republican defiance of the Church's prohibition of membership of the IRA did not mean that most IRA members were not devout believers in every other respect; such is the peculiar dualism concerning matters of politics and religion that exists in Ireland. Maud came from a very different tradition. Before the First World War, the Church had refused to co-operate with her campaign for school meals for children and she had argued vehemently against those priests who distrusted her work. In the 1930s she had lauded the example of Fascist Germany and Soviet Russia in providing comprehensive health care for women and children and had proposed a scheme which hardly differed from that which had now been rejected. Her indomitable younger self would surely have argued against the Church over this particular issue, which had always been so dear to her heart. Did she agree with her son's role in the controversy? She was by now too old to express publicly any disagreements. The most she ever admitted, in terms of possible different opinions with her beloved son, was to tell Micheal MacLiammoir, when he once asked if she was proud of Sean, 'Oh, he must go his own way. We all do in the end.'

The Mother and Child débâcle was a catastrophe for Clann na Poblachta. At the general election of 1951 only two deputies were returned for the party, whose period of triumph was over. For a brief while it had injected a note of radicalism and hope into Irish political life, but the former Blueshirt party with which it had been in alliance – now called Fine Gael – had its fortunes revived at the expense of its coalition counterpart. The next inter-party government did not include Clann na Poblachta. Sean MacBride scraped home with a greatly reduced majority in 1951 but in 1957 he lost his seat and by 1961, when he was again unsuccessful in regaining it, his political career in Ireland seemed to be at an end. However, once he turned his attention to the twin causes of human rights and peace, a new, increasingly illustrious international career developed. By the time of his death in 1987 Sean MacBride had achieved world renown as a major figure in the international movements for human rights and disarmament. Like his mother before him, the plight of political prisoners was always a major concern of his.[23] Maud thought he would become the President of Ireland. She never envisaged a Nobel Prize for Peace. At the turn of the century few people would ever have thought that the offspring of Maud Gonne and John MacBride could be associated with the cause of peace but, as Maud came to insist in her last years of life, 'peace and freedom are the only worthwhile things to strive for, and they are indivisible'. The fact that she also believed force might be necessary to achieve that peace and freedom does not invalidate her conclusion or lessen her achievements.

On 27 April 1953, after a painful last six months, Maud finally managed to go her own way. She was eighty-six and had longed to join all those friends whose loss she had mourned. In a letter to Francis Stuart, written after her mother's death, Iseult described 'Moura's' (her pet name for Maud) despair that her illness was making her 'selfish and materialistic'.[24] The only consolation for those who gathered to say their goodbyes to the person who had been at the centre of their lives for so long was the fact that Maud's last wish was now being realised. After she received the last sacraments she looked 'radiant, happy and young'. Her request for her baby's bootees was quietly whispered and then all was peace.

Her funeral was large, but restrained. There was not the political tension that surrounded the death of Constance Markievicz during the furore of the O'Higgins assassination. There was not the grief associated with untimely death. Her time had come and her passing was a relief for those who had witnessed the ravages of old age. So many of her friends had gone before her. Veterans from Inghinidhe na hEireann, Cumann na mBan and the IRA marched behind the hearse, but their numbers were now sparse. The O'Rahilly, a family friend, gave the funeral oration. He paid tribute to the courage, love of justice and persistence that Maud had possessed:

> It was over sixty years since she, with a minimum of association with Ireland, found herself amongst a people depressed, starved and treated with injustice. And injustice was one of the things which she could not tolerate.
> She realised that only by freeing Ireland from English rule could the lot of the people be improved and she devoted the remainder of her life to the Irish people.[25]

Amongst the many obituaries was a generous appreciation from the *Irish Times*, which was not a paper noted for any nationalist sympathies. It admitted that Maud's 'courage and dignity' and 'obviously earnest devotion to her cause . . . could not but command admiration even from her opponents'. Even that essentially pro-unionist organ mourned the passing of what it realised was the 'last of the romantic Republicans, who invested the independence movement with a colour and grace that have not been known since in Irish life'.[26]

Tributes poured in from all over the world: from former prisoners grateful for her work on their behalf; from Irish communities scattered around the globe; from countries now independent that had struggled for freedom when Maud Gonne was in her prime and ready to fight with anyone who was pledged to defeat British imperialism. And there must have been more than a few women, whose tears Maud had dried while they suffered the torments of waiting for news of their imprisoned children, who had cause to remember her quietly with love and gratitude on that day.

Those who had worked with Maud in the earliest years of the century remembered her insistence on women's rightful place within the heart of the nationalist movement. Most of them were long gone, although a few old comrades remained to mourn by the graveside. But what they remembered then, many more know about today. It is a legacy which must be ranked as one of her most enduring achievements. Unlike many of her counterparts, Maud's life was not a model of austere dedication to an idealistic cause. Her life was too multi-faceted and too contradictory for such an assessment. Neither did she ever claim to be a feminist. But as a woman who never wavered in her commitment to the struggle of the poor and oppressed, while also trying valiantly to maintain her independence and to cherish her family and friends, she holds an honoured place in the pages of women's history. Today, her personality remains as beguiling and as compelling as it was one hundred years ago, when the young Maud first began to work for the Irish cause.

NOTES AND REFERENCES

Full citations of works referred to are given in the bibliography. No date is given as n.d. I have used abbreviations for frequently cited books:

Maud Gonne MacBride, *A Servant of the Queen – SQ;* W.B. Yeats, *Autobiographies – Autobiographies;* W.B. Yeats, *Memoirs – Memoirs;* Nancy Cardozo, *Maud Gonne –* Cardozo; Samuel Levenson, *Maud Gonne –* Levenson; Finneran, Harper and Murphy (eds), *Letters to W.B. Yeats – Letters 1 or 2;* Kelly and Domville (eds), *The Collected Letters of W.B. Yeats* vol. 1 – *CL;* Allan Wade (ed.), *The Letters of W.B. Yeats –* Wade; Conrad A. Balliett, 'Micheal MacLiammoir Recalls Maud Gonne MacBride' – Balliett, 1977; Conrad A. Balliett, 'The Lives – and Lies – of Maud Gonne' – Balliett, 1979; Maud Gonne MacBride, 'Yeats and Ireland', in Stephen Gwynn (ed.), *Scattering Branches – Scattering Branches;* Joseph Hone, *W.B. Yeats –* Hone; Margaret Ward, *Unmanageable Revolutionaries –* Ward.

Frequent correspondents are indicated by initials: MG for Maud Gonne; WBY for William Butler Yeats; JOL for John O'Leary; LG for Lady Gregory; EM for Ethel Mannin; JQ for John Quinn; HSS for Hanna Sheehy-Skeffington.

Abbreviations for manuscript sources are: National Library of Ireland (NLI) for the Sydney Gifford Czira Papers; Sheehy-Skeffington Papers; Thomas Johnson Papers; letters from Maud Gonne to Ethel Mannin and miscellaneous letters from Maud Gonne. The New York Public Library (NYPL) for the John Quinn Papers and the Berg Collection, containing letters to Lady Gregory.

Chapter 1 The Colonel's Daughter

1 *Scattering Branches*, p. 17.
2 *SQ*, p. 12
3 Cited in Levenson, p. 414.
4 Elizabeth Coxhead, *Daughters of Erin*, p. 73.
5 Forty of Colonel Gonne's letters were preserved and are quoted from by Balliett, 1979, pp. 19–22.
6 Balliett, 1979, p. 21.
7 Tennessee Claflin, 'Virtue: What it is and what it is not', in Miriam Schneir (ed.), *Feminism: The Essential Historical Writings*, p. 147.
8 Balliett, 1979, p. 21.
9 *SQ*, p. 26.
10 Interview with Anna MacBride White, August 1988.
11 For further details of the Ladies' Land League, see Ward, pp. 12–35.
12 Balliett, 1977, p. 54.
13 Balliett, 1979, p. 23.
14 Cardozo, pp. 49–50.

Chapter 2 A Passionate Alliance

1 *SQ*, p. 84, quoting W.T. Stead in *Review of Reviews*, 7 June 1892.
2 *SQ*, pp. 89–91.
3 Balliett, 1979, p. 25.
4 Cited in Cardozo, p. 68.
5 Cited in Levenson, p. 64.
6 Padraic Colum, *Arthur Griffith*, p. 50. Maud, however, must have meant the Leinster Literary Society, because the Celtic Literary Society was only founded in 1893.
7 *Scattering Branches*, p. 19.
8 *SQ*, pp. 95–97.
9 Ellen O'Leary to WBY, 12 January 1889, *CL*, p. 134.
10 *Autobiographies*, p. 123.
11 *CL*, footnote p. 134.
12 *Memoirs*, p. 40.
13 WBY to Ellen O'Leary, 3 February 1889, *CL*, p. 140.
14 WBY to Katharine Tynan, 21 March 1889, *CL*, p. 154.
15 Katharine Tynan, *Twenty-Five Years*, p. 364.
16 Balliett, 1979, p. 27.
17 MG to JOL, *CL*, footnote, p. 192.
18 WBY to Katharine Tynan, 23 October 1889, *CL*, p. 192.
19 *Scattering Branches*, p. 20.
20 *SQ*, p. 120.
21 Balliett, 1979, p. 25.
22 *Annual Register*, 1890.
23 *Memoirs*, p. 45.
24 *Memoirs*, p. 46.
25 *Memoirs*, p. 46.
26 WBY to JOL, 14 December 1891, *CL*, p. 276.
27 *SQ*, p. 308.
28 Balliett, 1979, p. 31.
29 *Memoirs*, p. 48.

Chapter 3 Ireland's Joan of Arc

1 *Memoirs*, p. 50.
2 WBY to AE, 1 November 1891, *CL*, p. 266.
3 *Memoirs*, p. 58.
4 WBY to AE, 1 November 1891, *CL*, p. 266.
5 WBY to JOL, 9 November 1891, *CL*, p. 270.
6 WBY to JOL, 17 February 1892, *CL*, p. 285.
7 *United Ireland*, 2 July 1892.
8 *Memoirs*, p. 60.
9 Cited in Cardozo, p. 95.
10 *SQ*, pp. 154–155.
11 *SQ*, p. 161.
12 'Political Prisons: Outside and In', in W.G. Fitzgerald (ed.), *The Voice of Ireland*, pp. 112–113.
13 *Memoirs*, p. 107.
14 See K.R.M. Short, *The Dynamite War: Irish-American Bombers in Victorian Britain;* Sir Leon Radzinowicz and Roger Hood, 'The Status of Political Prisoners in England: The Struggle for Recognition', in *Virginia Law Review*.
15 *United Irishman*, 4 November 1899. (Thanks to Liz Curtis for the reference.)
16 Levenson, p. 97.
17 WBY to JOL, 16 October 1892, *CL*, p. 322.
18 MG to JOL, 4 October 1892, *CL*, footnote p. 322.

19 WBY to MG, *CL*, p. 341.
20 *Autobiographies*, p. 283. For his report as Hon. Sec. of the Committee, see *CL*, p. 358.
21 *Memoirs*, pp. 66–68.
22 *Memoirs*, p. 133.
23 *Memoirs*, p. 73.
24 Balliett, 1979, p. 29.
25 Cited in Levenson, p. 200.
26 *Scattering Branches*, p. 22.
27 *Shan Van Vocht*, August 1896.
28 Levenson, p. 118.
29 *Shan Van Vocht*, June 1897.
30 *Autobiographies*, p. 445.
31 Desmond Greaves, *The Life and Times of James Connolly*, pp. 89–90.
32 Incident mentioned in *Autobiographies*, p. 450 and *Memoirs*, p. 112.
33 *Memoirs*, p. 112.
34 *Autobiographies*, p. 447.
35 *SQ*, p. 275.
36 *Memoirs*, p. 113.
37 *SQ*, p. 275.
38 Samuel Levenson, *James Connolly*, p. 53.
39 *SQ*, pp. 277–278.
40 WBY to LG, 3 October 1897, Wade, pp. 287–288.
41 Levenson, p. 131.
42 WBY to AE, 22 January 1898, Wade, p. 294.
43 Desmond Greaves, op. cit. p. 103 and *SQ*, pp. 227–228.
44 Cited in Cardozo, p. 143.
45 *SQ*, p. 243.
46 WBY to LG, 14 June 1898, Wade, p. 299.
47 *Memoirs*, p. 61.
48 *SQ*, pp. 282–283.
49 Balliett, 1979, p. 26.
50 *Memoirs*, p. 114.
51 *SQ*, p. 286.

Chapter 4 A Daughter of Erin

1 *Memoirs*, pp. 131–134. See also Curtis Bradford, 'Yeats and Maud Gonne', in *Texas Studies in Language and Literature* III.
2 WBY to LG, 4 February 1899, Wade, pp. 311–312.
3 WBY to LG, 10 February 1899, Wade, pp. 312–313.
4 Cited in Cardozo, p. 161.
5 *United Irishman*, 7 October 1899.
6 *United Irishman*, 14 October 1899.
7 WBY to Lily Yeats, 1 November 1899, Wade, p. 326.
8 Sean O'Casey, *Pictures in the Hallway*, p. 311.
9 *SQ*, p. 302.
10 *SQ*, pp. 303–305.
11 *Irish World*, 10 February 1900.
12 WBY to the *Daily Express*, 3 April 1900, cited in Wade, p. 338.
13 *SQ*, p. 248.
14 Ward, pp. 47–48.
15 *SQ*, pp. 287–289.
16 Ward, p. 51.
17 Ella Young, *Flowering Dusk*, p. 70.

18 A History of Inghinidhe na hEireann by Sydney Gifford Czira, Introduction by Maud Gonne MacBride. Czira Papers, NLI.
19 *SQ*, p. 266.
20 Ella Young, op. cit. pp. 57–58.
21 Inghinidhe na hEireann by Sydney Gifford Czira, op. cit.
22 *SQ*, pp. 319–320.
23 *SQ*, p. 321.
24 *Irish World*, 23 February 1901.
25 John MacBride to Mrs MacBride, 20 March 1901, cited in Cardozo, p. 207.
26 *SQ*, p. 324.
27 *SQ*, p. 328.
28 *SQ*, pp. 329–330.

Chapter 5 Marriage

1 MG to WBY, 3 February 1902, cited in Cardozo, p. 217.
2 *SQ*, p. 343.
3 Maire nic Shiubhlaigh, *The Splendid Years*, p. 19.
4 WBY to LG, 3 April 1902, Wade, p. 368.
5 *SQ*, p. 344.
6 Balliett, 1979, pp. 31–33.
7 *SQ*, p. 349.
8 *SQ*, p. 349.
9 Cited in Balliett, 1979, p. 33.
10 *United Irishman*, 28 February 1903.
11 Interview with Louie Coghlan O'Brien, August 1988.
12 MG to LG, 28 February 1903, Berg Collection, NYPL.
13 LG to WBY, cited in Cardozo, pp. 232–233.
14 Cited in Levenson, p. 200.
15 Details of the protests contained in *SQ*, pp. 334–339 and Ward, pp. 60–63.
16 *United Irishman*, 18 July 1903.
17 Balliett, 1979, pp. 34–35.
18 Ward, pp. 63–64.
19 *United Irishman*, 31 October 1903.
20 *United Irishman*, 24 October 1903.
21 Balliett, 1979, p. 35.
22 Ella Young, *Flowering Dusk*, pp. 101–102.
23 Scrapbook shown to author by Sean MacBride, May 1987.
24 Police report shown to author by Sean MacBride, May 1987.
25 Balliett, 1979, pp. 36–37.
26 MG to JQ, 25 March 1908, NYPL.
27 Correspondence from Anna MacBride White to author.
28 *Sunday Press*, 15 January 1989. (Thanks to Mike Farrell for the reference.)
29 WBY to LG, cited in Hone, p. 212.
30 Mary Colum, *Life and the Dream*, p. 142.

Chapter 6 Exile

1 R.M. Fox, *Rebel Irishwomen*, pp. 120–121.
2 MG to EM, n.d., NLI.
3 MG to JQ, 19 January 1910, NYPL.
4 Levenson, p. 236; interview with Sean MacBride, May 1987.
5 MG to JQ, 3 November 1911, NYPL.
6 MG to JQ, n.d. (1914), NYPL.
7 Cardozo, p. 258.
8 MG to WBY, 26 June 1908, *Letters 1*, pp. 200–201.

9 Cited in Cardozo, p. 259.
10 MG to WBY, 26 July 1908, *Letters 1*, pp. 201–202.
11 Cited in Cardozo, p. 262.
12 Curtis Bradford, 'Yeats and Maud Gonne', in *Texas Studies in Language and Literature* III, p. 465.
13 Richard Ellman to Conrad A. Balliett, 27 February 1978. Balliett, 1979, p. 42.
14 Cited in Cardozo, p. 263.
15 *Memoirs*, p. 133.
16 R.M. Fox, op. cit. p. 121.
17 Sydney Gifford Czira, *The Years Flew By*, pp. 48–49.
18 MG to JQ, 19 January 1910, NYPL.
19 Cited in Cardozo, p. 268.
20 *Bean na hEireann*, April 1910.
21 MG to JQ, 22 April 1915, NYPL.
22 MG to JQ, 29 October 1910, NYPL.
23 Sydney Gifford Czira, op. cit. p. 52.
24 Ward, pp. 81–82.
25 MG to JQ, 16 March 1914, NYPL.
26 MG to JQ, 31 December 1910, NYPL.
27 MG to JQ, 19 February 1911, NYPL.
28 *Irish Review*, December 1911, pp. 483–485.
29 MG to JQ, 3 November 1911, NYPL.
30 *Irish Worker*, September and October 1914; Ward, p. 82.
31 MG to JQ, n.d., (1912).
32 Cited in Cardozo, p. 289.
33 Mrs Oldham to HSS, n.d., Sheehy-Skeffington Papers, NLI.
34 *Irish Citizen*, 15 June 1912.
35 *Irish Citizen*, 12 July 1913.
36 Ward, pp. 75–79.
37 R.M. Fox op. cit. p. 68.
38 *Irish Worker*, 1 November 1913.
39 MG to JQ, 29 December 1913, NYPL.
40 MG to JQ, 8 March 1914, NYPL.
41 Elizabeth Coxhead, *Daughters of Erin*, p. 62.
42 MG to EM, n.d., NLI.
43 J.H. and M.E. Cousins, *We Two Together*, p. 177.
44 Cousins, *We Two Together*, pp. 158–159.
45 Everard Feilding to WBY, 10 July 1914, *Letters 1*, pp. 292–293.
46 MG to WBY, 9 July 1914, *Letters 1*, pp. 291–292.
47 MG to WBY, 25 July 1914, *Letters 1*, p. 294.
48 MG to WBY, 26 August 1914, *Letters 2*, p. 303.
49 MG to JQ, n.d., (early 1915).
50 MG to JQ, 15 July 1915, NYPL.
51 MG to WBY, 7 November 1914, *Letters 2*, p. 308.
52 MG to WBY, 26 August 1914, *Letters 2*, p. 303.
53 MG to JQ, 15 July 1915, NYPL.
54 MG to JQ, 4 February 1916, NYPL.

Chapter 7 'Madame MacBride' Returns

1 MG to JQ, cited in Levenson, p. 297.
2 WBY to LG, 11 May 1916, Wade, p. 613.
3 MG to JQ, 11 May 1916, NYPL.
4 *Irish Times*, 16 July 1988. Unpublished letter from WBY to Florence Farr, giving Iseult's description of Maud's initial response; article on the Paget Collection, which was about to be auctioned. (With thanks to Mike Farrell for the reference.)

5 MG to JQ, 11 May 1916, NYPL.
6 MG to JQ, 8 October 1916, NYPL.
7 Received by JQ 4 June 1917 and included in Quinn Papers, NYPL.
8 MG to JQ, 4 June 1917, NYPL.
9 Hone, p. 303.
10 Hone, p. 307.
11 WBY to Florence Farr, *Irish Times,* 16 July 1988.
12 *Scattering Branches,* p. 32.
13 MG to JQ, 16 August 1916, NYPL.
14 Hone, pp. 307–308.
15 Hone, p. 308.
16 MG to JQ, 8 October 1916, NYPL.
17 MG to JQ, 24 November 1916, NYPL.
18 MG to JQ, 6 December 1916, NYPL.
19 Ward, pp. 119–121.
20 Ella Young, *Flowering Dusk,* p. 133.
21 MG to JQ, 30 July 1917, NYPL.
22 WBY to LG, 12 August 1917, Wade, pp. 628–629.
23 WBY to LG, 21 August 1917, Wade, p. 630.
24 WBY to LG, 8 September 1917, Wade, p. 631.
25 Hone, p. 310.
26 Cited in Cardozo, p. 319.
27 WBY to LG, 16 December 1917, Wade, p. 634.
28 Cited in Levenson, pp. 316–317.
29 Levenson, p. 319.
30 Levenson, p. 321.
31 Elizabeth Coxhead, *Daughters of Erin,* pp. 66–67.
32 Constance Markievicz to Eva Gore-Booth, 11 September 1918, Esther Roper (ed.), *The Prison Letters of Countess Markievicz,* p. 185.
33 Constance Markievicz to Eva Gore-Booth, 8 October 1918, *Prison Letters,* op. cit. p. 186.
34 Cited in Cardozo, p. 328.
35 MG to HSS, November 1918, Sheehy-Skeffington Papers, NLI.
36 Constance Markievicz to Eva Gore-Booth, 4 December 1918, *Prison Letters,* op. cit. p. 189.
37 MG to HSS, November 1918, Sheehy-Skeffington Papers, NLI.
38 MG to HSS, n.d. (1919), Sheehy-Skeffington Papers, NLI.
39 Interview with Maire Comerford, January 1975.
40 Interview with Sean MacBride, May 1987.
41 Cited in Cardozo, p. 330.
42 Interview with Louie Coghlan O'Brien, August 1988.
43 Brian Behan, *Mother Of All The Behans,* pp. 47–48.
44 Ward, p. 147.
45 Ward, p. 143.
46 Cardozo, p. 343 and Maire Comerford, unpublished memoirs.
47 Margaret Mulvihill, *Charlotte Despard,* p. 7.
48 MG to JQ, 21 February 1921, NYPL.
49 Aine Ceannt, *Irish White Cross.*
50 MG to Arthur Griffith, dated Good Friday 1921, NLI.
51 Handwritten notes from Sylvia Pankhurst to HSS, and MG to HSS, 1919, NLI.
52 MG to HSS n.d. (1921), NLI.
53 MG to WBY, 21 March 1921, *Letters 2,* pp. 377–378.
54 MG to EM, 8 January 1946, NLI.
55 Diana Norman, *A Terrible Beauty,* p. 215.
56 Constance Markievicz to Eva Gore-Booth, 26 November 1920, *Prison Letters,* op. cit. p. 254.

57 MG to JQ, 21 February 1921, NYPL.
58 Interview with Sean MacBride, May 1987.
59 Interview with Louie Coghlan O'Brien, August 1988.
60 Francis Stuart, Blacklist, Section H, p. 22.
61 MG to EM, n.d., NLI.

Chapter 8 Working for Peace

1 Eithne Coyle O'Donnell, unpublished memoirs, shown to author 1976.
2 Interview with Sean MacBride, May 1987.
3 SQ, p. 173; Jacqueline Van Voris, Constance de Markievicz in the Cause of Ireland, pp. 306–307.
4 Maud Gonne MacBride, 'The Real Case Against Partition', Capuchin Annual, 1943.
5 Leah Levenson and Jerry Natterstad, Hanna Sheehy-Skeffington: Irish Feminist. p. 147.
6 Letter from Maud Gonne MacBride, Eire: The Irish Nation, 22 September 1922.
7 R.M. Fox, Louie Bennett, pp. 76–78.
8 Francis Stuart, Blacklist, Section H, p. 65.
9 Interview with Sheila Humphreys O'Donoghue, May 1988.
10 Helena Swanwick, I Have Been Young, p. 329.
11 Helena Swanwick, op. cit. pp. 450–451.
12 In possession of the Coghlan family.
13 Cardozo, p. 353.
14 Correspondence from Lilian Dalton to Peter Beresford Ellis.
15 Scattering Branches, p. 25.
16 WBY to Olivia Shakespear, 5 January 1923, Wade, p. 697.
17 Cited in Levenson, p. 345.
18 Charlotte Fallon, 'Civil War Hunger Strikes: Women and Men', in Eire-Ireland, 1987, pp. 82–85. (With thanks to Bill Rolston for the reference.)
19 Margaret Mulvihill, Charlotte Despard, pp. 148–149.
20 Charlotte Fallon, op. cit. p. 84.
21 MG to EM, 15 May 1946, NLI.
22 Van Voris, op. cit. p. 332.
23 Stuart, op. cit. p. 104.
24 Mulvihill, op. cit. pp. 154–155.
25 C.S. Andrews, Man of No Property, p. 35.
26 Interview with Anna MacBride White, August 1988.
27 Interview with Louie Coghlan O'Brien, August 1988.
28 MG to Thomas Johnson, 23 September 1927, NLI.
29 R.M. Fox, Rebel Irishwomen, p. 13.
30 Andro Linklater, An Unhusbanded Life–Charlotte Despard: Suffragette, Socialist and Sinn Feiner, p. 234.
31 Cited in Levenson, p. 393.
32 Eire: The Irish Nation, 20 September 1924.

Chapter 9 'The Mothers'

1 Interview with Sean MacBride, May 1987; Catherine Rynne, 'Maud Gonne', in the Evening Press, 12 February 1968.
2 Charlotte Fallon, Soul of Fire, p. 136.
3 Jacqueline Van Voris, Constance de Markievicz in the Cause of Ireland, pp. 348–349.
4 Margaret Mulvihill, Charlotte Despard, pp. 158–159; An Phoblacht, May 1926.
5 Andro Linklater, An Unhusbanded Life – Charlotte Despard: Suffragette, Socialist and Sinn Feiner, p. 234.

6 Sean McCann (ed.), *The World of Sean O'Casey*, p. 65.
7 Article on the history of *The Plough and the Stars* in the *Irish Times*, 4 March 1989.
8 Sean McCann, op. cit. p. 168.
9 Sean O'Casey, *Inishfallen, Fare Thee Well*, pp. 178–179.
10 Francis MacManus, 'The Delicate High Head: a portrait of a great lady', in *Capuchin Annual*, 1960.
11 W.B. Yeats, *Uncollected Prose*, cited in Cardozo, p. 376.
12 Cited in Levenson, p. 358.
13 Levenson, p. 359.
14 Details on Bhikaji Cama from the India Office Library.
15 *An Phoblacht*, October 1932.
16 J. Bowyer Bell, *The Secret Army*, pp. 98–99.
17 *An Phoblacht*, July 1929.
18 J. Bowyer Bell, op. cit. pp. 101–102.
19 Ward, pp. 213–214.
20 Maud Gonne MacBride, 'How We Beat The Terrorist Proclamations', in *An Phoblacht*, 12 November 1932.
21 Seamus O'Kelly, 'Personal Recollections of Maud Gonne MacBride', in the *Irish Independent*, 31 May 1966.
22 *Republican File*, 28 November 1931.
23 *Republican File*, 2 January 1932.
24 *Republican File*, 9 January 1932.
25 *Republican File*, 13 February 1932.
26 Mulvihill, op. cit. p. 177.
27 Mulvihill, op. cit. p. 178.
28 Maud Gonne MacBride, 'Must We Fight Again for Ireland's Honour?', in *An Phoblacht*, 9 December 1933.
29 *An Phoblacht*, 19 March 1932.
30 *An Phoblacht*, 28 January 1933.
31 Leah Levenson and Jerry Natterstad, *Hanna Sheehy-Skeffington*, p. 166.
32 Levenson, p. 370.
33 Levenson, p. 371.
34 Interview with Anna MacBride White, August 1988.
35 Levenson and Natterstad, op. cit. p. 166.
36 Francis Stuart, *Blacklist, Section H*, p. 125. Balliett, 1979, p. 35, quotes from the deeds of Les Mouettes, which reveal only that Maud acquired the property in 1904 and sold it in 1926.
37 Interview with Anna MacBride White, August 1988.
38 Hone, p. 443.

Chapter 10 A Servant of the Queen

1 *An Phoblacht*, 9 December 1933.
2 *Republican Congress*, 9 June 1934.
3 *Republican Congress*, 28 September 1935.
4 Cardozo, pp. 384–385.
5 T.P. Coogan, *The IRA*, p. 116.
6 *Irish Press*, 9 November 1936.
7 *Irish Freedom*, September 1936.
8 Ward, p. 234.
9 Aine Ceannt, *The Irish White Cross*.
10 Seamus O'Kelly, 'Personal Recollections of Maud Gonne MacBride', in the *Irish Independent*, 31 May 1966.
11 *Irish Times*, 21 June 1937.
12 Seamus O'Kelly, op. cit.
13 Interview with Anna MacBride White, August 1988.

14 Interview with Louie Coghlan O'Brien, August 1988.
15 WBY to MG, 16 June 1938, Wade, pp. 909–910.
16 Cited in Levenson, p. 380.
17 *Irish Press*, 24 October 1938.
18 Cardozo, p. 394.
19 Interview with Anna MacBride White, August 1988.
20 MG to EM, 27 September 1949, NLI.
21 Hone, p. 473.
22 *Scattering Branches*, p. 25.
23 Hone, p. 474.
24 Hone, p. 470.
25 Cited in Cardozo, p. 376.
26 Andro Linklater, *An Unhusbanded Life – Charlotte Despard: Suffragette, Socialist and Sinn Feiner*, p. 257.
27 Interview with Sean MacBride, May 1987.
28 Levenson, p. 398.
29 Cardozo, pp. 396–397.
30 Michael Farrell, 'The Extraordinary Life and Times of Sean MacBride', Part 1, *Magill*, December 1982.
31 Cited in Cardozo, p. 400.

Chapter 11 A Prisoner of Old Age

1 MG to Brigid O'Mullane, n.d. (1946), NLI.
2 MG to EM, 21 April 1946, NLI.
3 Ethel Mannin, *Privileged Spectator*, p. 259.
4 MG to EM, 14 November 1945, NLI.
5 MG to EM, 2 July 1946, NLI.
6 MG to EM, 27 September 1949, NLI.
7 Balliett, 1977, p. 59.
8 MG to EM, 21 December 1947, NLI.
9 MG to EM, 23 January 1957, NLI.
10 Catherine Rynne, 'Maud Gonne', *Evening Press,* 12 February 1968.
11 Interview with Louie Coghlan O'Brien, August 1988.
12 Balliett, 1977, pp. 45–47.
13 Levenson, p. 401.
14 MG to EM, 3 May 1945, NLI.
15 Balliett, 1977, p. 47.
16 Cardozo, p. 395.
17 MG to EM, n.d., NLI.
18 Francis MacManus, 'The Delicate High Head: a portrait of a great lady', in *Capuchin Annual,* 1960.
19 MG to EM, n.d., NLI.
20 Part of the interview was released in 1966 by Ceirnuini Claddagh. The recording also included reminiscences by Helena Moloney and singing by Kathleen Behan.
21 MG to EM, 10 February 1948, NLI.
22 Noel Browne, *Against the Tide,* p. 96.
23 Michael Farrell, 'The Extraordinary Life and Times of Sean MacBride', Part 2, *Magill,* January 1983.
24 Cited in Cardozo, p. 409.
25 *Irish Press,* 30 April 1953.
26 *Irish Times,* 28 April 1953.

BIBLIOGRAPHY

Articles by Maud Gonne

'Responsibility', *Irish Review,* December 1911.

'The Real Criminals', *Irish Worker,* 1 November 1913.

'A Protest Addressed to AE', *Eire,* 20 September 1924.

'Political Prisons: Outside and In', W.G. Fitzgerald (ed.), *The Voice of Ireland,* Virtue, Dublin and London, 1924.

'Prisoners in the Free State', *An Phoblacht,* 12–19 March 1932.

'How We Beat The Terrorist Proclamations', *An Phoblacht,* 12 November 1932.

'Why Prisons Should be Reformed', *An Phoblacht,* 25 November 1933.

'Must We Fight Again for Ireland's Honour?', *An Phoblacht,* 9 December 1933.

'Fascism or Communism', *Ireland Today,* vol. III, no. 3, March 1938.

'Yeats and Ireland', Stephen Gwynn (ed.), *Scattering Branches: Tributes to the Memory of W.B. Yeats,* Macmillan, London, 1940.

'The Real Case Against Partition', *Capuchin Annual,* 1943.

Newspapers

An Phoblacht
Bean na hEireann
Eire: The Irish Nation
Irish Bulletin
Irish Freedom
Irish Times
Irish World
Prison Bars
Republican Congress
Republican File
Shan Van Vocht
Sinn Fein
The Irish Citizen
The Irish Worker
United Irishman
Workers' Voice

Articles

Balliett, Conrad A., 'Micheal MacLiammoir Recalls Maud Gonne MacBride', *The Journal of Irish Literature*, University of Delaware, vol. VI, no. 2, May 1977.

Balliett, Conrad A., 'The Lives – and Lies – of Maud Gonne', *Eire–Ireland*, vol. 14, no. 3, Autumn 1979.

Bradford, Curtis, 'Yeats and Maud Gonne', *Texas Studies in Language and Literature* III, Winter 1962.

Deutsch-Brady, Chantal, 'The King's Visit and the People's Protection Committee 1903', *Eire–Ireland*, vol. 10, no. 3, Autumn 1975.

Fallon, Charlotte, 'Civil War Hunger Strikes: Women and Men', *Eire–Ireland*, vol. 22, no. 3, Autumn 1987.

Farrell, Michael, 'The Extraordinary Life and Times of Sean MacBride (Parts 1 and 2), *Magill*, December 1982–January 1983.

Macken, Mary, 'Yeats, John O'Leary and the Contemporary Club', *Studies*, vol. XXVIII, 1939.

MacManus, Francis, 'The Delicate High Head: a portrait of a great lady', *Capuchin Annual*, 1960.

McKillen, Beth, 'Irish Feminism and Nationalist Separatism 1914-23', *Eire–Ireland*, vol. 17, nos. 3 and 4, Autumn, Winter 1982.

O'Kelly, Seamus G., 'Personal Recollections of Maud Gonne MacBride, *Irish Independent*, 31 May 1966.

O'Reilly, J., Doran, 'Maud Gonne', *Sunday Chronicle*, September–November 1948.

Radzinowicz, Sir Leon, and Hood, Roger, 'The Status of Political Prisoners in England: The Struggle for Recognition', *Virginia Law Review*, vol. 65, no. 8, 1979.

Rynne, Catherine, 'Maud Gonne', *Evening Press*, 12 February 1968.

Books

Andrews, C.S. (1979), *Dublin Made Me,* Mercier Press, Dublin and Cork.

Andrews, C.S. (1982), *Man of No Property*, Mercier Press, Dublin and Cork.

Behan, Brian (1984), *Mother Of All The Behans*, Arena, London.

Bell, J. Bowyer (1972), *The Secret Army*, Sphere, London.

Bourke, Marcus (1967), *John O'Leary*, Anvil Books, Tralee.

Brown, Terence (1981), *Ireland: A Social and Cultural History, 1922–79*, Fontana Books, London.

Browne, Noel (1986), *Against the Tide*, Gill & Macmillan, Dublin.

Buckley, Margaret (1938), *The Jangle of the Keys*, Duffy, Dublin.

Cardozo, Nancy (1979), *Maud Gonne: Lucky Eyes and a High Heart*, Victor Gollancz, London.

Ceannt, Aine (n.d.), *Irish White Cross 1920–1947*, Sign of the Three Candles, Dublin.

Colum, Mary (1947), *Life and the Dream*, Dolmen Press, Dublin.

Colum, Padraic (1959), *Arthur Griffith*, Browne & Nolan, Dublin.

Coogan, Tim Pat (1971), *The IRA*, Fontana Books, London.

Cousins, James H. and Margaret E. (1950), *We Two Together*, Talbot Press, Madras.

Coxhead, Elizabeth (1965) *Daughters of Erin*, Colin Smythe, Gerrards Cross.

Cullen Owens, Rosemary (1984), *Smashing Times: A History of the Irish Women's Suffrage Movement 1889–1922*, Attic Press, Dublin.

Czira, Sydney Gifford ('John Brennan') (1974), *The Years Flew By*, Gifford Craven, Dublin.

Davis, Richard (1974), *Arthur Griffith and Non-Violent Sinn Fein*, Dundalgan Press, Dundalk.

Donoghue, Denis (ed.) (1972), *W.B. Yeats: Memoirs*, Macmillan, London.

Fallon, Charlotte (1986), *Soul of Fire: A Biography of Mary MacSwiney*, Mercier Press, Dublin and Cork.

Finneran, Richard and Harper, George Mills and Murphy, William (ed.) (1977), *Letters to W.B. Yeats*, vols. 1 and 2, Macmillan, London.

Fox, R.M. (1935), *Rebel Irishwomen*, Talbot Press, Dublin.

Fox, R.M. (1943), *History of the Irish Citizen Army*, James Duffy, Dublin.

Fox, R.M. (1957), *Louie Bennett*, Talbot Press, Dublin.

Gogarty, Oliver St John (1988), *Sackville Street and Other Stories*, Sphere, London.

Greaves, C. Desmond (1972), *The Life and Times of James Connolly*, Lawrence & Wishart, London.

Greaves, C. Desmond (1979), *Sean O'Casey: Politics and Art*, Lawrence & Wishart, London.

Gwynn, Stephen (ed.) (1940), *Scattering Branches: Tributes to the Memory of W.B. Yeats*, Macmillan, London.

Haverty, Anne (1988), *Constance Markievicz*, Pandora Press, London.

Hone, Joseph (1942), *W.B. Yeats*, Macmillan, London.

Jeffares, A. Norman (1971), *W.B. Yeats*, Routledge & Kegan Paul, London.

Jeffares, A. Norman, and Cross, K.G.W. (eds) (1965), *In Excited Reverie: A Centenary Tribute to W.B. Yeats*, St Martin's Press, New York.

Kelly, John and Domville, Eric (eds) (1986), *The Collected Letters of W.B. Yeats*, vol. 1, 1865–1895, Clarendon Press, Oxford.

Levenson, Leah and Natterstad, Jerry H. (1986), *Hanna Sheehy-Skeffington: Irish Feminist*, Syracuse University Press, Syracuse.

Levenson, Samuel (1973), *James Connolly*, Martin Brian & O'Keefe, London.

Levenson, Samuel (1976), *Maud Gonne*, Cassell, London.

Linklater, Andro (1980), *An Unhusbanded Life – Charlotte Despard: Suffragette, Socialist and Sinn Feiner*, Hutchinson, London.

Lyons, F.S.L. (1978), *Ireland Since the Famine*, Fontana Books, London.

Macardle, Dorothy (1937), *The Irish Republic*, Victor Gollancz, London.

MacBride, Maud Gonne (1974) (1st edn 1938), *A Servant of the Queen*, Victor Gollancz, London.

MacCurtain, Margaret and O'Corrain, Donncha (eds) (1978), *Women in Irish Society: The Historical Dimension*, Arlen House, Dublin.

MacEoin, Uinseann (1980), *Survivors*, Argenta Publications, Dublin.

MacLiammoir, Micheal and Boland, Eavan (1971), *W.B. Yeats*, Thames & Hudson, London.

Mannin, Ethel (1939), *Privileged Spectator*, Hutchinson, London.

Marreco, Anne (1967), *The Rebel Countess*, Weidenfeld & Nicolson, London.

Martin, F.X. (1967), *Leaders and Men of the Easter Rising: Dublin 1916*, Methuen, London.

McCann, Sean (ed.) (1966), *The World of Sean O'Casey*, Four Square Books, London.

Milotte, Mike (1984), *Communism in Modern Ireland*, Gill & Macmillan, Dublin.

Moody, T.W. (ed.) (1968), *The Fenian Movement*, Mercier Press, Dublin and Cork.

Mulvihill, Margaret (1989), *Charlotte Despard*, Pandora Press, London.

Neesan, Eoin (1966), *The Civil War in Ireland*, Mercier Press, Cork.

Norman, Diana (1987), *Terrible Beauty: A Life of Constance Markievicz*, Hodder & Stoughton, London.

O'Brien, Nora Connolly (1975), *Portrait of a Rebel Father*, Four Masters, Dublin.

O'Casey, Sean (1972), *Autobiography: Book 2. Pictures in the Hallway*, Pan Books, London.

O'Casey, Sean (1972), *Autobiography: Book 3. Drums Under the Windows*, Pan Books, London.

O'Casey, Sean (1972), *Autobiography: Book 4. Inishfallen, Fare Thee Well*, Pan Books, London.

O'Faolain, Sean (1934), *Constance Markievicz or the Average Revolutionary*, Jonathan Cape, London.

Roper, Esther (ed.) (1934), *Prison Letters of Countess Markievicz*, Longmans Green & Co, London.

Schneir, Miriam (ed.) (1972), *Feminism: The Essential Historical Writings*, Vintage Books, New York.

Shiubhlaigh, Maire nic (1955), *The Splendid Years*, Duffy, Dublin.

Short, K.R.M. (1979), *The Dynamite War: Irish–American Bombers in Victorian Britain*, Gill & Macmillan, Dublin.

Stuart, Francis (1982), *Blacklist, Section H*, Penguin Books, London.

Swanwick, Helena (1935), *I Have Been Young*, Victor Gollancz, London.

Tynan, Katharine (1913), *Twenty-Five Years: Reminiscences*, Smith, Elder, London.

Van Voris, Jacqueline (1967), *Constance de Markievicz in the Cause of Ireland*, University of Massachusetts Press, Amherst.

Wade, Allan (ed.) (1954), *The Letters of W.B. Yeats*, Rupert Hart-Davis, London.

Ward, Margaret (1983), *Unmanageable Revolutionaries: Women and Irish Nationalism*, Brandon Books and Pluto Press, Dingle and London.

Whyte, J.H. (1971), *Church and State in Modern Ireland, 1923–70*, Gill & Macmillan, Dublin.

Yeats, W.B. (1952), *Collected Plays*, Macmillan, London.

Yeats, W.B. (1955), *Autobiographies*, Macmillan, London.

Yeats, W.B. (1972), *Memoirs*, Macmillan, London.

Yeats, W.B. (1982), *The Collected Poems of W.B. Yeats*, Macmillan, London.

Young, Ella (1945), *Flowering Dusk*, Dobson, London.

Younger, Carlton (1970), *Ireland's Civil War*, Fontana Books, London.

INDEX